DEFYING
Silence

DEFYING
Silence

A Memoir of a Mother's Loss and Courage in the Face of Injustice

Hera McLeod

Dedications

My friends and family, those "ride or die" people,
who were there during my darkest hours.

People who risked their lives trying to protect
my son and fight for justice.

My daughter's Estela and Isabel, the loves of my
life who both saved me and continue to
be my inspiration and my joy.

My sister Lara, my best friend, and the
smartest person I know.

My mother, my rock and co-conspirator.
My father, the fixer and inspiration when I need
to channel practical stoicism.

My Suno, the boy who made me feel like a
mom for the first time.

And finally—my son Prince, the true hero of this
story who changed me and the world in only 15-months.

I love you all and am so thankful you are in my life.
Thank you for giving me the strength to survive
and to defy silence.

Author's Note

Defying Justice is not about a serial killer nor is it an indictment of any specific person or people. Many characters in the story represent cracks in the system and any one of them could be identifiable with people in similar roles across the nation. It's a work of nonfiction based on the author's recollection and perception of true events. Some names, locations, and identifying details have been changed. In this story there are characters that represent many types of people, and sometimes the essence of multiple people – some kind and heroic and some not. The following names are pseudonyms: Dr. Becky Smith, Officer Timothy Jones, Officer Bailey, Tracy, Sammy, Eduardo Flores, Eduardo Flores Jr., Delores Flores, Mark McBride, Officer Karen Martin, Officer Kramer, Gideon Horowitz, Officer Jameson, Noah Levin, Josiah Henson, Chastity Carter, Ronan Bailey, Roxy Bailey, Frank Kaplan, Ron Borger, and Judge Justin Jude.

Preface

My 15-month-old son Prince was murdered by his father. The murder occurred on the heels of a 12-month long custody battle, full of damning evidence, which pointed to the dangerousness of Prince's father. In the decades since this tragedy, I've processed and analyzed the facts of this case—searching for both closure and justice. My son's father, Joaquin Rams, is fully responsible for his actions; however, there's more to this story than one sick and twisted man capable of killing his own child. This is the story of a family court and justice system that broke down, paving the way for a serial killer to gain access to an innocent child.

Pieces of my story were covered in newspapers, magazines, and television programs but this book is going to give you a deeper look into what happened from my perspective—as both a party to the case and an unofficial investigator. Joaquin got away with dozens of crimes before he killed Prince, and I was determined to see that his crime spree come to an end. Though Joaquin is in prison, there are lessons to learn from this story.

My story was a perfect storm of horrible wherein if just one variable of the equation hadn't been an epic disaster, we all could've survived to tell the tale. I'm not telling my story to attract people addicted to trauma porn, but instead to highlight the deep fractures in our justice system. I want the truths between these pages to ignite a fire inside you that compels you to be a part of the solution. And I want to take readers step by step through how this happened so that we don't keep repeating the mistakes that ruin families and take lives.

It's taken me over a decade to write this story because for years I was completely stuck in my own trauma—unable to process my feelings to the degree required to give the story its due justice. Though rage still courses through my veins, I've channeled this rage into advocacy. And through this work, I continue to parent my son by working to protect the children who come next.

During the custody trial, I started blogging about my experience. Writing started as a mechanism to help me process and heal from my own trauma, but I started hearing from other parents who were suffering through similar situations. They'd write to tell me how they finally felt seen, explain the parallels they saw between things in their experience and mine, and asking for help and advice. At first, I worried about my ability to help because I'm not an attorney or a therapist. But after talking to thousands of parents, despite for as much information as possible, I began to share with them things that I wish I'd known and done. One story, that illustrates many others in the same vein, came from a woman named Sara.

"I'm afraid to leave my son's father because I am afraid of having to leave my son alone with him."

It was three in the morning, and my phone pinged loudly to notify me of a new Facebook message in my inbox. I rolled over in bed, rubbed my eyes, and immediately got mad at myself for forgetting to put my phone on mute before getting into bed. As I lifted my phone to turn off the noise, I noticed this haunting message and couldn't look away.

"My son is only 11-months old. Is there anything I can do to make sure he's safe while still leaving this situation?"

Sara, the woman who'd sent me these messages, wasn't the first woman who reached out to me for advice since my very public, highly googleable, nightmare. Each time it happened, I found myself torn between wanting to give words of wisdom and being afraid that I wouldn't say the right thing.

"I am so sorry . . ." I wrote, trying to shake myself awake enough to tell her something helpful.

"Is he physically abusing you and your son?"

Though I suspected, I didn't want to assume. I'd learned over the years that not everyone has the same definition of abuse, but I often ask the question to try and understand the urgency of the situation.

"Well, it's more verbal abuse," she said.

"Emotional abuse is terrible, but if you're scared to leave your child alone with him, is there another red flag that you've ignored," I asked.

I felt a similar deep worry in my own gut before leaving my son's father, Joaquin. I suspected that she also hadn't considered emotional abuse a red flag, and that she was withholding additional concerns that would make her believe her son's father was also a physical threat. It is hard to admit to a stranger that you have witnessed both physical and emotional abuse and still didn't leave.

"He's hit my daughter in the head with his cellphone when she doesn't listen to him. I'm not sure this is abuse, but I don't think its ok because she isn't even his daughter," she wrote.

There it was—she wasn't clear on what constituted abuse, and whether her child's father had crossed that threshold. I think it's natural to not want to admit that someone you love, especially the father of your children, is abusive. Admitting this is also having to admit that your child will be abused and that you have essentially chosen this for them. What made it even more confusing was that he abused the child in the house that wasn't biologically his. While he hadn't yet hit the child they shared, her concerns were warranted. Someone who will abuse a child, whether they are related to that child or not, is not safe around any child.

"Sara, that is abusive. Whether the child is biologically his doesn't matter," I responded.

Sara responded with an emoji depicting tears and told me that she never knows if different cultures define abuse in different ways. Sara's boyfriend told her that because she was White, she was too nice. His use of race to excuse abusive behavior made my skin crawl. Luckily, when it comes to the law, I suspected that a judge wasn't likely to excuse abuse simply because the abuser happened to be Black.

Even though we live in a country where police are beating and killing Black people, often facing nothing more than a mild slap on the wrist and paid administrative leave, child abuse is still child abuse. What I didn't explicitly tell her was that there are judges that knowingly place children in the hands of child abusers every single day. But for her child, she needed to try—she needed to acknowledge this was happening—and she still needed to do her best to leave him and protect her child.

As if hitting her child in the head with his cell phone wasn't bad enough, this man was also self-destructive and potentially suicidal. Sara continued writing and disclosed that her son's father kept telling her that he didn't think he would grow old because of the way "his mind thinks" and that he would either get locked up or die. It was hard to deliver Sara the advice that I knew she needed because I knew it might tug on deep-seated insecurities and scare her more. The reality was that her presence didn't ensure the safety of her child. Not only did it not seem as though her son's father had concern for the safety of her older child (the one that wasn't biologically his), while she was physically present, but his own words implied that he isn't really all that concerned about his own life either. This is potentially the most dangerous kind of person because this is a person for whom self-destruction is part of his game plan.

In addition to not actually being able to protect her children as she intended, staying forced them to have more exposure to a man she knew was unstable. The longer she stayed would also imply to both the courts and her children that she condoned this abusive behavior.

"I know this is hard. I understand how you have justified staying for so long and leaving is not going to be a walk in the park. But if you intend to protect your children, and if this man is as violent as you have described, you owe your children the best possible chance at having a good life."

It was now four in the morning, and I could no longer fall back asleep. Every time I speak to women who remind me of myself when I was with Joaquin, I try to tell them things I wish I had been able to tell myself.

1. **Trust your gut:** Women don't trust their gut enough. Many people who have met Joaquin, have told me that they could tell something was off with him immediately. They aren't wrong, and their gut isn't more functional than mine. The difference was that I, like many other women, made the dangerous mistake of second guessing my gut.

Sara's gut was completely functional, but it was constantly being tested by someone who had initially earned her trust. This forced her to second guess her gut and push it so deep inside that she was not able to distinguish what was real and what was not. Though she wanted someone to validate her feelings, and explain that what she was witnessing was abuse, she knew she needed to get her children out of that situation long before I told her. Our gut often tells us everything we need to know.

2. **When people reveal who they are—you should believe them:** I remember at least one time in my relationship when Joaquin told me that he wasn't a "good guy." Intimacy often breeds disclosure, and it is not always positive disclosure. In fact, he revealed that as a young adult he had treated women horribly to the point where his own mother was disgusted with him. At the time, I falsely assumed that if he was telling me this, he must not still be bad.

In Sara's case, her child's father was showing her who he

was, and he was telling her. Healthy people don't go around telling others that because of their personality they believe they will end up dead or in jail. While it was most likely also a plea for attention, he was revealing one of the most helpful red flags of a bad relationship.

3. **A Psychopath never punches you in the face on the first date:** In the 2017 film "Get Out", directed by Jordan Peele, a psychotic White family lures an unsuspecting Black man into a nightmare. While things start out friendly and polite, the main character continues pushing past red flags until it's too late, and he is trapped in this house of horrors.

At some point in every abusive relationship, the target reaches the moment when they realize they're stuck in their own house of horrors without the keys to their car. If you wait too long, making excuses for all the red flags, you risk getting stuck. While leaving might always technically be a possibility, it becomes much harder when you're financially tied to someone or when you share children. My relationship with Joaquin lasted less than two years, but I'll never fully escape the damage he caused.

It was much easier for me to give Sara the advice that she should leave her abuser than it was for Sara to hear it. I was aware that I was giving her this advice from the safety of my home. She and her children were in danger, and the mechanics of leaving were a critical piece of the advice that I needed to provide. Toward the end of my conversation with Sara, she revealed that even though she blamed herself for getting into this mess—and for staying. She hadn't realized that the justice system might blame her as well. Since she hadn't left him yet and hadn't revealed to her friends and family what was happening in the home, she also didn't realize the long road that lay ahead. I don't know if Sara ever ended up leaving her abuser. She never reached out to me again.

Sara's story is representative of so many women who've lived and are currently living through abusive relationships. But for every woman who's experienced an abusive relationship, there are at least a hand full of trolls who would rather believe it could never happen to them then face the reality (and subsequent terror) that it absolutely could.

If I had a dollar whenever I heard someone say, "If my partner abused me, I'd be gone so fast he wouldn't know what hit him," I would be able to pay for my daughter's college education in one-dollar bills. Abusers don't generally come up to their targets and punch them in the face as a special form of "hello". Instead, they boil us like frogs in a pot. At first, it seems like you are taking a warm bath in paradise as they shower you with affection.

By the time they throw the first punch, the water has already risen to a boil, and you are so far entrenched in his abuse that you can no longer identify that you are even being abused. I read letters from women who'd been raped and were forced to share custody of their child with their rapist. One woman's face was burned after her child's father threw hot water on her. The judge in her case didn't believe the abuse she endured had any bearing on how her abuser would treat their children.

A Father cried on the phone with me, detailing how his children's mother routinely drove drunk with them in the car. They once called him for help after their mother drove the car into a pole in the school parking lot. He worried that one day the call would come from the police or the hospital instead.

According to the Center for Disease Control (CDC), 683,000 victims of child abuse and neglect were reported to child protective services (CPS) in 2015. Roughly 1,670 children died from abuse or neglect that same year. The CDC estimates that the total lifetime cost of child abuse and neglect is estimated at $124 billion each year. It's shocking that even with this data publicly available, courts seem to actively choose to ignore abuse as though a custody order will make all the risk of danger disappear.

My hope is that telling my story will arm people with knowledge that will help them fight for reform. Sure, this is *my* story—but know that much of what I experienced in family court wasn't unique to my case. These problems are systemic and elements of what happened to me—are happening to others every day, across the country. My Prince represents children everywhere who are in danger and routinely stripped of basic civil rights.

And to the parents, children, or witnesses who love them—may my story be the inspiration you need to speak up and the virtual embrace to comfort you in the lonely silence. This is the story of how I survived an abusive relationship with a serial killer, uncovered cracks in the American system, and set out on a journey seeking justice. And this is the story of Prince—the little boy who changed the world.

Chapter 1

Interrogation

I was about four years old when my father hung me by my ankles over the railing of the 12-foot-high banister in our house. He held me there until I stopped crying.

"Never show folks that you're afraid. Showing fear can be dangerous, baby girl," he warned.

My father, a Black man, grew up in Corinth, Mississippi in the 1950s and 60s. He believed that this obviously nontraditional, and admittedly a bit crazy, parenting lesson would make me tougher. Being black in Mississippi back in his day, offered no forgiveness for the weak. In stark contrast, I grew up in a predominately white, affluent neighborhood. Being "Mississippi Black" kind of tough wasn't a requirement in our suburban Sea Meadow neighborhood in Portsmouth, Rhode Island.

As a child, I mostly shrugged off my father's lessons as

some deep South, Black folk stuff. He never dared to do these things while my mother was watching. She surely would have reminded him that his children were not in immediate danger of being lynched. Despite the balance my white, Irish Catholic mother brought to my childhood, I learned at an early age that Black people didn't have the privilege to show fear the way that white folks did.

While as an adult I recognize these lessons as remnants of generational trauma, I didn't experience the type of situation my father was trying to prepare me for that night he hung me over the stairs until I was 31 years old.

The night I fled my son's abusive father, and the acute trauma in the years that followed, required a resilience—a calm in the face of chaos—and the ability to keep putting one foot in front of another despite the world erupting around me. Many people have asked me how I survived that time in my life, and there's no easy response to that question.

With a gun pressed to my temple, I had to reach deep into the stores of my life experience to find a courage inside myself that my abuser tried his best to kill. How I reacted in that moment was the difference between whether I lived or died. That night, and many times after, I've needed that "Mississippi Black" kind of tough.

July 2011

I used to think that a near death experience would cause my life to flash before my eyes like cartoon images flipping rapidly across a movie screen. But as my son's father pressed a gun to my temple—time slowed down. It was as though my brain was conserving energy in the event it had to figure out how to sustain my life. The words he spoke came at me as though he uttered them through some sort of distorted technical delay.

"Leave and I'll kill you, just like I killed Shawn," Joaquin said, lips slowly curling upward into a terrorizing grin while his cold-blooded eyes moved between me and our newborn son in my arms.

"TAP, TAP, TAP."

"Ms. McLeod? Ms. McLeod, can you hear me?"

Detective Jones was tapping on the table in front of me, attempting to get my attention.

"Huh?" I jumped in my seat, surprised to see the chubby, fair-skinned officer hovering just a few inches from my face.

Suddenly remembering that I was in a police interrogation room, I cleared my throat and apologized for the difficulty I was having being fully present. I plastered a fake smile on my face, desperately trying to stifle tears. Jones's breath smelled like old tuna fish, and his closeness made me feel like I was going to throw up.

'I'm not the man who was brandishing weapons earlier, but why do *I* feel like I'm being investigated,' I thought.

"OK, Ms. McLeod, why don't you start by telling me what happened tonight," Jones asked, thankfully moving back from my face to take the seat across from me.

Detective Jones stated his questions in such a monotone that it was as though he was reading from a script. As he prepared the recorder, I looked around the room. The walls looked like they were once bright white, but the years since fresh paint made them look like a pack of toddlers walked all over them with filthy gym shoes. The only furniture was a steel desk and two chairs—one for me and one for the detective across from me.

It was the middle of July, but the room was cold enough

for a heavy jacket. I clenched my jaw to keep my teeth from chattering and goose bumps covered my arms and legs. I was still wearing my pajamas—a tank top and a thin pair of casual, cotton pajama pants. Reaching for the water he'd placed in front of me, my arm shook so violently that some water spilled on my shirt before I could get it to my lips.

I looked down at my son, who'd been splashed with some water I'd just spilled, wondering what our lives would be like now. I was relieved that we got out of the house alive that night, but also terrified and deeply ashamed. I'd become the stereotypical victim of domestic violence who didn't leave soon enough. With every question, I felt like I needed to wash off judgment and the dirt and grime of sitting in that room.

I knew it would be hard to believe that I stayed because I wanted so badly to keep my family together. I wanted so badly for Joaquin to be the man I'd fallen in love with—the man I'd hoped to raise children and spend the rest of my life with.

'Hold Fast. Stay tough. Don't cry.' I gave myself a pep talk.

I wanted to cry and scream and worried my body language would betray my desire to remain in control. My father always taught me to remain calm. But this outward calm came at an emotional cost. The pain boiled under the surface and the degree of mental and emotional effort it took to suppress it took its toll. These culturally engraved trauma responses, often rooted in generational and historical trauma, are often misunderstood by the person on the receiving end—in this case, Officer Jones.

"As Black folks, we aren't given the luxury of losing our cool," my father told the child version of me.

My father tried to prepare us for a time when we'd have to convince an authority figure of our legitimacy. I needed this police officer to hear me, and I couldn't risk falling apart and not able to tell him what happened that night.

"Can my parents come in here with me," I asked, my voice shaking.

"I'm afraid we can't allow that," Jones responded, now tapping his pen loudly on the table impatiently.

Giving my report would have been a bit easier had the police allowed either of my parents to be present in the interrogation room. Their denial of my request made me feel uneasy.

Prince's diaper was full, and I worried it would soon leak all over my pajamas. I didn't have any backup clothing for either of us and hadn't thought to grab diapers before escaping to safety. I was lucky that Prince had such an easygoing disposition. He never seemed to care about a full diaper. He was the type of child who required me to constantly stick my fingers in his diaper to determine the situation inside. And as we sat there in the freezing cold interrogation room, Prince drifted in and out of sleep with his body curled up under one of my breasts.

I sighed deeply, trying to steady myself so that my voice didn't shake. And I began giving Jones my report.

The weekend began when Joaquin begged me to allow him to take my sister to a rap concert. My sister Lara was 19 years old, and almost as much as a daughter to me as she was my sister. She hated Joaquin and hated rap music. He creeped her out and on the rare occasion that Joaquin agreed to hang out with my family, he'd either picked on her or hadn't bothered to speak to her.

Joaquin continued pushing me for weeks, explaining that

he wanted to do something nice for her so that she wouldn't dislike him so much. I was tired, had just given birth, and wasn't strong enough to stand up to Joaquin. Feeling as though I had no choice, I convinced myself that maybe this concert would allow him to prove to my family that he was a good person. I was thankful that he seemed to *want* to repair things with my family.

"Why didn't your family like him," Jones asked.

"He was always trying to keep me from them, and perhaps his non-conventional appearance was off-putting as well," I responded, not quite sure how to respond or why that was relevant.

Now that Prince was in a deep sleep, I carefully placed him in the infant car seat next to me. Then, I rubbed my hands together trying to generate some heat and clasped them firmly under the table. I wanted this to be over, but I was also terrified that Joaquin would hurt us and wanted the police to know what happened. A million thoughts were running through my head about all the things I'd need to take care of, and I was still trying to process what happened just a couple hours prior. So, I continued . . .

Joaquin insisted that I take the children (his older son Sammy and Prince) with me to my parents' house during the concert. His reasoning for this was that my parents could help me with Prince. In the two weeks since Prince's birth I'd been the only one taking care of him at night, but I didn't fight him or pick at this flawed logic. I was too tired.

The night of the concert, Joaquin didn't answer my calls or text messages and went completely radio silent for hours. My sister came home to my parents' house alone and appeared distraught. She refused to tell me about the evening, and this left me anxious to get back home to ask Joaquin what happened.

Joaquin's older son Sammy, Prince, and I returned to the house. As soon as I settled into the bed to breastfeed Prince, Joaquin paced around us. His nervous tension bothered me, and I wanted him to sit still. I was struggling to keep Prince awake long enough to feed him, and more focused on the tiny baby attached to my breast than anything Joaquin had to say. He pushed me for details on what my sister had told me about the concert. I felt as though he was interrogating me when all I wanted to do was be at peace with my son.

"She didn't tell me anything," I told him.

I was irritated that instead of telling me how the concert was, he was more concerned about what my sister thought of him.

"Why don't *you* tell me how things went?" I turned the questions back on him.

I wanted him to explain what happened. From the way my sister looked when I saw her, in addition to her refusal to talk about it, I assumed that she still hated him. My phone started pinging with text messages, one after another. Joaquin's eyes darted to the phone, asking me who was trying to contact me.

"It's probably my mom," I said casually.

It wasn't out of the ordinary for my mother to text. We were close, and her constant texting didn't seem strange to me at all. Joaquin continued to hover over me and pace at the base of our bed, where his gun was set out in the open. Just as the text messages stopped rolling in, my phone rang. It was my mother.

"Hera, don't tell Joaquin what I am about to say. Just

listen to me. Your father and I are downstairs. Get Prince
and come down and open the door. *Don't* tell Joaquin."

Prince was in a milk-induced sleep on the bed, even
though there was a commotion brewing. I left him to go
downstairs to see what was going on. Joaquin stayed in the
bedroom with Prince.

By the time I got downstairs, Sammy, Joaquin's son,
had already answered the door. He was doing the dishes
when the doorbell rang and seemed just as surprised as I
was to see my parents at the door. Both of my parents
looked as though they were about to tell me someone
had died.

"Where is Prince?" my mom asked frantically.
"He's upstairs. What is going on?" I asked, still calm but
confused. My mother immediately started pushing me and
heading up the stairs.

"We have to get the baby." She was not raising her voice,
odd for my mom given the panicked look on her face.

I felt like a rag doll as she dragged me with her up the
stairs. I wanted to know what the hell was going on, but
clearly neither of my parents felt as though there was time
to explain.

When we got to the bedroom, Joaquin was holding
Prince. The way he looked at us scared me. It was
that look of rage that I had grown to dread. It made me
panic. This time, he was holding my son—my whole heart
—in his hands. My mother went to the side of the bed and
began to scream at Joaquin. She was crying, screaming,
and reaching for Prince. I was in such a fog that I
couldn't understand any of the words coming out of her
mouth. Joaquin started toward my mother as though he
was about to strike her, but

my father walked through the bedroom door just as Joaquin's hand neared her face.

My father's hand was in his pocket. I wasn't sure if he had a gun with him, but it wouldn't have surprised me if he did. It was clear my father intended for Joaquin to believe he was armed. Joaquin knew my father was a gun owner, and he also knew my father would not hesitate to kill him to protect us. When Joaquin's eyes shifted straight to my father's pocket, it was clear that he understood the threat.

* * *

"*Did* your father have a gun with him?" Jones's tone changed.

"No, I don't think so. The only gun I saw tonight was Joaquin's gun," I responded defensively.

* * *

My father calmly told Joaquin to give me the baby and get away from my mother. He insisted that Joaquin comply and told him he would sort it all out later. My father had perfected the ability to stay calm amid true chaos, and this was the epitome of the "Mississippi Black" kind of tough.

"You don't want to cause a scene," my father said, with a dark and menacing look.

Perhaps Joaquin was spooked by my father, because he backed down enough for me to grab Prince. My father's calm demeanor was a stark contrast to my mother's behavior. It was like watching two complete opposite ends of a spectrum, but each of them portrayed a poignant seriousness and immediacy. I struggled to remember whether I had ever seen my parents in this way.

With Prince in my arms, still sleeping peacefully, my

mom pushed me out the bedroom door. I felt like a rag doll, my body flopping as my brain tried to catch up. Without Prince in my arms, I'd have surely collapsed on the floor. Even in the brain fog, I clung to him and knew that my primary job was to keep him safe.

As my mom continued to prod me down the stairs, I kept asking her what was going on. Joaquin and my father followed us down the stairs. Time seemed to move in slow motion. My head darted in every direction, hoping to get some clues from the scene unfolding around me. But there was no time, and my parents weren't willing to have a conversation about it prior to getting Prince and I out the door.

I stopped halfway down the stairs and firmly told my mother I wouldn't move until she told me what was happening.

"He raped your sister, Hera," she said, her voice halfway between a whisper and a scream.

I could tell that she was trying to keep the information from Sammy, who was standing at the bottom of the steps. My mother's eyes appeared a mixture of pain and rage. She's always been a fierce advocate for her children, and I could tell that this rocked her to her core. The glass of my already fragile relationship with Joaquin shattered, and I felt as though I was physically bleeding from the news.

"We have to get out of here. Joaquin is dangerous, and, regardless of what you think, we are *not* going to let you stay here tonight," my mother said.

She'd tried to convince me to leave him several times before, and likely anticipated that I might resist coming with her. I felt as though someone had dumped a pail of ice-cold water on my head while slapping me in the face. I put up with months of abuse from Joaquin, but the knowledge that he would hurt my kid sister in this way revealed a monster to me that I hadn't realized had been there the entire time.

'Run,' was the next and only thought that came into my head. I needed to get my baby out of that house.

"I didn't touch her," Joaquin screamed as he chased us down the stairs.

"Hera, come on. Just talk to me, and I can explain."

'Why is he trying to speak to me after all this,' I thought.

There was no way in hell I was going anywhere with Joaquin alone after hearing that news. The fog that I'd been stuck in for the previous year was lifting, and I was finally able to see Joaquin for the soulless shell of a man he truly was.

My mom left the house first, and my father was beside me. He was keeping an eye on Joaquin. My father was stoic, but I knew there was a fire of rage burning inside of him just by the look in his dark and menacing eyes. He didn't move his gaze away from Joaquin. Just as I crossed the threshold of the front door, directly behind my father, Joaquin grabbed my arm. I fell backward. He pulled me back into the house, and I fought to stay close to the doorway. I was holding Prince, who was now awake and crying.

"Let go, Joaquin. Let me go." I screamed, shaking.

"Prince is staying with me," Joaquin said, now showing me his gun.

The closer I got to the door, the harder he squeezed on my arm and the closer the gun came to my skull.

I glanced over Joaquin's shoulder to see Sammy. I wanted to take him with us. Sammy looked panicked, too, as though he was waiting for an invitation to leave with us. I gestured for him to come, but Joaquin quickly reminded me that Sammy was not my son. Leaving him broke my heart, but I had to choose: try to save both children, risking them both—or leave with my legal son, in hopes that I could at least save one of them. Taking Sammy would have made me a kidnapper, and I knew his rescue would be short-lived. One of the most painful moments of my life was having to leave him behind.

"Now, Son, we talked about this. You don't want this kind of problem," my father warned, his southern drawl only slightly coming to the surface.

Joaquin's dark eyes returned to my father's pocket. He shifted his weight from one leg to the next, a nervous tick that I'd seen several times in the months leading up to this night. When he rocked back and forth, it seemed as though he was trying to keep himself from become unhinged. He hesitated, appearing to ponder his chances in a fight with my father as we waited.

"Fine, go," he said to me, "but I'll find you, and kill you—just like I killed Shawn."

I was momentarily stunned and paralyzed in the doorway. Shaking my head as though to jolt myself out of shock, I stumbled backward through the open doorway and ran into the night.

Chapter 2

Get Off the X

Before I met Joaquin, I was trained to determine whether someone was lying. I was 25 years old when I joined the Central Intelligence Agency. In training, we were taught that when we were "in the red zone" we needed to constantly be aware that threats to our life could come at any moment. When our lives were threatened, we were told that it wasn't our job to engage the threat. Our job was to get off the "X" and survive to report about it. We weren't soldiers—we were Intelligence Officers. A red zone sometimes meant that you were in enemy territory, but it could also mean that you were in a place that wasn't familiar. Even with all this training, I didn't consider that I could ever be in a red zone in my own home.

On my 28th birthday, I took a trip from Brasilia to Rio de Janeiro. I'd signed up for the 2008 Rio de Janeiro half-marathon on my birthday. A friend of mine who worked at the U.S. Consulate in Rio took me to dinner, along with another couple we knew, after my race.

We weren't close friends, but I was grateful for his friendship. He was one of the few other single Americans I knew in Brazil, and we always had a lot of fun together. Despite several uncomfortable moments when I suspected he might have been trying to turn our friendship into something romantic, I'd firmly placed him in the friend zone. Despite not being physically attracted to him, he was kind and intelligent. But at the time, kind and intelligent was not enough for me to risk a friendship over.

We decided to venture away from the touristy strip of Rio to try out a hole in the wall restaurant in an area none of us were familiar with. Though we'd all been trained on how to stay safe in a foreign country, we broke a cardinal rule on the trip home. Instead of calling a driver we knew, we decided to hail a taxi from the street. We'd all had a few drinks, and none of us thought twice about the dangers this posed.

The driver was relatively quiet at first. My guy friend and the other couple were staying several miles north of my hotel, and their places came up first along the route. The driver encouraged us to have him drop off everyone else first and promised to bring me to my hotel after dropping off the others. My legs throbbed in pain from the race earlier that day, so walking back to my hotel from my friend's apartment wasn't an option.

As soon as they all got out of the taxi, the driver locked the doors and sped off. At first, I wondered if he was just in a hurry. I actively shook my head to try to force myself to think clearly enough to process what was happening. He hadn't been in a hurry to drop off everyone else, so clearly something was amiss.

"*Onde voce vai?*" Where are you going? I asked him in my best attempt at a Brazilian accent.

"*Meu hotel esta na praia.*" My hotel was on Copacabana beach, and the driver was driving in the opposite direction.

"*Eu nao sabe d'onde sh'ta!*" He was screaming that he didn't know where Copacabana was, ridiculous given that it was arguably the beach with the most hotels in Rio.

He had a thick Carioca accent, which made his Portuguese more difficult for me to understand.

"*Me deixe aqui!*" I screamed, asking him to just drop me off, now raising my voice and starting to panic.

The driver was no longer stopping for stop signs and traffic lights. I needed to get out, and to get off the "X." He wasn't going to let me out willingly, so I had to act swiftly. The doors were locked, and he was driving fast. I grabbed one of my Nine West black pumps, which thankfully had enough of a heel to be useful and broke the window. The glass shattered all over me.

For a split-second, I thought about how painful it was going to be to climb out of this shattered window. Then I remembered that the alternative was being hauled off to a Brazilian favela and raped or killed. As soon as the driver was forced to slow down in traffic, I jumped out the window and rolled onto the street.

Almost immediately after my bloodied body hit the pavement, I started running. I now had one shoe on, leaving me lopsided, as I didn't have time to stop and search for the other shoe. I quickly pulled off the remaining shoe while continuing to run down the street. I ran three miles back to my hotel. When I arrived at the JW Marriott, thankful that

I had stayed at an American hotel chain, I collapsed on the lobby floor.

I was confident enough in my career to meet strangers in hotel rooms for intelligence debriefs, recruit foreigners to betray their country for America, and jump out of a moving cab to save myself. I was living a double life. At work, I was a fierce and passionate woman. In the office, I didn't have a problem speaking up. I was wildly confident about my intelligence and abilities in my professional persona. When it came to my relationships, I was not the same woman. I was submissive, silent, painfully self-conscious, and terrified of being rejected.

When I returned from Brazil, I was 29 years old. I don't regret the experience I had living and working abroad but traveling alone and living in a five-bedroom luxury apartment was lonely. By the time I returned, I was ready to stop traveling as much and establish roots in one place.

"You hold the women in your life to a way higher standard than the men you date," my friend Tracy said to me one evening over a bottle of wine, shortly after I returned from Brazil.

Tracy and I met in fourth grade. She was often brutally honest, which sometimes got her into trouble in middle school when she would inform someone that they had gained a few too many pounds or tell people their outfit didn't quite match. While her personality was off at times, I could count on her to tell me things others would be too afraid to say. She was also the type of person who never seemed very concerned with how her words cut.

I sat silently sipping my wine as she continued to chastise me for putting up with complete bullshit from the men in my life.

"No, I don't," I retorted.

I knew she was right, but I was so ashamed that I was unwilling to own this truth.

I didn't put up with any bullshit from people outside of romantic relationships. My tendency to drop friends frequently when they threw up red flags of bad behavior wasn't true for the men in my life. Though there was truth in her words, her comments hurt. I felt emotionally naked and physically curled into myself as she spoke.

I was almost 30 years old, and I still hadn't experienced *real* love in a romantic relationship. Though I'd been in several long-term relationships, but none of them were particularly healthy. They all eventually came to painful endings when I realized that the other person didn't love me as much as I loved them. This long string of failed relationships left me feeling undesirable—unlovable.

When I was in my mid-twenties, I met a man I was sure would eventually be my husband. I loved him so much that the thought of us not being together physically hurt. After dating for two years, I started talking to him about how I was ready to get married. I dreamed of my wedding day, and I longed to have a family of my own. I thought he wanted this, too, but one autumn morning I learned we had two completely different understandings of how our lives would continue.

We were at brunch in Adams Morgan, a trendy neighborhood in Washington, D.C., when we saw two children playing on the sidewalk while their parents waited for the hostess to call their name. I looked at the children and smiled, excited that someday I would be a mother and get to experience that type of joy.

My boyfriend said, "Ugh, aren't you glad we don't have kids?"

My heart dropped, and with it came my jaw.

"What do you mean . . . aren't I glad?" I asked, now steaming with anger.

He dropped this significant bomb too late into our relationship. And this relationship was a clear example of how I projected love, safety, and happiness onto the man I was with. His comments made it clear that he didn't see this relationship as I did. But for too long, I'd assumed we felt the same way about our future.

He went on to explain that he felt as though children didn't fit into his lifestyle. They were messy and required too much attention. I probed him further, only to learn that he never wanted marriage or children at all.

"Why didn't you tell me this two years ago?" I asked him.

I often spoke about how I wanted children, and I wondered how he could have missed that fact about me.

"Well, I just assumed that we would one day break up, and then you would have children with someone else," he said casually, in complete disregard for the woman who was now sitting in front of him crying.

I was temporary to him, and he had no remorse for wasting the time I could have spent on finding someone who wanted to be with me forever.

I wish I could say that I left him at the restaurant that morning and got on with the rest of my life, but I didn't. I sat there through brunch in silence as he talked to me like we hadn't just come to a crossroads in our relationship. He moved to Florida a few months later, and to no one's surprise he didn't propose before he left.

Just after I returned from Brazil, I ran into him in the building where I worked. As soon as our eyes met in the hallway, I pondered whether it was too late to run in the opposite direction. Seeing him reminded me of how in love with him I had once been, how heartbroken I was when he didn't choose me, and how even years later it seemed as painful as the last day I saw him. It was too late. The moment I stood there gave him time to recognize me. He ran over and hugged me. As soon as his arms wrapped around me, I stiffened up. I hated him now. Realizing I wasn't returning the enthusiasm of his hug, he quickly stepped back and awkwardly smiled.

"Hera, it's so nice to see you," he said with a toothy grin.

I stood there awkwardly, praying that my fake smile hid the pain I felt deep in my gut.

"I've wanted to tell you that my relationship with you made me a better man," He uttered, seemingly completely unaware of how his words cut me like a sharp sushi knife.

As I stood there, rooted in the ground and unable to force myself to politely excuse myself, he continued to tell me about his wife and son. It was his belief that our relationship was the impetus for more adulting and helped him realize how important it was for him to marry.

It's not often that I am at a loss for words, but in this moment, I truly had none. I simply turned and walked away, leaving my pride and what was left of my broken heart on the marble floor of the building's main foyer. I imagined myself slapping the smile off his face as I walked away.

Shaking my head, I felt like a complete idiot for having allowed myself to fall in love with a man who had a naked picture of himself hanging on the wall above his bed.

Feeling like an old maid was an irrational fear, but it

consumed a lot of my energy at the time. The desire to be loved the way I was capable of loving and my need to be truly cared for in a romantic partnership was palpable. I wish I could go back in time and shake some sense into that version of myself. I'd tell her she had time, and to stop settling for the men who were like undesirable public bathroom stalls. She deserved so much better than she thought she did.

Chapter 3

Perfect Target

Click—click—swipe left—swipe left—swipe right.

Internet dating wasn't popular back in 2010. Sure, lots of people were doing it, but nobody wanted to admit they were. It wasn't like today where there are dating apps for just about every category from religious affiliation to racial preferences. In Washington, D.C., the traditional, old-school style of dating where you'd strike up a conversation with a potential mate at the grocery store or the local coffee spot was tough. A transient city where people are always busy and reaching for the next career milestone, I just wasn't meeting anyone.

When I first signed up for a dating website, I felt as though I'd hit rock bottom. Back then, apps weren't as prevalent as they are now so signing up meant creating an elaborate profile on the website. If someone messaged you through the site, you'd get the message through your email prompting you to go check the dating site to respond.

With a glass of red wine in hand, I thought, 'Damn, Hera, I cannot believe it has come to this. It's like you are mail ordering a husband.'

The full-bodied wine wasn't bold enough to disguise the anxiety pit in my stomach over this entire process. Despite the commercial attempts to make online dating seem popular, there seemed to be a palpable shame associated with having to resort to the internet to find a man. And no matter how much I tried to convince myself this was the way people dated, I remained deeply embarrassed that I hadn't just been able to meet someone in college, at work, or strolling the aisles of the grocery stores.

I'd waited patiently for Mr. Right, but he hadn't been hanging out at the grocery store waiting to chat with me in the cheese aisle or walking his dog in my neighborhood ready to strike up a friendly conversation. I wasn't ready to accept that I wasn't going to have my own fairy tale and going online felt like the furthest thing from a romantic story. It felt like I was giving up on traditional love, but the horror I felt at the thought of being single forever (and never having children) was motivation enough to try. My biological clock was ticking so loudly that I could just about hear it ringing in my ears every damn day.

In the initial few days, I had a handful of matches. Some of them I immediately ruled out for either being shorter than me (5'6" and under), scary looking, or having no picture at all. I hoped that I would be less vain, but I kept thinking, 'If I am not even mildly attracted to this guy in a picture, there is a low probability that we will vibe in person.'

It also continues to amaze me the number of men who

post selfies next to urinals in public bathrooms, but I digress. I continued to read through the personal profiles of the men who Match.com, praying I'd find someone interesting enough to date.

As the weeks wore on, I got more comfortable with the idea as I saw several attractive guys, but the process was tedious. I felt like I was searching for a tiny needle in a haystack of weirdness. The string of dates before I met Joaquin were particularly terrible, and in hindsight even comical:

- The Racist Drunk, who had seven drinks within the first thirty minutes of our date. Clearly toasted drunk, he shared with me that he was disappointed upon meeting me because he had assumed I was white from my pictures. He wasn't attracted to Black women.

- The Handsy Man who made me feel like a prostitute. Despite his grammatically correct profile, he didn't speak a lick of English. He also had such a problem keeping his hands to himself that I made up an excuse to flee from the date.

- The Baby Mama Seeker seemed to have promise in the beginning. Then the date turned into an awkward interview about how many babies I'd be willing to give him.

- The Gigolo, who initially seemed to have promise. The first date went well with lots of laughing and talking. On the second date, however, it became clear that he was more interested in having his first sexual experience with a black woman than pursuing a meaningful relationship.

By the time I met Joaquin, I was exhausted and close to giving up on Internet dating. It was turning into that part-time job I dreaded, and I didn't think I could handle many more epic failures. I met Joaquin on Valentine's Day week in 2010. The Washington, D.C. area was in the middle of "Snowmaggedon," a storm so big the city affectionately gave it its own name. Snowmageddon dumped several feet of snow on my broke city, which caused the city's small snowplow budget to dry up before my street was plowed. I had serious cabin fever. I was so desperate for human interaction, and coffee, that I walked a mile in thirty inches of snow just to get coffee and chat face to face with another human.

After being stuck in the house for several days, with only the one venture outside for coffee, I went Online to check my email. I noticed a message that came from a profile I hadn't viewed. Joaquin hadn't included any pictures, which would explain why I hadn't come across his profile first. He also claimed to be 26, which put him outside of the dating range I had specified (28-35). In his email, he said that if I was interested, he would send me a picture upon request. I was bored and figured I would at least check out a picture of him since he was brave enough to initiate contact.

There were several things about Joaquin's profile that should've struck me as strange. For one, he claimed to be the opening act for several popular musicians, but he was nowhere to be found Online. In particular, he bragged about how he would be opening for Jay Z at the Verizon center a few weeks after we first spoke. I had a lot of time on my hands that weekend, so after viewing his initial pictures I was intrigued enough to begin an email conversation:

"Cute pictures, but why do you keep your hair so long?" I asked.

"Wow, I guess it's an image thing . . . but thanks for the compliment," he replied.

"So why are you on match.com? Isn't it a little weird meeting folks this way?" I was still self-conscious about resorting to online dating myself, and one of my first questions was always why someone decided to try it.

"Yes sweetie, it is hard as hell. My good friend and publicist met her husband online, so this was more her idea than mine, but I figured what it gonna hurt?"

"So, you are only 26 and you already have a child? How old is he, and do you have a relationship with him?" I hadn't considered dating someone with a child before, and this was a topic I wanted to dig into immediately to determine what kind of father he was.

"My son is eight and I have full custody, but don't you think this is something we should be talking about in person? So why online for you?"

Even over email, it appeared as though I'd struck a nerve with my question about his son. Since I didn't have a child, nor had I ever dated someone with one, I worried that I was being insensitive with my direct line of questioning.

While I didn't have the backstory of how Joaquin ended up a single parent, the fact that he was raising his son alone gave him some legitimacy in my mind. I wasn't used to seeing men parent alone, so I made a lot of assumptions about how Joaquin was as a man because he had custody. I assumed that parents who were unfit automatically lost their children.

Trying to lighten the email exchange a bit, I responded.

"LOL, but yeah, I ask about your son because I am curious. I'm trying online because I want to meet folks that I don't meet in my normal circles. I'm not a fan of clubs, nor would I want to meet someone in a bar that I was at all serious about. Soulmates are still something I believe in, and I guess I just am not sure I will meet him just out and about."

I was sharing too much and immediately felt the need to defend why I was online dating, as though the man I was talking to hadn't *also* been on match.com.

After I revealed that I was searching for my soulmate via email, Joaquin asked if we could talk on the phone. He told me that he was searching for the same thing I was, and that he was excited to hear my voice. Joaquin was skilled at mirroring—everything I said I wanted, he also mentioned wanting. When I would tell him what I wanted from a relationship, he would explain that he wanted the same. When I would tell him a story about how a relationship had gone wrong, he would immediately follow it up with a story that sounded almost the same.

Being bored, and still stuck inside, I entertained a phone call and tried to keep an open mind. Chatting on the phone with someone who hadn't included a picture in his profile was typically something I wouldn't do. I always felt that if I was brave enough to share my picture, the men should too. But from the initial messaging back and forth, I was curious to know more about him.

From that initial back and forth, there was something about conversation with him early on that felt easy. Though he was careful about certain topics, like his son, words used to flow with him, and he always seemed to have a some-what plausible response to everything I questioned. He was engaged and confident in a way that many of the men I was meeting weren't.

Typically, I'd match with someone and after it was clear the only messages the person was capable of sending were things like "good morning" and "how was your weekend", the conversation would die a painfully, silent death.

While Joaquin offered to send photos in his first email, and almost immediately sent some after I responded. Most people dating online are putting themselves out there with a photo in their profile: they should be able to expect this of their potential dates as well.

Pro tip daters: If a person doesn't show clear (and recent)pictures of themself with their true name attached, there are several things to be aware of. They could be married, dating several people serially, cat fishing, or they don't want previous victims of whatever nefarious behavior they are trying to perpetrate to identify and flag their profile.

Roughly five minutes after I emailed Joaquin my phone number, he called. In those first interactions, it was as though he was anxiously awaiting my response to his next move because there was hardly ever a period of lag time between when I would respond to him and when he would send addi-tional communication.

"So why is someone like you are dating Online?" He asked.

If I was confident about my decision to date this way, maybe I wouldn't have been so pained by this question. I thought I'd answered this during our email exchange, and this follow-up seemed almost a dig. It reminded me of the times I had been questioned about my relationship status by my coworkers at the U.S. Embassy in Brazil. Several of them thought that the fact that I was in my late 20s, and still single, an appropriate topic for lunch or casual office chatter.

"Well, you're dating online, right? What does that say about you?" I fired the questions back.

From the first phone conversation, Joaquin was an amazing storyteller. He could go on and on for hours about his internet business, career aspirations, and his "budding" music career. The passion in his voice when he talked about his dreams was contagious. I didn't question his authenticity because he seemed to have a story and an explanation for everything. He spoke as though he knew exactly what he wanted out of life, and he was successfully pursuing his dreams. Chatting with him on the phone offered me an interesting escape from snowstorm television binging. I was surprised that I was able to spend hours on the phone with a stranger.

As soon as the streets cleared, we agreed to meet in person at a shopping mall in Virginia. The mall was about six miles from where I lived in Washington, DC. As I walked into the mall, I was nervous. Taking deep breaths to calm down, I called my friend Lisa for moral support as I waited.

"I don't think I can handle more of these bad dates, Lisa," I complained as I stood and watched the door.

Every time a man about 5'9" walked in, I would search his face to see if he could be Joaquin. Lisa told me that I needed to relax and just have fun. I was pacing and, in my head, hoping he was the same person as I saw in the picture, and I'd spoken to on the phone.

While still on the phone with Lisa, I spotted Joaquin walking through the door, and I panicked. He only vaguely looked like the pictures he had sent.

"Oh my gosh Lisa, something isn't right. He's here, but he doesn't really look like the pictures. He looks almost like a different person—or maybe just older?!"

I was word vomiting into the phone, and Lisa told me that if it didn't feel right, I should just turn in the other direction and walk away. As soon as I picked my jaw off the ground and pondered that as an option, he caught my eye and started walking toward me. No, not walking—waddling. His pants were about three or four sizes too large, and the crotch hung so low that he appeared to just rock side to side as if struggling to walk correctly.

"Oh no, he just spotted me. I gotta go."

I got off the phone with Lisa. He caught me standing there, and my Christian guilt made me freeze as though my feet were permanently welded onto the marble floor. The first thing I noticed was his hair. It was a little past his shoulders, shoe polish-like jet black, and bone straight, as though he had run a flat iron through it one too many times. He was so pale that I could see his veins in his forehead. His coloring was like a vampire, and the overall appearance sent chills down my spine.

He walked with a limp that reminded me of a character out of a low budget 1990s gangster movie. I'd had such a good conversation with him on the phone during the storm, and this false sense of closeness made me feel as though I owed him this date. I internally scolded myself for judging him on the way he looked. I was always taught not to judge someone based on their appearance. What confused me about this common Christian teaching was that what it really meant was not to judge someone based on physical attractiveness. There was nothing in Christian teachings, though, that would have scolded me for being frightened by someone's off-putting appearance. Joaquin's basic features were not what made him unsettling: it was the entire package that seemed off.

I wanted to be nice, and instead of protecting myself, I was more overcome by the guilt I would feel if I chose to walk away. My gut told me to run. I didn't listen to my gut.

"Why do you keep your hair so long?" I blurted out almost immediately as I walked up to him.

As soon as the question came out, I wanted to stuff it back inside my mouth. I had already asked this question over email but hadn't been completely satisfied with his answer. His hair was so shocking; I was completely caught off guard.

"Wow, you're direct," he said, "It's part of my image, and I am not allowed to cut it because it is written into my contract with the record label that I keep it this long."

He'd said this before, but the in-person version was so shocking that I couldn't stop the words from leaking out of my mouth.

"That doesn't make any sense. I can't imagine a record label being able to dictate how you wear your hair," I said.

What I wanted to say was that I couldn't imagine anyone would insist that he keep his hair looking like that, instead of a style that looked a bit more mainstream. I didn't know anything about the music industry and shrugged his statement off as something I might not understand as an outsider.

As he continued to talk, his appearance didn't match how he presented himself verbally. His confident presence made him intriguing. I searched his face, trying to boil away the strange costume he was wearing. He had on gray sweatpants that were so baggy the cuffs folded over his timberland boots and dragged on the ground. He wore a baggy t-shirt over the top of the sweatpants, and a black leather jacket that would have fit someone well over six feet who weighed about 300 pounds. Only about 5'9" and no more than 160 pounds fully clothed with boots and all, I strained to imagine what he really looked like under all those oversized clothes.

Just like on the phone, he was different, and I was drawn to learning about him and why his appearance didn't seem to match the person I'd spent hours with on the phone.

There was a strange sadness in his eyes, and he looked at me with an intensity that I had never felt before. His gaze seemed to look into my soul. Despite his extremely off-putting first impression—there was an energy about him that felt almost addictive. I wanted to hear more of his stories because listening to them felt like I was listening to a movie.

We decided to go have lunch, and while he was free with his stories and his flattery—his attention was focused on me. He hung onto my every word as I shared with him what had brought me to online date. His gaze made me feel comfortable, and nearly as suddenly as I had panicked over his appearance, I relaxed in a way that I hadn't with anyone else. His jet-black eyes reflected the light of the room. He stared at me without looking away as he listened to me explain what I was looking for in a relationship. He continued to mirror my words back to me, convincing me that we were looking for the exact same things. Almost as quickly as I panicked about his initial appearance, his charm relaxed me and caused me to push my initial impression of him to the back of my thoughts.

I was surprised at how easily conversation flowed between us. We laughed through animated descriptions of the horrible Internet-generated dates we'd been on. Joaquin described one date that gave me the misconception that we shared similar morals. He explained how one woman he dated admitted to him that she used the money her parents gave her for college to get breast implants.

"If she treated her own parents that way, I was worried about how she would treat me," Joaquin said.

As he finished his story, I casually glanced at my watch. The waitress started hanging around our table like a buzzard waiting to swoop down and eat a dead animal. She was probably frustrated that we were staying so long and wanted to close out the tab, so she could go home. We completely lost track of time. I was shocked that this man who had creeped me out only a few hours earlier was someone I wanted to keep hanging out with.

Walking to our cars, we discussed where we could go next. I suggested we go to Washington, DC because that was back in the direction I loved. While this particular mall was only a 20-minute drive from my house, I hated Northern Virginia. It was stale, suburban, and lacked the vibrant life that DC had to offer. I also wanted to be closer to home if the date was going to carry on into the evening because I worried the streets would ice over after dark.

"I can't go to DC." Joaquin looked concerned at the prospect of having to cross the border into DC.

I immediately wondered if I made a mistake about him, and worried he was about to tell me he was running from the police in the district.

He gestured toward his car and explained that he carried a weapon. In Virginia, he had a carry permit. He was not allowed to carry in DC. My gut told me to stay away from him, but, for the second time that day, I ignored it. There was nothing wrong with this, I thought. Then, I tried to rationalize this strange explanation. My dad had guns, and he was normal—he was not a murderer. Owning guns doesn't make someone a killer, but I wondered why someone who was not carrying a weapon for work would carry one around in his car. I also wondered what circumstances would prompt anyone to obtain a concealment permit.

Confined to Northern Virginia if we were going to continue with the date, we drove separately to a nearby bowling alley. The bowling alley was crowded, so as we waited, we sat on the sidelines and continued to talk. I teased him about his singing career and told him that if he was really a famous singer, he should have no problem showing me his skills in the middle of the crowded bowling alley.

His eyes darted around the room, and he hesitated for a moment before clearing his throat loudly. To my surprise, he started singing loudly. As the terribly off-key notes came out of his mouth, I smiled awkwardly and shifted in my seat. I was both embarrassed and regretful that I asked, but also amazed at his strange confidence. He sang an obscure song from a popular boy band that I recognized—claiming he wrote it. A fact that would have been easily discovered as false with a simple internet search. I wanted to believe him. If I wasn't already hooked by his intense gaze and lavish demonstrations of attention and affection, this entire scene would have been creepy.

After he was finished singing, he looked at me intensely. He expected a compliment.

A few moments of awkward silence . . .

"Wow," I muttered.

It was the only thing my brain would allow me to utter. My polite side was shoving a sock in the mouth of my honest side. More awkward staring. The look of confusion on his face showed that my facial expression was betraying polite.

"I, um, well that was impressive." I was referring to his confidence.

I shrugged off the lack of talent, thinking that maybe voice machines had gotten to the point where they could just completely change someone's voice. I was impressed that he was brave enough to get up in front of a large crowd and sing, especially since he didn't sound amazing. I was also flattered that he would do this simply because I had asked.

After bowling, we finally went our separate ways after almost six hours together. Driving home, I should have been focused on the icy roads through the pot-holed streets of DC. Instead, I was more focused on how that date made me feel. I hadn't been looked at the way he looked at me in my entire life. His eyes pierced my skin, and it felt as though I was being stripped naked with just his simple gaze. I felt vulnerable, and scared.

Though uneasy, there was also something about his attention that was intoxicating. Instead of butterflies, I felt as though bats were flying around in the pit of my stomach. Part of the reason I struggled to pay attention to the road that night was that I kept trying to determine what about Joaquin made me like him so much. Upon first gaze he had scared me, but I quickly ignored my gut and gave him a chance. As soon as he turned on the charm, it was as though he had put me under a spell. I was hooked in a way that I didn't understand.

Falling for someone isn't supposed to be scary. It isn't supposed to hurt, be traumatic, or be emotionally painful. I didn't know that when I met Joaquin. I confused his intensity as chemistry, though it was more likely that he had found an attractive target.

Chapter 4

The Great Resignation

Two weeks after the Snowmageden of 2010, I resigned from the CIA. Two weeks before my resignation, I was sitting at my computer on what seemed a usual day on the Langley compound. I was writing up an in-depth report and had spent the last few hours completely engulfed in my notes from the meeting that had generated the report. A message popped up on my screen, interrupting my focus.

"Did you see that agency wide notice that just went out?" Samuel, a coworker, and friend typed.

"Um, no . . . I am crashing on this report that I need to finish by close of business," I responded.

"I think you need to take a look at it," Samuel said.

"Dude, just tell me what it says. I only have a couple of hours before I need to get this thing out," I sighed exasperated.

"There was a terrorist attack in Khost, Afghanistan. One of our classmates was killed," He typed.

I stared at my screen for several minutes. I wasn't sure I wanted to know who it was who had died. The realization that it could have been any of us was terrifying.

"Hello?" Samuel typed.

"Sorry, I just . . . do you know any more information?" I asked.

"It was Elizabeth," Samuel responded.

Elizabeth had slept in the bunk bed three feet away from mine in the barracks during paramilitary training. She wasn't in my platoon, but when she saw that I was struggling with weapons training, she offered to help me practice so that I could pass the test.

Her death made me re-evaluate my future with the agency. I was tired of being lonely, and life in the CIA left me feeling like a United States Government investment rather than a person that was truly valued. I was still wildly patriotic, which my service had been unable to beat out of me, but I wanted more for my future than the lonely life of being a single Case Officer could provide.

Taking the job with a defense contractor was my first step out of what felt like a career and life trap. As a Case Officer, being always "on" but never able to truly be myself was the norm. So many parts of my life were in compartments that no longer seemed healthy. Many of the friends I'd made in the service I'd have to walk by in public without acknowledging.

But in many ways, moving to a defense contractor was like being horseshoed back to that life. With a resume that didn't make sense to most people outside the intelligence world, making connections inside the agency building was one of the few obvious ways out. Once the defense contractor discovered my intelligence training, the interview was simply a formality.

In the month it took for my paperwork to process, I had ample time to spend getting to know Joaquin. We'd find a way to grab food together in between commitments, and he'd talk about how, even though he was busy with work and taking care of his son, he wanted to make time for me.

He invited me to one of his favorite restaurants, an old Diner, which caused me to tease him mercilessly. It was hardly my definition of fine dining. On this day, I felt as though I'd walked into a country western movie, and I was one of the main characters. As soon as we walked in the restaurant, it seemed as though all conversation stopped, and everyone turned to stare at us as we walked to our seats.

The town he lived in was not diverse. We were the only two people under the age of 65 at the restaurant. We were also the only non-white patrons in the establishment that day. Joaquin was pale enough to occasionally pass for white, but if you looked closely, you could tell he was Puerto Rican. Bristow, VA, is considered a suburb of Washington, D.C., but though its only about an hour away from the city—it felt like a different world culturally.

Washington, D.C., was an educated, socially conscious, bustling city. In D.C. you could walk into any restaurant and hear diverse and passionate political conversation. As a Black woman, walking on the streets of D.C., I was comfortable. Nobody looked twice at me in a suit, because being an educated Black woman with a job wasn't an anomaly. In Bristow, things seemed to move at a slower pace. You were more likely to hear a conversation about the cattle on someone's farm, or the new development that had been built up on Mr. Jones's old land, than anything political in nature. It wasn't everyday folks in Joaquin's neighborhood saw a Black person, let alone one wearing a suit.

At the time, I assumed people were staring because we looked different from the demographic that typically hung out at this restaurant. Looking back, I wonder if it was simply that we didn't look like we belonged together. I looked professional, headed to a work meeting. He was dressed in baggy clothes, still easily four sizes too big for him, and had a dew rag wrapped around his greasy, jet-black hair. His hair was uniformly dark and appeared over-processed.

Despite the attention we were getting, it wasn't hard to focus my attention on our table. Joaquin spoke to me as though I was the only person in the room. He made it feel like the world was disappearing around me. We had strange yet riveting conversations, ranging from me picking fun at his hair to the definition of bisexuality. He made me laugh, and I was intrigued by his experiences and stories. No matter how crazy the story sounded, he always made it seem as though it had happened.

During brunch, he showed me a picture of his son. Sammy was a gorgeous kid, with warm brown skin—big black curls—big brown eyes and dimples when he smiled. My heart melted every time Joaquin talked about him. I loved children, and while I hadn't considered dating someone who had a child before, I never worried that I would have a hard time loving a child who was not biologically my own. Since I hadn't had any experience in Family Court, I assumed that if a parent had custody, then that would mean the courts vetted the parent thoroughly.

"Where is your son's mother?" I asked innocently.

I assumed I would hear that they shared custody, and

maybe a small tidbit about why their relationship hadn't worked out. The question seemed natural, given that we were already on the topic of his son. As I waited for an answer, Joaquin shifted uncomfortably in his seat.

"Sweetie, that is a little personal for this stage in our relationship, don't you think?" he retorted.

I cringed when he called me "sweetie," but wasn't yet ready to tell him how much I hated that word.

"No, I don't, actually. I think it's a natural question, as it takes two people to have a child." I was stunned at his defensive response.

Joaquin began to rock back and forth in his chair and quickly deflected the question by saying that she was out of the picture. There was more to this story, but I let it go because clearly this topic was a sore spot for him.

Later that day, I was going to visit a high school friend in Texas. Joaquin and I knew we wouldn't see each other for weeks, so in the empty parking lot of the Old Diner, we said our goodbyes. He pulled me close to him. I put my arms around him and under his jacket. It was so cold we could see our breath in the air, but we held each other tight, looked into each other's eyes, and shared a passionate kiss. Then, he noted that he had to run back inside to grab something he had forgotten. I got in my car and drove away.

Joaquin called me ten minutes after I left, claiming that everyone in the restaurant told him that we looked like a couple that had been together for years. He went on and on about how the older people in the restaurant told him that it appeared as though our love was meant to last. According to Joaquin, several people had watched us through the window. He was proud, but this entire story made me uncomfortable. We hadn't been dating that long, and there was something a bit unsettling about strangers staring at us through the window of that old Diner.

At the time, I believed that what he told me was the truth. Learning that most of it was not likely true almost makes it more impressive because he was so convincing. He could talk for hours about his concerts and the celebrities he opened for. One time, he answered the phone and claimed a popular musician was on the other line. Joaquin proceeded to carry on an hour-long, one-way conversation with himself while I sat on the couch nearby.

At first, there was something that seemed incredibly refreshing about Joaquin. I previously dated the ivy league graduate who dressed in a suit, who had a stereotypical cookie cutter job. I was attracted to what Joaquin presented as an entrepreneurial spirit, and I never felt as though he was trying to show off his intelligence. I was more intelligent, more educated, and came from more opportunity than Joaquin. These were facts that we never fought about. He would ask for me to help him edit things, and he initially appeared to respect my intelligence. Being with Joaquin allowed me to feel like when I left work, I could completely turn it off. He had no experience with my line of work. Instead of bringing home stress from work, I left it at the office because telling him about it would just confuse him.

I met his 10-year-old son a couple months after we started dating. Initially Joaquin told me he was 8, but his son later corrected him. I continued to press Joaquin for more information on his son's mother. It was clear that he never talked about nor visited her. Sammy also never spoke to me about his mother. After I made it clear that I wasn't going to let the question about Sammy's mother go, Joaquin told me she died in a car accident, and I had no other data points to believe any other version of the story.

I loved children, and Sammy was initially easy for me to deal with, though I was suddenly thrust into the role of mother to a child I barely knew. Joaquin kept him in the house and discouraged him from going outside to play. Joaquin claimed to be wildly protective over his son, but his involvement in his son's life seemed to taper drastically after I became involved. After only a few months of dating, I was the person who fielded all the calls and emails from Sammy's teachers, and Joaquin began expecting me to shuttle Sammy to all his activities.

Just as I started to feel as though I was being taken advantage of, Joaquin started talking about marriage. He professed his love and often told me that he didn't think he could live without me. My relationship with Sammy started to change as well. I fell into a parental role quickly cooking meals, helping with homework, and trying to bring Sammy out of his shell.

I noticed that Joaquin got angry at Sammy for things that seemed silly, and I started feeling intensely protective over him. If Sammy didn't respond to a question the way that Joaquin wanted, he would scream at him. If he was supposed to be practicing piano and stopped for any reason, it was cause for punishment. It began to make sense why Sammy lied about things at school. His lies seemed to come from a place of fear, because Joaquin never seemed satisfied with his achievements. Since Joaquin was often disengaged from what happened at school, his son usually got away with withholding the truth. This was especially true since it appeared that Joaquin was perfectly comfortable with the women in his life taking responsibility for his son's education.

"I guess I should start saying I love you now, huh?" Sammy said to me one evening as I was making dinner.

The statement shocked me, and I was initially not sure how to respond. Love should never be something a person feels entitled to—it must be earned.

"No, you should never feel as though you have to say that to anyone, Sammy. I wouldn't want you to say that to me unless you felt like you did. Please don't feel like you have to force that feeling just because me and your father are together." Sammy thanked me, smiled, and then walked away.

He came back a few minutes later, popping his head through the doorway.

"Hera, I like you. A lot. You're nice to me, and I hope you stay."

As he walked out, I recognized that despite my irritation with the sudden responsibility Joaquin required of me, I had grown to really like Sammy, too.

That summer I spent with Joaquin, he spent money as though he made millions. He had a huge five-bedroom house, an expensive luxury SUV, and I saw him pay $10,000 for a home entertainment center during one unplanned trip to an electronic store. The very next week after the entertainment center purchase, he bought $15,000 worth of studio equipment for his in-home recording studio.

"What do you think about the new television?" Joaquin asked, looking for validation.

The sour face I made was hard to hide, never having been good at 'fixing my face'. I didn't feel comfortable offering him advice on how he should be spending his money, because I still hadn't seen where the money was coming from. I had no idea how much money he made.

Having not spent the kind of money he spent in a day since the down payment on my condominium, which was close to the amount he spent in the store that day, who was I to comment on this type of casual purchase.

"Well, I don't spend the kind of money you do. I don't even make that much in a month," I responded.

Joaquin's face lit up. This seemed to be exactly what he wanted to hear from me. Breathing a sigh of relief, I was glad he wasn't looking for me to be a voice of reason. I thought it was completely frivolous to spend that sort of money on a television but seeing him throw down a credit card as though he had a constant flow of loads of money reminded me that everything is relative. Maybe this wasn't a lot of money for him, and who was I to tell him how to spend it?

I knew it was poor form to ask someone how they made their money, but the fact that he asked my opinion on the purchase gave me the courage to dig a bit.

"You must not be worried about money. I guess your music career is going really well," I tried to bait him into giving me more information.

Initially Joaquin was defensive. He defended the purchase by bragging about having a successful government contracting business. I raised an eyebrow, and then immediately caught myself. I didn't want him to see my skeptical face, and then get more defensive.

"Oh, well okay then," I mumbled.

I chose not to push further but wondered how someone could run a "successful" government contracting business while also pursuing a music career full time.

Every time he would tell a crazy-sounding story—that

he was opening for a popular music artist, for example—he always assured people they could google it. He went into that electronic store that day, telling any salesman who'd listen, about how he was going to be opening for a huge R&B artist soon. Not satisfied with his strange and vague description of where all his money came from, I decided to google his name. I found no mention of him being connected to any of the artists he claimed to have opened for. And of course, he was also not mentioned as being part of the any R&B tours that summer.

Though a bit nervous that my questions would trigger a similar defensive response to the previous time I asked about money, I decided to take the chance. I was genuinely curious why he would claim all these things, and even ask people to google his name, when he knew they wouldn't actually find any evidence he had done any of these things. Attempting to give him the benefit of the doubt, and hoping I was wrong, I claimed that maybe I hadn't conducted the search right. I asked him if he could show me the Google search, he claimed I would be able to find online about his previous concerts.

At this request, Joaquin flew into a rage. "Don't you trust me? You probably just didn't google it correctly."

In hindsight, this should have been the type of red flag that made me walk away from this relationship forever. But I was already invested enough in the relationship and still really wanted to believe the best in him at the expense of my gut.

This was a clear example of gaslighting. Joaquin knew there was nothing online to find about him, because he had not done the things he bragged about. Instead of owning up to the lie, he turned the situation around and made it appear as though there was something wrong with me. He was right about one thing—I didn't trust him. This was obvious by my audacity to google him in the first place. My instincts were right to question him. If he were an honest person, my attempts to vet him wouldn't have made him question me.

His rage that day was so strange, and scary, that I walked out on him mid-conversation. I drove back to my condo in DC determined not to see him again.

'What the hell is wrong with this dude,' I thought.

I asked him a simple question, after he *told* me to google him to verify his claims. Why was he getting so weird? Though we'd only been together for a few months, I was angry and sad. Tears ran down my face as I punched the steering wheel of the car. With one hand on the steering wheel, and the other poking around the car for a spare napkin or tissue to wipe my tear-stained face, I couldn't help but second guess my feelings. Had I done something wrong? I had fallen in love with this fairytale, and the thought of having to let it go gutted me.

It was a long drive to DC. Having time to think made me more upset. Even considering Joaquin's strange behavior, I was thinking about how terrified I was at the prospect of starting over again. I didn't want to go back online, suffer through endless amounts of bad dates, and I didn't want to be single and childless at 35. It seems silly now that the thought of staying with someone who was showing signs of an unstable personality presented as a better idea than starting over and taking my chances in the dating game. I wish I could go back in time and convince myself that it was best to keep driving and never turn back.

Though in these early moments of our relationship there were red flags, that seem so clear in hindsight, Joaquin knew how to always make me question my own recollection of events. At the end of an argument, I left feeling terrible and as though I was the person who needed to apologize. The times when it was clear he lost his temper, he had the ability to retreat almost immediately and profess his love for me. This is emotional abuse. Men like this can turn a confident, completely stable woman into someone who questions her version of reality on a regular basis.

"I just can't live without you. I love you so much. That is why I get so upset when you hurt me," Joaquin frequently said.

By the time the bright red flags started flying, I'd fallen in love with him. He'd tell me about his troubled childhood, his hopes, and dreams, and gushed about how much he loved his son. According to his recollection of his life, he'd been hurt by close family and friends and longed to be loved and accepted. I didn't want to be someone else who hurt him.

I began to have a hard time distinguishing truth versus the twisted reality that Joaquin was creating inside his house. The first couple of months with him had felt so magical, I spent the rest of the relationship trying to bring back the version of Joaquin that I'd met in February of 2010. What I didn't realize was that this version was not the real version of him, and the real version was slowly seeping out in the moments of rage and terror would start to become more than just a rare occasion over the latter half of our relationship.

The loudly ticking biological clock began to audibly tick in my ears again. Tears ran down my face, and I began to doubt myself. Had I been accusatory, and was this the reason he got so upset? Was there a reasonable explanation for his behavior?

'No, Hera, this is crazy. You are not wrong for leaving this fool,' I thought, trying hard to give myself a pep talk.

Just when I had nearly talked myself off the ledge of forgiving this hot-head, Joaquin called. I glanced over at the phone and grabbed the steering wheel tighter. My first instinct was to not answer it. I let the phone ring a few times before my curiosity got the better of me. I wanted to hear him apologize for acting crazy, and I needed him to validate my feelings.

Answering with a simple hello, I tried hard to hide in my voice the fact that I'd been crying.

"Why did you walk out on me?" he asked, hurt in his voice.

Shock caused a long pause in my ability to respond. Was he really going to keep turning this around on me? He didn't call to apologize at all. I pushed back on him, telling him that he was acting irrational. Joaquin then started to twist the story. He explained that he was previously in an abusive relationship, and that I was starting to remind him of his verbally abusive ex-girlfriend. The rational part of my brain caused a visceral reaction to being compared to an abusive ex after he'd essentially raged on me hours prior.

As I sat on the phone with him, I was shocked into silence. I couldn't believe that his memory was so different from my own. Had we really been in two completely different conversations? He claimed he didn't have a hostile reaction, and that he explained calmly why I'd been unable to find information. He also accused me of not trusting him and argued that he had given me no reason to distrust him.

By the time I hung up the phone, I doubted my own recollection of our conversation.

'Were we in the same conversation,' I asked myself.

It seemed like everyone around me was happily married with children. I hadn't met my person and the man I thought would be my forever partner didn't want to get married when I was ready. I was painfully self-conscious in relationships because even though I wasn't even 30 years old yet, I'd internalized negative messages in our culture around a woman's worth being connected to affirmation by a man. And that if I wasn't yet married by the time that I was 30 years old—it must mean there was something wrong with *me*.

I spent the next 24 hours thinking about what occurred, wondering if the relationship had deteriorated beyond repair. It was clear from our conversation that if I was going to continue in the relationship, I would have to accept responsibility for a fight I'd been so sure I wasn't at fault for starting. My conversation with Joaquin, and his accusations, had gotten in my head and mixed with my own insecurities.

Society, with her crazy pressure and unrealistic views, is a traitorous Bitch. And she was in my ear, reminding me of that clock that was loudly ticking in my ear. Instead of protecting myself, I chose to run full speed ahead toward someone who had given me no reason to trust him. I chose to continue following the fairy tale, even though it had already started to unravel around me.

Chapter 5

The Mask

I don't remember the first time Joaquin and I had sex. It was so forgettable that I have a hard time wondering how this wasn't a powerful enough data point to make me wonder whether we had enough physically chemistry to last as a couple. I wanted to be with someone with whom I had sexual chemistry, and somehow, I tricked myself into believing I was satisfied with our sex life.

At this time in my life, I'd firmly settled into the role of caregiver in all my romantic relationships—often at the expense of my own pleasure and many times also at the expense of my own self-care. It took may years of therapy for me to identify how easy it was for me to feel responsible for the care of others even if it meant the utter destruction of myself. When this type of relationship imbalance occurs, it's easy to miss the red flags popping up all around because you are too focused on caring for that other person.

Sex was always only about him and his needs. Everything Joaquin suggested somehow played into his own personal fantasy. It didn't matter to him whether what he suggested turned me on. If I shot down something he wanted to do, he would call me a prude and chastise me for ruining his ability to be turned on. He seemed to get pleasure out of pushing me past my comfort zone and was on a mission to see how far I would go.

Prior to my relationship with Joaquin, I'd only ever assumed there was one type of abuse. I naively believed that if your partner wasn't punching you in the face, it wasn't *really* an abusive relationship. But Joaquin's initial abuse was way more insidious than physical abuse and it left no visible mark for someone in my family or my friends to discover.

The first sign of coercive control and emotional abuse came through our sexual relationship. At first, I felt great about it because he acted as though he found me sexy. But over time, he used sex as a weapon for humiliation and always tried to push my boundaries in ways that scared me.

Sex with him became something that never felt safe, but I still craved his attention because the rules of our relationship dictated that if he wasn't into it—there was happy that I lost track of how fulfilled I was. When he was happy or pleased with how I had allowed him to treat me sexually, he would shower me with compliments, and it was in these moments that I felt as though he cared about me. When he was upset, and didn't want sex, it immediately made me feel self-conscious and undesirable.

A few months before I turned 30, Joaquin and I were

sitting on the couch in his bedroom. His son was home and in the next room. Sammy had a regular habit of walking in without knocking, and the lock to the bedroom door was broken. Joaquin started to initiate sex. I was panicked. I also knew we didn't have protection, and I didn't want to get pregnant or get a sexually transmitted disease. One of my clear boundaries was that I never wanted to have unprotected sex outside of marriage.

"Joaquin let's not do this right now," I pleaded.

I pushed him off me. This seemed only to fuel his excitement. He grabbed me around the waist, pulling me so tightly that it took my breath away.

"What would you do if I just took it?" he whispered in my ear, so close that I could smell his breath.

I didn't want to have sex with him, but I wasn't sure how to get out of the situation safely, either.

"Please don't," I whispered, now holding my breath, and praying that he would listen to me.

The more I protested, the more excited Joaquin became. Knowing his son was in the other room, I whispered my protests and tried to nudge him away from me. As he grew more insistent, I thought about how in college during a Rape Aggression Defense (RAD) class I took, they told us that if we thrust our hips quickly to the side, we would have a chance to fight off an aggressor. In this moment, that advice seemed ridiculous.

His grip was now growing painful. At some point in the struggle, I froze. I was both afraid and too weak to stand up to him completely. He tore off my clothes, and I lay shivering on the couch. I stared at the ceiling and prayed for this moment to end. I loved him, and I thought he loved me. I was now completely unsure. I didn't consider this rape at the time. I knew him, we were dating, and I had willingly gone into his bedroom and laid down with him. I was also still completely unwilling to consider that he didn't love me as much as I loved him.

We'd had consensual sex before, and there'd been plenty of times when he didn't want to, and I never pushed him. But like another unspoken contract, this interaction told me that I was his to do with whatever he wanted, and my wants and needs didn't matter.

Though I know there was little I couldn't do in that moment to stop it, I still hold incredible guilt that I experienced that and still didn't leave. Things got markedly worse after that night, as though he'd beaten his way through an invisible wall and now the floodgates of hell were open. Like in that one ruthless act of sexual violence, he'd realized that he could do anything to me.

After years of therapy, I've learned that early in relationships—social contracts are formed. I'm not talking about formal ones where you sign on the dotted line, but instead, the contracts that show others how they are allowed to treat you. When conflict arises in a relationship, even something as small as someone not holding the door for you or helping you clean the dishes after you've made dinner, how each person behaves in those moments will lay the foundation of the relationship. And as I've learned through mistakes in all types of relationships, if you don't speak up and hold firm boundaries on how you wish to be treated from the beginning—don't expect to start later without a level of conflict likely to end the relationship.

My 30th birthday fell on a holiday weekend. I'd been working hard on a customer deliverable, often pulling 16-hour days, and staying at the office well past 9 pm. I needed a break, and I desperately wanted to feel settled on this birthday. Growing up, I attached ridiculous expectations to this date. I believed that by 30 I'd have my own family. Even though in reality my relationship was far from a good one, I was still desperately holding onto the fantasy version.

It's insane how tightly held my belief in the significance of my 30th birthday was back then. I was truly terrified that 35 years old was just around the corner and that if I didn't make this relationship work somehow, I'd end up alone and childless forever. Fooling myself into thinking I vibed with Joaquin.

I wanted to celebrate my birthday with a trip. Joaquin, complaining that he hadn't received a check from an alleged appearance at a big name concert, said he didn't feel comfortable spending money. Given the fact that only a few months prior he had dropped nearly $30,000 on studio and entertainment equipment, I wondered if he just didn't want to spend money on *me*.

Determined to not be unhappy on this birthday, I booked a trip to a popular, upscale resort in Virginia. The resort sat on a prestigious golf course, and I thought this would cheer and excite Joaquin. Joaquin loved golf and claimed his son was a golf protege. After much convincing, Joaquin agreed to help me pay for half of the trip. He said he would reimburse me once he received his check from the concert.

Up to the moment we got into the car to drive to the resort, Joaquin was noncommittal about the trip. He claimed that he could be called any time for a modeling shoot in NY or to join a concert date. Once we were on the drive, his story shifted again.

"A television station wants to do a reality show with me and my son," he claimed.

I found this odd, given how he always claimed to be a private person. How would he deal with cameras in his face when someone asked about the story behind Sammy's mother? Whenever I asked, he claimed he was so devastated over her loss that he couldn't bear to speak of her.

As soon as we arrived at the hotel, Joaquin stepped into character. He told everyone from the concierge to the bellhop about how famous he was. He encouraged people to google him and read about how he was on the Rihanna tour. I was starting to doubt these claims, given how my own searches had come up empty. I still, however, refused to believe that he was flat out lying about his career. Instead, I chose to assume that he was embellishing and that maybe he was just an aspiring artist. Maybe he was trying to sound bigger than he was because he was ashamed that he hadn't done as well as he'd hoped.

But the grandiose stories kept getting more elaborate without a shred of evidence that any of it was real. Deeply worried that none of it was real, I also hung onto hope in the moments of happiness between us—even if few and far between.

My 30th birthday was drama filled, and I felt as though I was dodging personality land mines all weekend. Sammy was having trouble with the golf course, and Joaquin acted like an angry coach. At one point, Joaquin threw the club at Sammy's head because he was unhappy that Sammy had missed a shot. I spent most of the day running interference between Joaquin and his son, reminding everyone that we were there to relax and have fun.

When I wasn't dodging emotional landmines, I was

happy when I looked at my new family. I enjoyed having Sammy around, and I felt as though for the first time we were a family. Other vacationers assumed that Sammy was my son, despite the irritation that came over his face when unknowing strangers told him how much he looked like me. We were an instant family, and the feeling of euphoria that this fantasy gave me was blinding. I wanted the image of what we looked like to outsiders to be real—so much so that it was like I was acting in a film of my own life.

As the weekend grew more uncomfortable, and the television crew never showed up to film Joaquin's fictitious reality show, I continued to tap dance around Joaquin. Instead of doing things I was interested in, I allowed him to drive all our activities. If Joaquin wanted to go to the pool, we went to the pool. If Joaquin wanted to eat, we ate. That night, Joaquin wanted to have sex. We had sex on the balcony of the hotel on his insistence. I felt dirty, and I was angry at myself for not pushing back enough on Joaquin's desires. When I pushed back, he always pushed me harder. He seemed to enjoy controlling me, and that weekend I was not strong enough to keep pushing back. Every time I compromised myself for him, a part of my identity and resolve died.

A month after our trip, I took a pregnancy test. When I saw the two pink lines, indicating pregnancy, I threw up all over the floor. Something I'd wanted my entire life—to be a mom—was happening. But this was *not* how I'd wanted it to happen. And while I'd been actively ignoring my gut for months, I also knew (deep down) that Joaquin was not the man I'd wanted to raise a child with.

Weeks passed before I told anyone. Over the course of that week, I took five pregnancy tests. Each time I took a test,

I got another positive. I initially convinced myself each time that it must have been a faulty test. One night, after I had spent several days googling what a positive pregnancy test looks like, Joaquin grabbed my phone. He looked through my search history, and his eyes grew wide. He flew into a rage so quickly that I didn't initially understand what set him off.

I jumped up from the bed, certain he was going to hit me.

"Why didn't you tell me you were pregnant?" he yelled, his eyes turning bloodshot.

A large vein throbbed on his forehead. The fire in his eyes made him look like a stranger, and this was terrifying. I couldn't tell whether he was more upset about the baby, or about the fact that I'd kept it from him. This was the first time I witnessed him completely unhinged. In prior experiences, his rage always seemed controlled enough to pull back when I reacted poorly in response. But this time was different—like something inside him snapped and the mask was now completely down.

"I, I wasn't sure yet," I responded, trying to keep my voice calm as if that would cool his rage.

I was now cowering in the corner of the room, to avoid a physical altercation. I started to cry and asked him why he was so angry. Almost as quickly as the rage came, Joaquin did a complete 180-degree mood change. He smiled and explained that he was only angry that I hadn't told him. I wasn't entirely convinced. This sudden shift of emotion, as soon as I suggested that the baby made him angry, was unsettling.

I should've walked out of that house that night—and several times prior. But society was back in my head and on my shoulder. This time, she was reminding me that children need fathers and that I'd laid my bed and it was now time to lay in it.

This mad man who'd just raged on me was now the father of my unborn child and the desire to believe he was a good man underneath the surface quieted any further attempts to dig for the truth. Now, I was afraid that if I found out he was a fraud—it would force an action I was unwilling to even consider. I stopped asking questions about his business activities, because he continued to get upset when I tried to make sense of his stories. The checks Joaquin claimed the record label owed him still hadn't come. There isn't a conscious day I can remember when I realized they'd never come—but sometime after I became pregnant, I entered a stage of acceptance and stopped expecting his story to come together.

Looking back on this time, I wish things had been clearer. I wish my family, my friends, and my coworkers had been able to see bruises. I needed someone to save me from the hell I was in because I'd gotten to the point where I couldn't save myself from it. It might seem like a cop out because clearly my legs worked, but over time I knew that leaving wasn't something I could easily do without presenting a level of danger.

'At least he doesn't beat me,' I thought to myself, to convince myself there wasn't an acceptable reason to leave the father of my child.

Joaquin's 9mm handgun became a permanent fixture on the dresser in his bedroom. I'd known he had a gun from our first date but didn't start seeing it until he found out I was pregnant. It was also after the pregnancy that he started picking it up when we'd argue or when I wasn't doing something he wanted me to do. That gun was an ever-present fixture in our relationship, like the third wheel that could end my life at any time.

Though I'd stopped asking Joaquin about his past or his career, he continued a campaign to prove his legitimacy. I never found a shred of digital evidence to back up his claims, but Joaquin started introducing me to people who verified his stories. The first set was the Flores family. Mama and Papa Flores appeared to head up a lovely family. They invited Joaquin and I over to their house for dinner one evening. They spoke of Joaquin fondly and referred to him as their nephew. In addition to pretending to be family, they told me stories of times when they would see Joaquin in concert.

I remember feeling an incredible sense of relief as they'd share stories about him performing that were so detailed it was hard to question their validity. Joaquin would laugh, recalling a moment on stage and one of them would respond affirmatively and add more detail to the story.

The Flores family was thrilled when they learned about the pregnancy. I felt so much acceptance from them and they acted joyful about welcoming me into their family. I trusted them. They seemed like good people, and they went out of their way to make me feel comfortable. A little over a year after I met the Flores family, I learned that they weren't related to Joaquin. Joaquin met their son at a fast food restaurant when he was in high school and worked the drive thru window.

As the months passed, none of the concerts he claimed to be on tour with materialized. He claimed he was on tour to everyone who would listen to him, including the random cashier in the grocery store. On the night that tour he claimed to be a part of came to our town, Joaquin was frantic. He paced the house, claiming that he wouldn't know until the last minute whether he was going to be called to perform. I was nervous for him, and still anxious about a day when I might see one shred of evidence that he was telling the truth. Of course, Joaquin never received a call.

Every time I started to wonder if I was crazy to stay with him, given that I was starting to have a strong inclination that he was not truthful about his career, he would present another character witness. This time, he introduced me to an attorney named Greg. Joaquin claimed Greg was his entertainment attorney, and Greg didn't correct him in my presence. Haven's website showed that he was an insurance attorney with offices in Northern Virginia. While it was odd that Joaquin would choose an insurance attorney to represent him in the entertainment industry, I shrugged this off as something I wouldn't understand, being unfamiliar with this line of work. And like the Flores family, Greg had stories of when he'd seen Joaquin in concert and spoke openly about entertainment contracts, he helped Joaquin negotiate.

A few months after I found out I was pregnant, Joaquin started pressuring me to move in with him. Money became an obsession, and he was frantic about it. A man who'd spent thousands of dollars on frivolous entertainment paraphernalia was now acting like he was about to lose his home. It was such a giant shift from the flashy, carefree spender that I'd seen just a few months prior.

The big check was always just around the corner, and he explained that it would be best for our family if I moved in. He wanted me to start helping him pay his mortgage too. I questioned why he suddenly didn't seem to have money, but he always had an excuse: he was down on his luck; contracts were slow; his agent wasn't doing her job; he hadn't been paid for a tour, etc. He began spending every day in his home studio, screaming into his microphone. At this point, I knew the music career wasn't real—at least it wasn't currently. We'd been together almost a year at this point, and I didn't see one shred of evidence (other than the lawyer and family who'd corroborated his stories) that he was a professional musician. It was no longer a good relationship that kept me there: it was my fear of leaving—for what that meant for my son, his older son, and for me.

Joaquin seemed to get more comfortable using my money and insisted I start paying all his bills. His mortgage was almost twice my own.

"Joaquin, how much money do you think I make? I can't pay for your entire mortgage," I argued.

Our biggest fights typically centered on money as his expectations for what I earned outpaced reality. I was still maintaining my own residence in DC, while also now helping him pay for his house. I simply didn't have enough money to support our entire family on my own—not with the lifestyle he insisted on living.

Upon hearing that I couldn't and wouldn't pay his entire mortgage, he began pacing back and forth. With the gun in his hand, that unwelcome third partner, he also started to rock side to side every time he'd reached a corner of the room. I remember this fight vividly because his eyes scared me. The man that once had depth and passion in his eyes, now looked completely void of love and care. The constant back and forth rocking, like the movements of an adult trying to sooth themselves akin to a baby searching for calm. As his words sped up like a panicked and uncoordinated dance, his body movements mirrored the pace.

The day prior to this argument, an older couple named

Ronan and Roxy had come to the house asking him for money he owed them. While he consistently referred to them as close family friends, they only surfaced during times when they were determined to cash in on debt. I wondered if their visit was what spurred Joaquin's insistence that I cover the entire mortgage bill.

"I assumed you'd take care of these bills," he was now screaming.

Joaquin's rage continued, and I sat silently wondering what he wanted me to do or say. Did he think that I made more money than I was reporting to him? Was he with me because he thought I would financially support his music dreams?

"You know . . . I also have my own bills that I am responsible for paying," I said, only slightly louder than under my breath.

Joaquin's face contorted, and he genuinely looked both confused and perhaps just uninterested in any bills that I had that didn't include his expenses.

"This isn't fair, Joaquin. This doesn't feel like a partnership," I continued, growing more courageous as my anger surged.

He stopped pacing, looked right at me, before beginning to throw things around the room like a toddler in the middle of developmental fit. Shoes, books, a laptop, a couch pillow. At first, he was just throwing things around, but then he started throwing things at me. I shielded my head while maintaining eye contact with the gun that remained in the hand that he wasn't using to destroy the room.

"I will never forgive you for this," he screamed.

When backed into a corner, he'd either shift the story or fly into a fit of rage. And my comment, pointing out the imbalance in our relationship and clearly noting that he wasn't financially contributing to the family wasn't something he could twist. Because there weren't any checks, and he needed my money to survive. So, anger, gaslighting, and coercive control by scaring me were on the menu that night.

I was terrified enough that night that I tried to leave. Every instinct in my body was screaming for me to get out, except for that one voice of social pressure telling me that I needed to stay with the father of my unborn son. But even though I wanted my son to have a father, it had gotten to the point where I didn't feel safe. And my concern for my son was enough to mobilize me.

I waited for him to leave the bedroom, then I gathered everything I could get my hands on quickly and jumped in my car. I started driving south, not sure where I was going. I drove several hours south from where we lived, deep into Virginia.

On the car ride south, I grappled with my fear of staying and my fear of leaving. Things had gotten too out of hand to remain in the naïve space of thinking we'd be a happy family. My life shifted to survival mode. How would I get us out of this—now thinking of not only myself but also my son.

And then there was the question of mental health. Even with the various red flags that I'd ignored at the beginning of our relationship, Joaquin didn't seem at all like the man I'd fallen in love with. And the only framing that my experience would allow was that he'd suffered some sort of mental health break. And I had guilt about what kind of person would leave the father of her child when he was having a health crisis. Then there was Sammy, the boy I'd grown to love who was now my son's brother. And while I'd only known him for a year, he felt like my son—a son that I had no legal claim to. If I left Joaquin, Sammy wouldn't be coming with me.

I stayed in a hotel that night and drove to my parents' house the next day. I wanted so badly for my parents to talk me into leaving Joaquin and tell me that I'd be safe there with them. But with the thin layer of information that I was willing to offer, they weren't going to do that. I didn't tell my parents the truth that day. I told them we'd argued about money but left out the details that I worried would make my father want to kill him. I left out how he'd thrown things at me, the rage, and the gun.

Joaquin hadn't made a good first impression on anyone in my family. My parents had a visceral reaction to his appearance, and my mother never got over it. She thought that his large clothing was like a costume and assumed from the first day she met him that he had something he was trying to hide. My father, on the other hand, was able to move past his clothing and seemed to try and give him a chance. Joaquin's Mercedes truck gave my father the impression that he was successful and led him to take interest in Joaquin's stories about his business activities.

I appreciated how hard my father was trying with Joaquin, and when they'd go golfing together and come back laughing and smiling—it felt like things would be okay. But I knew if I told my father the whole truth, there would be no going back. They'd never accept him again and though I feared who Joaquin had become, I wasn't ready to fully walk away from my son's father. There was a part of me that wanted it all to be just a bad dream and to wake up to the man I'd met a year prior.

"You need to go back and work this out Hera. He is the father of your child, and you chose him," my father told me.

To understand my parents, you must understand the community where we lived and the values we held. While in many ways my parents are complete opposites—Black man from the deep south and White woman from the north—they both grew up in highly religious households. My grandfather on my father's side was a preacher in a historically Black church, and my mother's family was deeply Irish Catholic. Had my parents known the extent of the abuse I suffered; they would've have instructed me to return. With the sparse details I provided, they believed they were encouraging me to keep my son's family together. Financial trouble wasn't a good enough reason to leave the father of your child.

I left my parents' house feeling defeated and ashamed. I was ashamed that I didn't have the courage to be honest with them or perhaps the real shame came from not yet having the courage to leave Joaquin.

Despite his behavior the night before, I ended up being the person who apologized. Joaquin complained and accused me of being hurtful because I'd accused him of taking advantage of me financially. I left the conversation wondering whether I was going crazy, and why I hadn't remembered things the way he had. His consistent gas lighting and the ease with which he twisted reality in his recollections made me feel as if I was in a horror house full of mirrors. In every mirror, things looked different but in none of the mirrors was a true reflection of me.

Chapter 6

Unhinged

Month by month, I watched my body change as the baby slowly developed into a little person. With every exciting milestone, my joy was strangled by relationship-induced anxiety. Months before, Joaquin made a big show of asking my parents for my hand in marriage. At the time, I was elated by this gesture. Finally, someone chose me. I was so in love with the fantasy that my racing mind and carried-away heart didn't stop to analyze the person who'd claimed me. The huge gestures of public affection also worked as a mechanism to disguise how rotten our actual relationship had become.

As the months passed, I started to wonder why he asked them when he hadn't bothered to propose. My anxiety brain was in a deep spiral, focused on the respectability politics of marriage instead of what the hell I was doing in this horrible situation.

Why had he bothered asking for my hand if he had no intention of marrying me?

Wasn't now a good time?

If he had intended to make me his wife, shouldn't he do it before I gave birth to our child?

His delay in proposing made me angry, and I was starting to resent him for it. Though I still wasn't large enough to be obviously pregnant, I became increasingly more self-conscious as strangers would look from my belly to my finger. Every time they spotted my bare ring finger, I could swear I saw judgement or general discomfort in their demeanor. It made me feel like I was embodying the image of the Black Welfare Queen—single and pregnant via her "baby daddy" who wasn't her partner.

The Christmas season was around the corner, and Joaquin was now completely reliant on me financially. The promises of the check that would never come, the concert he would never perform in, and now the proposal I wondered if I would ever get just made me angry and resentful. I went in a matter of a few months from being a single, 29-year-old woman without children to a woman who was now financially responsible for Joaquin, his son, my unborn child, and a house I didn't even own. Joaquin continued pressuring me into renting out my condo so that I could pay his mortgage instead of my own.

I woke up every day at 4:45 in the morning to beat traffic and drive an hour and a half to work. Often nauseous and exhausted from the pregnancy, I would get home after 6:00 in the evening, and both Joaquin and his son would ask me what I would be cooking them for dinner. I can't remember a single time when Joaquin offered to cook dinner for me.

A few weeks before Christmas, my company held an epic holiday party. I was still working for a beltway defense contractor, and the party was held at a local Museum. They had chocolate fountains, dozens of different food tables featuring cuisine from all over the globe, and somewhat creepy human-shaped ice sculptures placed throughout the museum.

While I was excited about this lavish party, Joaquin knew that my main motivation for attendance was to secure my position with the company. That night was all about political and corporate connections, and I needed to be there for as long as it took me to make them. I'd have to tell my boss in a little over a month that I was pregnant and would need to take maternity leave. I hadn't been at the company a year yet, and I'd only been on my new team for a little over a month. It wasn't going to be possible for me to hide the pregnancy for much longer.

While I was at the party, making up excuses for why I wasn't drinking, Joaquin called every 15 minutes to ask when I would be home. His calls increasingly annoyed me, as I was painfully aware that my career success was the only thing our new family had to rely on. He was completely unaware of how corporate America worked and didn't understand why I couldn't just leave to hang out with him.

After an hour of his incessant phone calls, I decided to head home. On the drive home, I thought about how I'd arrived at this place in my life. Before I was pregnant, this was a situation that would have been somewhat easy to leave. While I'd gotten close to his son, he wasn't my responsibility, and Joaquin's bills were certainly not something I would have signed onto before I was carrying his baby. But now, I felt trapped. I was angry at myself for not fighting harder and insisting that he wear protection. I didn't know how, or if, I would ever free myself from this horrible situation.

When I walked through the door, the first thing I saw was Sammy with a huge smile on his face.

"Why are you still awake?" I asked, looking around the front foyer of the house for Joaquin.

Sammy giggled, motioning for me to follow him, and walked toward the kitchen. When I rounded the corner into the kitchen after him, I saw Joaquin and a huge bouquet. I was confused and could barely hear anything that Joaquin was saying. Joaquin's giant pit bull, who spent most of his life in a cage, barked loudly from the room next door. I turned toward the dog, bending down to greet him to calm him down. As I raised back up and turned around, Joaquin pulled a small ring box out of his pocket. I immediately started crying and was overcome with emotions entirely inappropriate for this type of situation.

I had dreamed of this moment, but what was playing out in front of me was not ever part of my dreams. I dreamed that this would be an intimate moment between two people, that both of us would be ridiculously happy, and that I would be sure about spending my life with this other person. It wasn't any of those things, but with the pregnancy and my new somewhat self-imposed responsibilities, it felt like a necessary next step. My emotions felt like they were splattering everywhere and in all different directions.

I was crying tears of relief—because he'd finally followed through with one thing he'd promised.

Tears of sadness—because this wasn't the man of any-one's dreams in his current form.

Tears of shame—because I knew I shouldn't still be in this situation.

"What's wrong, aren't you happy," Joaquin asked, examining my face.

"Yes, I'm just surprised—but yes, I'm happy," I responded dishonestly.

Joaquin just stood there with the ring. I tilted my head, waiting for him to say something.

"Um, aren't you going to get down on your knee? Are you going to ask me?" I asked him.

I was trying desperately to make this scene at least some-what romantic. I couldn't believe that I had to coach him. Hadn't he seen a proposal in the movies?

"Uh, well . . . will you marry me," He finally asked.

Still struggling to hear over the deafening barking from the dog, I agreed to marry him. It was far from the romantic proposal I had imagined, I tried to take comfort in the fact that at least—perhaps—my son would have the hope of a traditional family.

After the proposal, I wanted to take pictures. But Joaquin insisted that he not be connected to me on the internet. When I asked why he was being so weird about announcing to my friends and family that we were engaged, he said his record contract didn't allow him to get married. So, the pictures I took on the night of our engagement were of me alone, which was authentically how I felt in those moments.

When I should've been wondering how Joaquin afforded to pay for a wedding ring, instead I was relieved that the ring provided the outward appearance that everything was fine within our home. Nothing about our relationship got better after he proposed. If anything, it only temporarily halted my anxiety.

Joaquin's mental state continued to drastically deteriorate the closer we came to our son's birth. He got more frantic about money, and his moods grew more unpredictable. Both Sammy and I continued walking around the house, worried that we would step on one of the invisible landmines that would cause Joaquin to fly into a rage.

One night, after a long and exhausting day at work, I heard screaming from the basement. I ran to the banister to hear what was going on. Initially, fear caused my legs to feel as though they were deeply rooted in the hallway carpet.

'I shouldn't get involved,' I thought, worried that he would turn on me if I attempted to insert myself into the middle of an argument he was having with his son.

The screaming got louder. I heard loud crashing, and the screams turned to loud, gut-wrenching cries. A small piece of my conscious knew I was potentially putting myself, and my unborn son, in physical danger by intervening. This realization didn't stop me from acting, because I wasn't physically able to stand there while my son's brother was beaten. It felt as though his cries physically pulled me toward him. I ran down the stairs, skipping several on the way down. I was afraid, and my heart felt as though it was going to beat out of my chest.

Peering through the basement door, I saw that Sammy was crying in the corner of the room, turned toward the wall, shivering and sobbing. Between sobs, he asked to go live with his grandparents. I looked frantically around the room, trying to find Joaquin before going to Sammy to comfort him. Joaquin sat on the couch, watching his son with a menacing look in his eyes. With an eerie calmness, Joaquin chastised his son. He cursed at him, called him names, and looked as though he was on the verge of popping off and slapping both me and Sammy any second.

I knew that to help Sammy I needed to first stop the ticking time bomb that was Joaquin. As quietly as possible, shaking with fear, I approached Joaquin. Outstretching my hand, I asked him to take my hand and leave the room so that I could talk to his son.

"I am going to sit right here," Joaquin snapped, refusing to take my hand.

"Please, Joaquin. You need to get out of here. Things are too intense, and you both need to calm down. Please go upstairs," I pleaded with him, fighting back tears.

I argued with Joaquin for several minutes and eventually prevailed. Joaquin left the room, stomping like a toddler up the two flights of stairs that led to our bedroom.

As soon as the door to the basement closed, and I was reasonably sure Joaquin was in a completely different part of the house, I approached Sammy.

"He's going to kill me. Just like he killed my mother. I want to live with grandmother because at least she doesn't . . . she doesn't hit me," Sammy sobbed.

Sammy's words shocked me into silence.

His mother? Kill him like he killed his mother? Why would he say this?

I wasn't sure what to say to him. While I didn't think Joaquin could kill anyone, I knew he'd hurt him and I didn't blame Sammy for wanting to run—because I, too, wanted to run. Joaquin told me Sammy's mother had died in an accident, but was this the truth?

"It's OK. I'm here," I tried to assure him.

"You don't know him like I do," Sammy said, now breathing heavily.

The sobbing ended. He now appeared to be trying to get himself under control. He was right. I didn't know Joaquin. He was also right to be skeptical about my ability to protect him. I was working twelve-hour days, and only awake for about two hours at night after getting home from my long commute. I wanted to protect him, though, and I also needed to believe Joaquin wouldn't kill anyone. I needed for him to be wrong, to continue living the fantasy I had fallen in love with.

When Sammy and I went back upstairs, Joaquin was still angry. We heard things crashing around his room as he kicked and punched the walls and the furniture.

"Go to your bedroom," I warned Sammy, patting him gently on the back to comfort him.

He didn't argue with me. He was smart enough to know that anywhere within Joaquin's line of sight wasn't safe for him. Sammy looked down at the floor, eyes red from crying and shoulders hunched over defeated, and walked into his room.

After closing his door, I took a deep breath. I stared at the door to the bedroom I now shared with Joaquin. I was terrified of what I would find on the other side of that door. I knew that by trying to protect Sammy that night, I might have hell to pay when I entered the room.

'It's going to be fine. This was just an argument between the two of them. Everything will be fine tomorrow.' I was giving myself a pep talk.

I wanted to believe that this evening was not a scene that would become our normal. My mind was racing, thinking about how to help the two of them—how to make sure

Sammy was safe and cure whatever was going on with Joaquin.

I slowly opened the door, trying to shield myself from anything Joaquin might be throwing. By the time I entered, Joaquin was sitting on the bed. His face was still angry, his eyes bloodshot, and he had the gun in his hand. He was mumbling to himself about what he was going to do to Sammy, and how angry he was that he'd lied to him.

Immediately jumping into fix-it mode, I didn't chastise Joaquin for hitting his son. Instead, I told him he needed to calm down, and we would settle things in the morning. I rubbed his back, trying to make him feel better. I prayed Joaquin wouldn't notice how violently my hands were shaking. One I got Joaquin to lay down, I took the gun from his hand and placed it back on the dresser.

That night I didn't sleep. I had so many things I wanted to ask Joaquin. Where was Sammy's mother? Why did he mention going to live with Grandma? I needed to know what really happened to her. Why had Sammy been so convinced his father would kill him? And what happened between the two of them that night in the basement? I laid there the entire night with my eyes open, too afraid to move.

As soon as it hit an hour that was reasonable enough for me to explain an early start to the commute, around 4:30AM, I hopped out of bed and quickly dressed. I needed to get out of that house and looked forward to throwing my mind into work that day. I texted Joaquin later that morning, telling him that I was going to stay at my condo that night. I needed time to think, and I wanted to get a full night of sleep before confronting Joaquin with the questions now consuming my thoughts. The condo was now officially on the rental market, and I knew that I only had about a month left to enjoy it before I'd need to rent it out. I'd gone from spending the entire work week at the apartment to only a couple days a week there. I worried about renting it because it'd been my escape from the chaos of this new life.

After I left work that day, I noticed that I had ten missed calls from Joaquin. In addition to missed calls, I had a text from him telling me to call him as soon as possible. On the drive back to my condo, I dialed his number. He didn't answer. I was so tired that I didn't bother to question where he was and what he wanted me to call him for. I needed sleep.

I walked through the door to my condo and felt immediately as though a large weight had been lifted off my shoulders. My condo was only 600 square feet, but the warmth of those walls enveloped me like a large blanket. I loved that condo because it was the first place I owned. It overlooked Rock Creek Park in Washington, D.C. It was a perfectly wooded area in the middle of a bustling city, nearly opposite the suburban war zone I wanted to escape. I felt safe and thought immediately about how much easier it would be for me to just stay there instead of ever returning to Joaquin's house. Then, in the very next second I remembered my unborn son. The choice to stay or return suddenly didn't seem as easy.

As I sat down on my couch, my cell phone rang. It was Joaquin. The tension in his voice immediately caused my heart to race.

"I was arrested today. I just got back from the police station," Joaquin hissed.

His words stunned me. There was silence on the line. I didn't know what to say. All the fear and anxiety that had been calmed by walking into my condo came rushing back.

"What happened?" My mind raced with the desire to follow that up with about 50 more questions.

Joaquin's voice was flat on the other end of the call. He explained that social services and the police showed up at the house earlier that day to arrest him. When Sammy went to school that day, the school guidance counselor, and nurse noticed signs of physical abuse from the night before. Sammy had a giant ring mark in the middle of his back where Joaquin punched him. Although Sammy asked the police to allow him to stay with his maternal grandmother, who had bi-monthly visitations with him, social services made the decision to place him back in Joaquin's house until they completed their investigation. Until the trial, Sammy received a protective order against Joaquin. This was supposed to ensure that Joaquin wouldn't physically harm his son.

In an official police report from December 14, 2010, the officer who arrived on the scene to question Joaquin reported the following:

> *"On the above date and time, responded to [the Elementary School] in reference to a domestic assault and battery. Upon my arrival, I met with [Sammy] who advised his father had struck him with his hands, feet, and threw shoes at him because he did not practice golf long enough. [Sammy] had a visible bruise on his back. I spoke with Mr. Rams, who advised he spanked his son because he was caught in a lie. Mr. Rams advised that his son moved, and he struck his back. Mr. Rams had a large ring on the striking hand, that he forgot was on his hand, which caused the bruise. An emergency protective order was requested and granted. Mr. Rams was given a domestic violence pamphlet. Case clear arrest."*

On the arrest report, there were several options that the officer could have chosen regarding the disposition of the case: active, inactive, unfounded, arrest, and exemption. This officer believed it was a clear case of domestic violence, and he chose to arrest based on the physical evidence on Sammy's back. Though the police chose to arrest, it was still determined that placing Sammy back in the home was appropriate—so long as Joaquin received a pamphlet on domestic violence.

After hearing the news of the arrest, I got back into my car and headed toward Virginia. Shortly after Joaquin called, social services called me to ask for my account of the incident. I told the social worker that I hadn't been in the room with them when any physical abuse occurred. I explained that by the time I came to the basement the two of them were not standing near each other. I confirmed that Sammy had also reported to me that his father hit him. The social worker informed me that they were returning Sammy to the home but asked that I remain in the home as part of the safety plan.

By the time I returned to Virginia, Joaquin was at the house with his "cousin"—Eduardo Flores. Eduardo picked up Sammy at school once social services determined it was safe for him to return home. While Joaquin claimed to be related to this man, they didn't look anything alike. In contrast to Joaquin's skinny, small, and pale frame, Eduardo was well over 6 feet and dark skinned. He was a man of few words. I wasn't entirely sure whether Eduardo spoke English well, or if he just didn't have anything to say when I was around. Of course, it also could've been that Eduardo knew Joaquin well enough to know that I was only a temporary fixture in his life, one he didn't need to bother to get to know. He always looked confused and showed up whenever Joaquin needed someone to use. I later learned that Joaquin and Eduardo shared a bank account, and the car that Joaquin drove was registered in Eduardo's name.

Eduardo looked uncomfortable when I walked into the house. He was standing next to Joaquin in the kitchen, and Sammy was upstairs in his bedroom. A few minutes later, Eduardo caught my eye, mumbled a few words under his breath, and excused himself to leave.

"How is he doing?" I asked Joaquin, referring to his son.

"What, how is *he* doing?" Joaquin immediately looked angry.

I'd stepped on a landmine and winced at the emotional lashing I was about to get.

"I was the one who had to spend all day in jail because he decided to lie on me," Joaquin screamed.

His improper grammar made me flinch. It was strange that in this moment, his grammar was what I decided to focus on.

'Um, was he physically lying on top of you?' I thought, still fixated on this ridiculous statement.

"Are you even listening to me?" Joaquin noticed my blank and exhausted stare.

My mind was wandering—my defense mechanism. I didn't want to be standing in this kitchen talking to him about this, and I was so confused and distraught that my brain wasn't working properly. I was also exhausted because I hadn't been sleeping properly in longer than I could remember.

"What happened to Sammy's mother?" I blurted out the question, immediately regretting this poor choice in moments.

The question popped out of my mouth quicker than my

brain could think better of it. I knew this was a sore topic given how Joaquin had avoided mention of Sammy's mother previously.

"What did Sammy say? What did he tell you while you were in the basement?" Joaquin paced around the kitchen.

When he stopped pacing, he started to rock again. He seemed unable to keep himself still, and it made me more nervous. His behavior reminded me of the night we'd fought about money when he'd waved his gun at me frantically. The night I should've left and never looked back.

"He told me he was afraid you would kill him, just like you killed his mother," I admitted, my voice shaking.

Joaquin continued pacing, now silent and biting his nails. I worried he was going to hit me. This was the worst time for this conversation. No matter how much I wanted to pull back the words that had escaped my mouth, that ship had already sailed.

"Sammy is a liar. He's just angry at me because I disciplined him," Joaquin seethed, fists clenched at his side and eyes blood shot.

I slowly backed away from him toward the door.

"OK. Sammy told me he was having nightmares, maybe we should have him see someone," I suggested.

I wanted to say more, but my fear wouldn't allow me to continue the conversation. Joaquin called Sammy over to him and pulled him by the shirt within inches of his face.

"What is the nightmare," Joaquin asked, his tone angry.

"Uh, it's . . . my mother falling out of a window, and someone pushes her," he responded, looking at the grown and trying to pull himself from Joaquin's grasp.

"It's me in the nightmare who pushed her right? You

think it's me." Joaquin stared his son down, still holding the collar of Sammy's shirt in his fist.

Sammy didn't respond to him about the nightmare, which was smart given that Joaquin seemed to already know the answer. Joaquin then spent several minutes asking Sammy why he'd lied to the school about what happened. I watched the two of them go back and forth while Joaquin clearly tried to change the narrative and rewrite history, as though he was attempting to re-program his son to agree with a version of history that exonerated him. By the end of the exchange, Sammy seemed confused and defeated. I felt responsible for his protection but wasn't even sure I was able to protect myself.

Sammy's behavior was deteriorating at nearly the same rate that Joaquin's anger was surging. Sammy started to lie about his schoolwork, and he would often lie about other things around the house in what seemed like an attempt to get out of trouble. One time in particular, his teacher emailed to tell me that he hadn't written anything on paper during an in-class assignment. When I questioned him about this, he told me that the teacher was not being truthful. I showed up at the school ready to go to bat for him with this teacher only to find out that Sammy was the one who wasn't telling the truth.

I knew Joaquin hit Sammy that night and Sammy had physical evidence to back up his version of events. Despite the evidence though, the further we got from the incident the more Joaquin's version of what happened that night morphed. At first, he'd admitted to hitting him (though he claimed it was an accident) but eventually he told everyone he hadn't touched him, and that Sammy had made the whole thing up.

I worried that Joaquin could tell that I didn't believe him. He knew I was there that night, after all. Or perhaps, he'd convinced himself of this revised version of the truth. Perhaps my lack of concern over his brief stay in jail was a giveaway that I wasn't fully on board for a truth that didn't include an acknowledgement of abuse. Shortly after Eduardo left the house, Joaquin called Sammy down to the kitchen and asked him to tell me what happened in the basement. Sammy, eyes still red from crying, gave Joaquin a confused look.

"Go on, Sammy. Tell her what really happened last night." Joaquin physically pushed him through the kitchen doorway, so he could be closer to explain.

"Dada was mad that I wasn't practicing golf. He caught me watching videos instead. He got mad and punched me in the chest and on my back. Then he told me to take off all my clothes, and he put me outside in my underwear. It was cold." Sammy's voice shook as he recounted his version of events.

"None of that happened, Sammy. Why are you lying to everyone?" Joaquin stared at Sammy; fists still clenched. Sammy's face continued to show confusion and fear.

"Maybe I imagined it," Sammy's voice trailed off as he looked nervously at his father, recoiling from Joaquin's clenched fist.

"Go to your room and think about what you're going to tell the court. You're not allowed to come out of your room until you stop lying," Joaquin yelled after Sammy as he walked back to his room.

That night, I searched online frantically for one shred of information about Sammy's mother. I didn't know her name, but I kept searching for any articles linked to Joaquin that might shed light on how she died. Nothing connected

Joaquin to any murders. I wanted to believe that Sammy was merely angry at his father and was using his mother's death to hurt him. There were a lot of unknowns and Joaquin's behavior as of late certainly put me on guard but moving from the belief that the father of your child is suffering from depression to acknowledging that he might've had something to do with a murder is a leap I was unable to take in my mind.

Joaquin's story about what happened to Sammy's mother was also inconsistent. Initially he claimed she had died in an "accident". Now he was admitting she was murdered. He explained his belief that she was killed by someone she didn't know, and that it was simply a random act of violence in a bad neighborhood. Claiming they'd been in a relationship at the time of her murder, he noted that he didn't talk about it because he was grief stricken. He said they never found the person who killed her.

In the days that followed, Joaquin continued emotionally terrorizing Sammy in an apparent attempt to get him to recant his story about the abuse. Though social services told him he wasn't to speak to Sammy about the incident or instruct him on what to say to the judge, Joaquin launched a full-on psychological war against his son. He took away everything in Sammy's room and told him he couldn't get it back until he told the truth. When Sammy asked Joaquin why he hit him, Joaquin told Sammy his memories were false and that he was making things up. After several weeks, I wasn't sure Sammy knew what the truth was after all the psychological terror.

Amidst this chaos, Joaquin's gun remained a prominent presence in our lives. It sat on the mantle and when he was upset, he'd pick it up and use it as a tool for coercive control, ensuring that everyone in the house complied with whatever he wanted.

"I have a legal right to carry this, and I will protect myself if I need to," Joaquin warned.

When he took out his gun, he'd often look me right in the eye, as though he wanted me to feel threatened by its overt presence in our bedroom. If Sammy had the protective order, Joaquin was no longer legally allowed to carry the concealed weapon in public. This gave him another excuse not to leave the house at all anymore. He began staying inside all the time, claiming he was depressed about the looming court date and playing video games day in and day out. I will never understand the logic behind taking someone's concealment license, while allowing them to remain armed. CPS put a child who'd clearly been abused back into a house with his armed and dangerous abuser, expecting that removing a concealment license would make any type of difference.

As the trial for the abuse allegations neared, Joaquin became more and more frantic. He stopped sleeping, stopped showering, and played video games for the entire time he was awake during the day. His eyes had dark circles under them, and he was starting to lose teeth. His breath was foul, and his teeth had what looked like months of plaque buildup on them.

He looked like a completely different person than the mad I'd met almost a year prior. I no longer initiated anything romantic with him but was afraid to reject his advances. On one occasion, when I'd recoiled when he tried to kiss me—telling him he needed to push his teeth—he pinned me down and forced himself on me. Afterward, I ran to the bathroom and threw up. This was one of the multiple occasions when I gathered my things and left the house.

I stopped being able to speak freely with friends and family while I was inside with him because he'd lurk behind me.

"Don't tell our business to your family," he'd scream.

I stopped hanging out with friends because I didn't want to leave Sammy alone with Joaquin and I didn't want them to ask about how things were going with us. My frustration with Joaquin's lack of employment continued, and when I brought up how he'd completely let himself go and didn't even seem to be trying, he claimed he'd had a stroke and was sick. Given his appearance, I believed this. And every time I'd think about leaving, there was a part of me who believed it was wrong to leave a partner because of illness—which is what I thought was happening to him.

As part of the court order, Joaquin was required to attend family therapy with Sammy. Joaquin found a therapist, Dr. Becky Smith (Dr. Becky), who eventually wrote a letter to the court that stated she believed Sammy lied to the school about the abuse. The charges were dismissed. Dr. Becky never told us that Sammy hadn't recanted his story. In a deposition years later, Sammy testified that he never understood why the charges against his father were dropped.

After the child abuse charges were behind him, Joaquin's mental state never returned to normal. In January of that year, I got a terrible bout of food poisoning from something I'd eaten at work. I rushed to Joaquin's house because I was afraid to be alone, given the pregnancy. When I told Joaquin that I didn't feel well, he immediately said he needed to stay away from me because he couldn't get sick. I woke up vomiting during the night. I crawled into the bathroom and screamed for Joaquin to come help me.

When Joaquin finally came upstairs, he peeked his head

in the door and threw a pot at me. "Don't mess up my carpets," he snapped as he slammed the door on his way back to his video games.

I slept on the bathroom floor that night, crying and throwing up. Joaquin left me there for more than 24 hours without checking on me again. That night was the first night it truly sunk in that I'd probably end up a single mother. The man I'd fallen in love with, partially due to the love he showed when speaking about his son, had really been incapable of compassion and didn't seem to want to take care of anyone except himself. And sometimes, didn't even want to care for himself.

In February 2011, I finally folded under Joaquin's near constant pressuring and rented out my condo. I couldn't afford to pay both mortgages. I moved out to suburban Virginia full time with Joaquin, to a place I'd never in a million years have bought a house. That Virginia town embodied everything I hated about suburbia. It was full of chain restaurants, cookie-cutter and vanilla neighborhoods, houses that were too large, and nowhere in walking distance I wanted to go. I felt trapped there and having to give up my condo felt like I'd lost my only haven away from the chaos.

I was paying for his mortgage (which was considerably more expensive than my own), his second mortgage, his housing association fees, and all the groceries. Though he'd proposed months earlier, no wedding date was set, and I was no longer sure if I even wanted one. The hormones of pregnancy, along with the added financial stress, eventually put me over the top. When I raised my frustration with Joaquin, he went into a rage. I was also worried he'd hit me—or shoot me. And I was angry with myself that I couldn't see my way out of this hell.

When I finally mustered the courage to tell him that I no longer wanted to be in this relationship, that this wasn't what I'd signed up for—and this wasn't healthy for me or my unborn child, the rage came out. But this time, the threat he made stopped my cold.

"If you leave, I'll take the baby, and you will have to fight me to get him back," he threatened.

I'd already worried about losing Sammy, a boy I had zero legal claim to—but now I had to worry about him fighting me for my unborn child too. I couldn't fathom leaving a baby in this house without me there to protect him. I was so afraid of this that I couldn't walk out the door.

My fairy tale was long over, and the fog was lifting rapidly. I was trapped in a hell that was somewhat of my own making and the fear of leaving my two boys in that house alone kept me a prisoner.

Chapter 7

Boiling Over

Joaquin started carrying the gun around the house as though he was chasing invisible demons. He talked to himself and spent most of the time in the basement. I didn't try to convince him to come upstairs because when he wasn't there, Sammy and I could live in relative peace. I never knew what Joaquin was so afraid of or if he just set out to scare us into submission.

The closer we came to the birth of our son, Joaquin's darkness continued to intensify. I started to notice strange things in the house. He told me his mother died of a heart attack before I met him. She'd lived in his house before she died. When I first arrived in his home, his mother's room had a single rosary hanging on the doorknob.

Joaquin said that she put it there before she died. He claimed she was very religious, and that he didn't have the heart to remove it after her death. In the months before I gave birth, though, I noticed that all the doors suddenly had rosaries. Every day, more rosaries seemed to pop up in the house. Joaquin wasn't religious and would never admit what was going on with the rosaries.

"Why are there rosaries on all the doors Joaquin?" I asked one evening.

"It's none of your business what I do in my own home." Joaquin shot me his now familiar menacing glare.

Since I was paying for everything in the house, this statement infuriated me. I turned away from him and bit my tongue, acutely aware that arguing wasn't safe. Things had gotten so strange that if clowns popped out of the closets, I probably wouldn't have been shocked. Sammy noticed the rosaries too, just shrugging his shoulders when I pointed out new ones I'd discovered.

Joaquin began pointing out my pregnancy weight gain, saying that I was no longer attractive to him. This was his lead in before telling me about what I could do to recover his affections.

"I think you should have sex with the lawn guy," Joaquin said one day, out of the blue.

I was sitting on the bed reading an article online. I slowly looked up from my computer, hoping that I'd see him laughing and claiming this was a bad joke. I wanted to ask him what the hell he was thinking. I wanted to scream at him, remind him of the fact that I was pregnant with his child, and tell him how this made me question whether he cared about either of us.

Instead, I muttered, "Excuse me, what!?"

"Well, if you offered to have sex with him . . . maybe he wouldn't make us pay him," Joaquin explained.

He was completely serious. I stared at him, wondering how he could ask me this. I stared back at him, trying to search for the man I'd first met—who I wouldn't have imagined would turn into this shell of a human sitting across from me. He'd initially acted like he wanted to be in a committed, monogamous relationship and I thought he knew the type of woman he'd picked in me. But his suggestion made me wonder whether he knew me at all.

"So let me get this straight—you're asking you the pregnant mother of your child to have sex with the gardener, so you don't have to pay him to cut the grass?"

My clarifying question hung in the air between us, as we both stared back at each other as though we were at opposite ends of a boxing ring. I was grossed out, feeling a very real wave of nausea bubbling to the surface.

"Well, I think it would be hot. If you love me . . . you'll do this," Joaquin argued.

"If I love you . . . I'll agree to prostitute myself for some sort of sick fetish of yours," I responded, feeling the heat on my face as the anger boiled inside me.

I was sure that he must've been able to see that I was clearly not on board with this brainchild of his. Tears welled up in my eyes as he just stared at me with a disgusted look on his face that matched mine. I felt dirty and unloved at even the suggestion of doing this. What had I gotten myself into with this man?

Joaquin was obstinate in his insistence that he wanted an open relationship because he'd get pleasure from seeing me have sex with other men. In the year that we'd been together by this point, this was the very first time he mentioned this fetish.

"If you don't do this, I'm no longer attracted to you," he threatened.

I hadn't stood up for myself in our entire relationship, but this was something I was not going to compromise on. I was never going to do this, though I suspected my disagreement could mean the end of our relationship. As Joaquin began berating me, I remained silent for several minutes as he droned on and on about all the other women who'd agreed to have this type of relationship.

"Don't you think it would've been appropriate to mention this a year ago, or perhaps before I was pregnant with your child," I asked, still seething.

"Lots of couples are swingers—don't act like this is a strange request," he defended.

"Then why didn't you make sure you found a woman who wanted to swing with you—someone who'd also think that was hot," my voice was raising, as my eyes darted to the gun that was resting on the dresser beside us.

Joaquin also looked to the gun and the corner of his lip curled into a smirk.

"I'm not doing that while I'm pregnant with our son. So, stop asking," I said, lowering my voice to cool the argument brewing between us.

My survival instincts kicked in when I recognized the familiar rocking and pacing that Joaquin started. I didn't want the gun to become a part of our conversation and with Sammy in the room next to use, I also didn't want him to hear us screaming at each other. That child had enough terror as of late and didn't need to add our adult drama to his plate.

"OK, I'll think about it. But not until after the baby,"

I lied, hoping that punting this conversation a few months would give me time to find a way out of this mess.

As soon as this conversation ended, I immediately buried my head back in the sand. I couldn't allow myself to consider what I'd do when the baby was born, and he'd asked me again. I couldn't love a man who was willing to share me, put my health at risk, and humiliate me in that way.

After the argument we had about prostitution, or "swinging" as he called it, he stopped touching me completely. Given how I'd felt about him in the past few months, a part of me welcomed this as peace—but we'd become like bad roommates. I suspected he thought I'd eventually give into his deviant sexual desires, but what he didn't know was that I no longer wanted him to touch me.

I was lonely and afraid, desperate to feel loved and safe—but knew deep down that neither of those things were possible in *this* relationship. What surprises me to this day was my ability to disassociate from the trauma occurring inside our home on a regular basis. I was disconnected from the trauma regularly, and it was that disconnection that allowed me to get up and go to work every day. I'd wait until I left the house to call friends and family and the moment I stepped across the threshold of the front door; it was as though the essence of the old me came back for the day. I put the trauma in a box and wrapped the box in excuses and explanations that allowed for a small thread of hope—hope that one day we'd get back to who we were together as a family, instead of who we'd become.

Most nights, I slept alone. Joaquin claimed he had insomnia, and he would spend the entire night in the basement playing video games. Some days, I wouldn't see him at all. Others, he would emerge from the dark, dungeon-like basement to ask me to make him dinner.

One night, roughly two months before my son was born, I woke up panicked. I was unable to catch my breath, as though someone was strangling me. It was in the middle of the night, and though it felt so real, at the time I was sure I was having a nightmare.

'Why can't I wake up?' I thought, as I struggled to breathe.

I tried to move and grab the pillow from my face, my breath caught in my throat like a caged animal desperately trying to break free. I clutched my stomach, terrified that I'd lose the baby if I was unable to catch my breath.

Finally able to sit up, shoving the pillow off my face, I came face to face with Joaquin. He'd been standing over me this entire time. And instead of attempting to console me, he had a devilish grin on his face as though he was mocking me.

"What are you doing," I screamed at him, tears rushing down my face and clutching my chest to try to catch my breath.

"You must've had a nightmare," he said with an eerie calmness.

But this wasn't a nightmare, because he was standing right there, and I felt someone—or something pressing a pillow to my face.

Was I losing my mind? I hadn't seen him enter our room at night in weeks. Why was he there now, and why had he just stood there when I was clearly in distress? Had it really been a nightmare? The worse things got, the more I tried to excuse the bizarre things that were happening around me. As quickly as the though entered my head that Joaquin was trying to kill me and our unborn child, Joaquin offered and explanation.

"It must be the pregnancy hormones. They are really messing with you," he said before walking out of the room.

I didn't sleep that night and never got another restful sleep again in that house. But I wanted to believe it was a nightmare, accepting that perhaps it *was* pregnancy hormones, because I could survive nightmares.

* * *

The weekend before American Independence Day on June 30th, 2011, I went into the hospital to be induced. It was a few days before my delivery date and the doctor's discovered that I had elevated liver enzymes, which if left unattended could cause the baby distress. Since we were so close to the due date, it made the most sense to just induce to avoid any possible harm to Prince by waiting the few extra days.

I had mixed emotions that evening. I was afraid, of the labor and the inevitable hardship I would face raising this child with a deadbeat father. I was afraid because I knew I would be doing this alone. Joaquin wasn't a partner. It was surprising he had even agreed to come with me that night.

As soon as the labor pains kicked in, Joaquin fell asleep in the recliner that was in the hospital room. I hobbled to the bathroom on my own, walked to the ice machines alone, and suffered through five hours of labor without a sole person by my side. I was in too much pain to be angry, but I did laugh at the irony. Here was a man who always complained of insomnia, and the one night I needed his ass to be awake, he was passed out asleep.

As the sun came up, a nurse came in and announced that I was dilated enough for her to believe that the baby would be here soon. At the presence of someone else in the room, Joaquin sprung awake and pretended he'd been awake all night. Seeing how quickly he could spring into action, acting like an entirely different person, was astonishing. He worked hard to give everyone in the hospital the illusion that he was a good father and partner. I'd been so consumed in the drama within our household in the months that proceeded, that I hadn't stopped to view how he put on the mask with ease before removing it when he was with me and Sammy.

He'd hooked me with that version of himself and in some ways, watching the nurses swoon was validating. It reminded me of what I'd fallen in love with a little over a year prior. And what for the last six months I'd been desperately trying to bring back in him. There was a time when I was unsure which version was really him. At first, he never let me see the monster. But covering who he really was must've been exhausting. Because now, I rarely saw anything but the monster.

When the nurses left, Joaquin disappeared for what seemed like hours. I wondered if he left the hospital, giving up on me completely. This thought, sadly, was not the worst-case scenario after the hours I'd just spent alone in labor.

When he finally returned, he brought a gaggle of nurses, all beaming and cooing. Joaquin then put on a huge show and acted like he was re-proposing to me in the hospital room. While these women were blinded by his show, I knew this was all about him as he attempted to essentially hijack my labor. He had this insatiable need to be always the center of attention. If the world wasn't revolving around him and his needs, he'd do something to ensure he captured the attention back.

As Prince started to make his appearance, Joaquin

grabbed my camera. We'd discussed photos and video prior to entering the hospital. I'd been adamant that I didn't want any photos or videos showing my naked and exposed body.

"Please don't take the video from that angle," I begged.

While I wanted to capture the birth of my son, I wasn't comfortable with my vagina being on camera. Joaquin, of course, didn't listen to what I wanted and continued filming.

I swallowed the lump in my throat to refocus on the moment with my son, promising myself I'd take the camera back at home and ensure he couldn't use the images to control me.

When Prince was born my attention turned completely to him. When they laid him on my chest, I looked at him and whispered, "Hi," with tears streaming down my face.

Though I'd just met him, I felt like I'd known him my entire life, and it was hard to remember my life before I was his mom. Prince came out singing, which is why the name suited him from the moment he entered the world. My heart danced as Prince's eyes and head searched for me, from the other side of the room, as he heard my voice. As I sat there nursing my son, I put all the drama that had been brewing in my relationship with his father to the side. It was as though my feelings of resentment and anger melted right off my shoulders.

All I could do was stare at Prince and tell him how happy I was to see him. This little boy became the love of my life, and at least in that moment, nothing else seemed to matter. I only spent one night in the hospital with Prince. I was thankful for this because I hated hospitals, and I was exhausted. I was so excited when I got to put Prince in the car seat to leave. He looked so tiny, and I couldn't believe he was mine.

I shifted between staring at him lovingly and being terrified and anxious about my ability to protect him.

As soon as we got home, I went upstairs to the bedroom with Prince. Joaquin left us there and disappeared to the basement with his video games. I didn't see him for an entire day after we arrived. I wasn't supposed to be climbing stairs, but I didn't have a choice. I needed food so that my milk supply didn't dry up.

The first time I went to get food Joaquin emerged from the basement and said, "Do you really think you should be eating? Shouldn't you be trying to lose all that weight?"

Even though I'd come to expect this type of behavior from him, it still crushed me every time. Our son was only a few days old, and instead of spending time holding him and talking to him, Joaquin was more concerned with terrorizing me. Standing at the top of the stairwell, I started crying. I felt dizzy and held onto the banister.

"I need to eat, Joaquin. What, are you trying to kill me and your son by starving us?"

I was tired, and I needed him to know how terrible he was being. As I pushed back with my words, Joaquin grew angrier.

"Look, I am trying to help you. I don't know why you insist on treating me so bad," he retorted.

He continued ranting, and I realized that to make it stop I'd need to be the person who apologized. Instead of pushing back as I should have, I tap danced and did whatever it took to calm him down. I turned and went back to the room, without food. When Joaquin went back to the basement, Sammy popped his head in through the door.

"I'm going to get you food and then I will come back and hold Prince for you so you can have a break," he said.

Sammy saw the tears forming in my eyes as I thanked him. When he returned with some yogurt and a bagel, I hugged him and reminded him that he was my "Suno"—a nickname that I gave him to let him know that he'd always be my first child. My "Son" and "Uno" for the Spanish number one.

Flashing his dimpled smile, he said, "I love you too."

As Prince struggled to stay awake, staring intently at his brother, Sammy started reading to him from his schoolbook.

'How will I ever leave this child,' I thought.

Though I was acutely aware that I wasn't legally his mother, Sammy *felt* like my son.

Chapter 8

Police Report

Officer Jones, who'd been quickly writing, looked up. He appeared to be studying my face. The way he was looking at me made me nervous. I smiled again. I wanted him to be less serious and prayed he'd give me a signal to show me that he was happy with my level of detail thus far. I wanted for this interrogation to be over. I wanted to take my son home, and I wanted to go to sleep.

'Stay calm, Hera. Don't show fear. You must be tough.' I continued giving myself a pep talk.

If I let myself truly feel the weight of this situation, I'd fall apart in front of this stranger. I couldn't let that happen.

Before this night, I hadn't had much experience with police. I grew up in the type of place where you could leave your keys in the car, the doors unlocked, and it would still be there in the morning completely untouched. The only time

I interacted with police officers was when they visited my small, Catholic elementary school to tell us about how they protected the community. I learned from this early age that if we ever had a problem, we should call them for help. They were the good guys.

"Wow, that is a lot. You seem calm given what happened," Jones said, now looking skeptical.

Smiling, I said, "Yeah, maybe . . . but I am trying to get through this and go home."

The thought never occurred to me that night that my composure, what I believed was necessary, could've been working against me. It also never occurred to me that I wouldn't be believed after reporting what was the worst experience of my life up to that point. My perception of how I came across that night seemed incongruent with the perception of the officers around me. It is possible that they expected to see a woman sobbing uncontrollably while recounting her story. Maybe expected that I'd have an emotional breakdown in front of them. This was not going to happen—it wasn't how I was wired.

Despite my smile and calm demeanor, I was terrified. Every time I closed my eyes, I saw Joaquin's gun and felt it pressed to my head.

'It's going to be OK,' I naively thought. 'The police will protect us.'

As I struggled through my story, I believed with all my heart that if I could just tell Officer Jones what happened, he would make sure Joaquin would not hurt us. I shifted in my seat, incredibly uncomfortable. My sore breasts told me that Prince would be awake soon, looking for food. I was mortified that I was going to have to find a way to feed my son in front of this officer. And my butt was sore from sitting on that metal chair for what seemed like hours by this point.

"Sorry, can I turn my chair toward the opposite wall? I need to feed my son, and I didn't have a chance to get a nursing cover," I asked.

I already felt naked telling my story to this officer. It wasn't just that my son needed to eat, and that I didn't want him to see my breast: it was easier to continue the story with my back turned to the officer. That way, I wasn't distracted by his reaction to my story.

With the same awkward reaction many men had to breast feeding, quickly averting his eyes and wincing, Jones quickly assured me that turning my chair wouldn't be a problem. Prince's big brown eyes looking up at me gave me the strength to continue. His cooing made me smile and reminded me why I was talking to the officer in the first place.

As Jones returned to taking notes, I continued my story.

After leaving the house safely, my attention returned to all the things I had left behind. I needed to go back to get my things. Baby things, my clothes, but, more importantly, my work computers. I couldn't leave company proprietary information with that man. I knew that I couldn't just go back into the house where Joaquin threatened to kill me, so I had called the police. I told them that there had been a domestic incident, that he had threatened to kill me, and that I needed police to come so that I could safely go back into the house and get some things for me and my baby.

"Please, I need help. I just fled my home with my two-week-old baby. I need to go back inside and get some things for the baby, but my son's father just threatened to kill me, and I am afraid to go back inside without protection," I pleaded over the phone.

My parents waited with me in the car as I called the police. While I wanted to scream on the phone about how Joaquin had raped my sister, my sister was in Maryland and told us that she was too afraid to come back to Virginia.

"This isn't an emergency. You need to call the non-emergency line, ma'am," the 911 operator said and promptly hung up.

An hour after my call to the non-emergency line, an officer arrived around the corner from Joaquin's house, where we were waiting after I called the non-emergency line. I wondered what sort of incident *would* warrant an immediate call. If I had called them while the gun was pressed to my head, would they have come immediately? But calling 911 while the gun was pressed to my head, holding Prince in my arms, would not have been possible.

I worried that Joaquin was now completely unhinged and pictured him waving his gun around the house and pacing in a rage. Was Sammy safe? What would the police find? I knew Joaquin wasn't going to go to sleep. He didn't try to call me after I left.

When the police arrived, they seemed calm, and their demeanor made me feel as though this was a regular day on the job for them. By this point, my parents and I were upset that it had taken so long for them to arrive. Instead of letting me enter the house, the police made us wait on the lawn for over two hours. Prince hadn't been changed in hours.

When they finally allowed us to go back into the house, I asked the officers if they wanted to come with me while I gathered some things. They told me that they didn't need to come with me, as I was clear that I was just going to collect things for the baby and for work. I ran through the house and grabbed clothes, shoes, and my work computers. While I went to get my things, the police sequestered Joaquin in a room at the front of the house.

It was hard to remain respectful to the officers. I understood that I was not able to pop off, telling the officers how angry I was that they made us wait on the lawn with a newborn baby. So, I bit my tongue and thanked them politely for allowing me to enter the house that I had been paying for during the months preceding this incident. I was getting increasingly frustrated by this scene. When I called the police, I assumed they would immediately help me get my things and that we would be out of there within thirty minutes. My sense of entitlement was likely obvious, and the officers didn't seem to share my belief of how they should have responded to my call of distress.

As I walked out of the house, the officers were speaking to my father outside. He was telling them that Joaquin had raped my sister. Now that we were out of the house, my father was more animated. Still exuding the type of emotion, the officers might have expected given our story, as that was not his way, my father was now using his hands while recounting to the officer what occurred that evening.

"Well, she is going to need to come back to Virginia and report this," one of the officers said.

Lara, by phone, said that she wanted to be left alone and that she was afraid to even come into Virginia. This is where Joaquin lived, and he had threatened her life if she told anyone. The officers continued to insist that she come and report a crime, despite our efforts to merely safely leave the scene. I didn't realize that we didn't have to comply with their demands. Reporting a crime is not something that anyone should feel forced to do.

While my father spoke to the police, I checked on Prince. He was sleeping in the passenger seat of the car, only a few feet from my father. Listening to my father explain what brought him to the house that night made me feel as though my heart was being torn out of my chest. I felt an overwhelming sense of guilt that I hadn't been able to protect my sister from Joaquin. Joaquin was pushing hard to have access to her that night, and I felt terrible that I was unable to see that he had nefarious intentions.

Up until this moment, it seemed like my poor choice in a partner had mostly impacted me. I could rationalize, excuse, and ignore the abuse that was directed toward me. I was not able to ignore Joaquin's attack on someone I loved.

From the moment I heard the news, there was not one second when I doubted my sister. She was and is a woman of integrity, and even at the young age of nineteen, I knew that her word was the truth. One major strength of growing up in a Christian community was that we all had a strong moral compass. While those Christian beliefs also sometimes allowed us to give people multiple chances that they didn't deserve, we were not liars. Joaquin, on the other hand, had given me plenty of reasons to doubt him. Joaquin hadn't earned my unquestioning trust—my sister had.

Joaquin seemed at home in this level of chaos. Later I learned that he didn't waste any time before calling his attorney, Mark McBride. McBride was a tall, lanky white man with longer arms than the average person. Whenever I saw him walk, I couldn't help but imagine I was in the middle of a jungle. McBride appeared whenever Joaquin was in trouble. When Joaquin had been accused of child abuse, McBride was there wheeling and dealing.

McBride sprang into action and immediately began creating just the amount of smoke and clouds the officers needed to come to Joaquin's defense. I was shocked to learn that police allowed McBride to be in the room when my sister was being questioned.

Before becoming a defense attorney, McBride worked as a prosecutor in Virginia. He seemed to know all the players, and he weaved in and out of that local legal scene with disconcerting ease. They let him take part in the investigation, as though he were still a part of the prosecutor's office.

Since I called the police for help, it never occurred to me that I might also need legal representation. I'd never called the police before that night because I'd never been in this kind of danger. As I was pouring my heart out to Jones, Joaquin was likely enacting his own defense strategy. *He* had been in similar situations before, and I suspect he knew exactly what would work to use law enforcement against the very people he'd just victimized.

After I gave my report to the police, I asked if I could go back to the house to get more of my things while they interviewed Joaquin. The police told me that I was welcome to go back into the house after they finished their investigation inside. Prince and I waited in the car outside of a shopping center down the street for several hours while the police finished combing through the inside of the house Joaquin and I had shared.

I was exhausted, still wearing the same clothes from the day before. The sun was now up, and I hadn't been to sleep. I looked down at Prince as I sat nursing him in the car. I felt terrible that he had to live through this only after two short weeks outside the womb.

Thankful that he was too young to understand what was going on, I did wonder if he was still able to sense my anxiety. Was it seeping into my breast milk? At this stage in his life, he wasn't even aware that we were two different people yet. This wasn't the experience I wanted my son to have, and it is certainly not how I imaged he would start his life.

Trying to avoid this very situation was one of the reasons I was somewhat content living in denial with Joaquin. I was afraid to face the reality that I would be raising my son alone and that there was something seriously wrong with his father.

We sat in car waiting for what seemed like hours, but it could have been significantly less. My mind wandered, and I drifted in and out of a half-sleep state. Once the police were finished searching the house, I went back and filled my car with as much as I could. Only able to fill a small car, I had to leave behind thousands of dollars' worth of my things that I would never be able to retrieve. I prioritized the baby things. Though much of that was replaceable, I felt an intense urge to make things as comfortable as possible for Prince without thinking at all of what I would need for myself.

While I was back on the second trip, I grabbed the camera that had the video with the birth of my son. I didn't give this a second thought, as I had purchased this camera months earlier. It was mine, and the video of my body in labor was certainly mine.

After learning that I was uncomfortable with the amount of nudity in the birth video, Joaquin teased me that he was going to upload it to YouTube just to embarrass me. While

I had allowed Joaquin to push my limits, I had reached my tipping point. I would be damned if I was going to let him terrorize me in this way, so I grabbed the camera on my way out and threw it in my purse. As I was wrapping up packing the car, I received a call from Officer Karen Martin.

"We are done questioning Mr. Rams, ma'am. He is going to be coming back to the house now," she said.

"He isn't being charged?" I asked, confused.

"Ha, no, of course not," Martin giggled, reminding me the girls in my fourth-grade class when they'd talk about boys.

'Uh-oh, that was quick,' I thought, worrying that Joaquin had flexed his superficial charm.

Obviously, this wasn't something she should've giggled about, but my surprise that he hadn't been charged seemed to tickle her.

Shortly after leaving Joaquin's house, another officer called and instructed me to go back to the station for further questioning. At this time, I trusted the police and wanted to do anything in my power to comply with their requests and assist them. While in the interrogation room, Office Kramer asked me if I had a camera. At first, I said no. I was confused, and I had no idea what they were talking about and what they wanted with my personal property.

I asked him to clarify what camera he was talking about. He explained that Joaquin told them I took his camera. Now I was really confused because I didn't know that Joaquin owned a camera. Officer Kramer then said he saw me take a camera.

"Really? The officers didn't even come upstairs with me last night. How would you have seen me take a camera?" I then looked in my purse and pulled out the camera with the birth videos.

"Is this the camera you're talking about?" My face twisted with confusion and irritation, which was painful given how incredibly exhausted I was now.

"Yes, that is the camera. That camera belongs to Joaquin," Officer Jones insisted.

As soon as Jones said that he believed the camera was Joaquin's, I got nervous.

"Why are you asking for this? I don't want Joaquin to have this. It has my birth video on it, and it doesn't belong to him. I don't want him to put it on YouTube," I was frantic, triggered at the loss of control and safety that turning over those images threatened.

"Don't worry, ma'am," said Kramer, "There's evidence on this camera. We aren't going to give it back to him."

After they claimed there was evidence, I willingly gave it to them.

This interaction at the police station was the first indication I had that something was amiss. This time, after talking to Joaquin and his attorney, McBride, the attitude of the police toward me seemed to change. Instead of asking me questions about my experience, the tone in their voices made me feel as though I was being accused of a crime instead of reporting one. Their questions indicated they had information they weren't sharing with me. The feeling that I was missing out on something important made me feel uneasy, but I was too tired and emotionally spent to try to diagnose the problem.

After giving the camera to the police, I walked, confused, and exhausted, back to my car. I hadn't slept in over 24 hours, and my mind was racing with anxiety and fear.

"Hey, whose car is that?" asked Jones as he ran down the paved path after me.

"Um . . . mine sir," I responded.

"Well, Joaquin says that car belongs to him," Jones said aggressively.

"Sir, I purchased this car and pay the insurance. The title is in my name, so if Mr. Rams has an issue, he can take me to court. I don't appreciate him trying to get you to do his bidding. I also don't appreciate your insinuation that I took something that doesn't belong to me," I retorted.

"Well, you can expect that he will come after you for that car," Jones responded smugly.

"I am more concerned about my son, sir," I said before continuing to my car.

"Well, ma'am, I don't think you have to worry about this guy coming after your son. He is going to come after that car, though," Jones explained.

How these officers were acting was confusing. I'd been the person who reported a crime, but now I felt like I was under investigation. And I still couldn't figure out why a police officer would follow me to my car to tell me that my ex-fiancé was going to come after me for a car I legally owned. I felt like I'd entered the twilight zone and was unable to determine if how I felt was related to the fact that I hadn't slept that night or if something was seriously amiss with that department.

Still naïve about how our justice system worked, I left the station believing that would be the last time I would have to step foot in this small town in Virginia. Clearly unable to go back to Joaquin's house, with a renter now in my condo, the only reasonable place for me and Prince to go was home to my parents' house in Maryland. I was incredibly grateful to have that option. I knew that my father was potentially one of the few people Joaquin was afraid of, as evidence by how he cowered in front of him the night I left.

As soon as I crossed over the border into Maryland, I let out an audible sigh of relief.

"We survived, Prince," I said aloud to my sleeping son. I knew he couldn't understand me, but I wanted to tell him anyway. I needed to tell someone.

When I turned in my camera to police, I was encouraged. I still believed that they were collecting evidence against Joaquin, and I wanted to do everything I could to assist with their investigation. I didn't know what they wanted with the camera but assumed that it would be used to help prove that he was a criminal.

Days later, I felt a deep sense of hopelessness as I learned the real reason the police asked for that camera. Unbeknownst to me, or my sister, Joaquin filmed the rape. Instead of questioning why Joaquin would do something so vile, not to mention that surreptitiously videotaping something of this nature is illegal in the state of Virginia, the police accepted his version of events. Joaquin insisted that he filmed my sister to prove that he didn't rape her. I was astounded those police couldn't seem to understand that this asinine explanation only proved that the rape was premeditated. If the sex had been consensual, he wouldn't have had to videotape parts of it to prove it wasn't rape.

Since the police couldn't find this video, they decided to hand the evidence over to Joaquin's attorney. McBride insisted that he had an IT guy who could recover the video. This was a clear violation of chain of custody for police evidence. Joaquin (along with an IT "expert" they never identified in court) mysteriously recovered the illegal video that

Joaquin had taken. The police were never able to prove my sister was on the video or whether it had been edited.

The police didn't seem to realize that there wasn't a moment that day when I would have had the time to view the contents of the camera, determine what was on the camera, and erase anything. I spent most of that evening and early morning at the police station. The rest of the time was divided between sitting on the front lawn in front of officers, nursing my son, and trying to get as many of my things that I could carry out of the house. Joaquin had drained my finances in those last few months, and I was devastated that all the baby items I had collected to make my son's nursery would be gone forever.

Joaquin told me he didn't touch Lara. If I *had* seen a rape video, I would have turned it into the police for that reason alone. To me, the existence of a video would have proved that he was lying. What was also strange, and confusing is that none of the officers bothered to ask Joaquin why (if he believed the sex was consensual) he decided to take a secret video in the first place.

None of this made sense, and the very fact that the police believed this man whom I knew to be a liar both angered and confused me. There was nothing about my past that would have led anyone to doubt my credibility. I had served my country as a Case Officer for the Central Intelligence Agency. I had to go through an incredibly rigorous background check to even step foot inside the CIA. I was both educated and accomplished. Joaquin, on the other hand, was not at all clean when it came to the law.

Given the irrational nature of Joaquin's bizarre, concocted story—perhaps with fine touches by his attorney—that my sister and I must have tried to set Joaquin up that night, what didn't make sense was why the police went along with it.

The day after I gave the police the camera, they called Lara back to Virginia, saying that they had additional questions for her. Still believing we didn't have a choice but to comply with their requests, and too naïve to insist on having our own attorney present, she returned. We all still believed that complying with the police was always a good idea.

Before she arrived, they had already decided that they were going to arrest her for making what they believed was a false report. It didn't matter to them that they had compelled her to come to Virginia and make the report in the first place. It didn't matter to them that they couldn't even prove where that video had come from, when it was taken, or even if it was her in the video. Her attorney was never given the opportunity to view the video, nor was he allowed access to the audio recording of Lara's statements to police, conveniently lost due to "technically difficulties" with the department equipment.

Two weeks after Lara's arrest, I learned that the police had put out a warrant for my arrest too. I waited weeks for my attorney to find out why I had been arrested. I replayed that night over and over in my head, trying to think of something I could have done that would have led to an arrest. I always came up short because all I had done that night was cooperated with the police. When I learned that they were charging me with obstruction of justice, I was still unclear as to why they were bringing these charges.

When I asked why the police would go so far as to charge Lara for reporting a crime that they compelled her to report, I was told that we had both wasted their time, and that I shouldn't have called them that night. Fighting in court to exonerate myself cost me more than $50,000. What I paid to defend myself was more than financial; I paid the price emotionally as well. I will never trust the police again, and our justice system will always give me a dangerous level of anxiety. I can no longer even drive next to a police officer without the threat of a panic attack. I fear that another day will come when I might need to call the police. The next time, I am not sure if I will be able to make the call.

I was finally free of the prison where I had lived for months, but I was thrown into a new prison. I was broken, and my sense of justice shattered. I called the police for help, and now I was the one forced to prove my innocence. I was merely a tiny reflection of myself, and I felt neither strong nor tough. I didn't save myself the night I left; I was saved by my love for my son. I was also saved by my courageous sister. Had she not told me what Joaquin did to her, I might not have had the courage to leave on my own. The people I loved kicked me into survivor mode, but I was *just* surviving.

Chapter 9

Detox

After leaving Joaquin, my son Prince was the glue that kept me from breaking into a million pieces. He had a sweet disposition even as an infant. Except for his sheer hatred and disdain for the car seat, able to scream like the possessed child in the exorcist for hours if not removed, he was a relatively chill baby. If he had a boob in his mouth and Adele's tunes in the background, he was in complete bliss. He could sleep anywhere, which was a good thing considering how much running around we did in the months after he was born.

Since I was spending every dime I had on attorneys, additional childcare costs weren't an option. Prince came with me everywhere—legal offices, the department of motor vehicles, and passport services, too. When he wasn't with me, he was with my mother. Neither of us felt safe leaving him with someone we didn't know considering the circumstances.

I often felt as though I was spinning around like a top, and without my family I would have spun completely out of control. My father, not the emotional type, gave me a car so that I could sell mine to afford legal fees. Being able to stay with my parents and save on rent and childcare enabled me to pay for attorneys.

My mother was by my side through the entire ordeal. She loved Prince as though she had given birth to him herself. The two of them would go on adventures together while I was at work, which frequently included secret trips to the local donut shop for a strawberry donut. They kept the donut trips to themselves for almost a year, until Prince flipped out one day inside a donut shop when I didn't realize he expected me to get him a strawberry donut.

I relied so much on my family and friends during this time. They listened without judgement and offered a shoulder to cry on whenever I needed one. I must've been somewhat insufferable during this time, as my thoughts were consumed with scheming of ways to show the court the monster, I now knew Joaquin to be. I also needed to show my attorneys, many of whom I am convinced just didn't understand the true danger until it was too late. My son's safety depended on my ability to expose the real Joaquin. It also relied on my ability to predict Joaquin's every move, something that I now understand to be impossible.

Having never been in any legal trouble, I turned to the only attorney my family knew—business attorney Gideon Horowitz. I had no idea what I was doing.

"We are going to need a fairly large retainer," Gideon said.

"Well, I am willing to pay what's necessary to protect my son. I've just sold my car, and I have about $30,000 from the sale," I replied.

My parents owned a salvage yard, and my father got me a used car from the yard to drive so that I could sell mine and pay attorneys. He hated the idea of coming to the attorneys' offices and the courthouse, but he did what he could to contribute to Prince's safety fund.

Gideon's face lit up at the mention of the money I had in savings.

"You should put the entire thing in a retainer. We'll need to use all of it, and that way if Joaquin sues you, he won't be able to take the money," Gideon said, with a gleam in his eye.

I was desperate to save my son, and I didn't know where else to go. Instead of researching a proper Family Law attorney, I gave $30,000 to Gideon. Gideon spent all $30,000 before we even went to trial.

I often wonder what sort of person *is* prepared for this type of experience. Maybe if I had known someone who had been through something similar it would have helped, but then I wonder how often others find themselves in Family Court with someone who has a personality disorder.

Most Family Court cases settle out of court, according to several Family Court studies. Some studies report as high as 90-percent of cases never make it to trial. This means that most people don't get to the point where they need to rely on a stranger to decide their child's fate—and most family court attorneys are rarely required to litigate. Prince's case, though, wasn't the first time Joaquin had gone through the Family Court system. The first time he was in Family Court was with his older son's mother, Shawn Mason. The second time Joaquin was in Family Court was to fight Shawn's mother for custody. By the time he entered Family Court with me, he had experience navigating this kind of system.

A week after leaving Joaquin, I filed for full custody of Prince in Maryland. Instead of receiving a response to my custody case, I received an email from Joaquin's attorney. McBride's letter didn't mention Prince at all. Instead, the letter asked me to return my car to Joaquin.

"Any delay in returning the vehicle to Mr. Rams is a substantial detriment to his well-being, as you know Mr. Rams does not currently have a vehicle at his disposal. Mr. Rams hopes to reach an amicable resolution of this matter, without the intervention of the courts. Please contact me as soon as possible to work out arrangements to return the vehicle."

Being left without a vehicle was detrimental to Joaquin's well-being? I shut my laptop with such force that I'm surprised it didn't shatter. The fact that I ever met Joaquin was detrimental to my well-being, and the fact that Prince shared DNA with this man was detrimental to his well-being. I wanted to laugh, cry, and scream all at once. I did all three—first laugh, then cry, then scream—one after the other.

This email felt like a threat and given how closely McBride was working with the police (as evidence by police turning alleged evidence over to him)—was legitimately scared.

Joaquin seemed to get sick enjoyment from litigation. He often gave too much thought to thinking about how he could sue people for perceived injustice. This should've been a clue that he was no good. In true Joaquin fashion, he tried to launch several lawsuits against me in Virginia after I left him. One of them was an attempt to sue me for the car McBride had written about in his email. Joaquin couldn't present any evidence that he owned my car, but I paid my attorney to fight it. If I had chosen not to fight it, possibly what Joaquin hoped, I risked having the court make a ruling in Joaquin's favor.

After spending thousands, and still not resolving the car case, Gideon sent me an email explaining that it was not cost effective to continue to fight the car case.

"Just to go to Virginia to handle trying to dismiss for lack of service, it took me 4.5 hours and $1,575," he stated.

After taking my money, he suggested I allow him to hire someone in Virginia to handle the car suit for another $1,500. Years later I learned this case could've been resolved with a letter requesting dismal of the case on the grounds that I owed the car outright and Joaquin didn't possess a shred of evidence to the contrary. An experienced attorney would've known this.

But even after all I'd been through with Joaquin, I still wanted to trust people. I had to believe in the good of most people, as it was too scary to go through life thinking that Joaquin was *not* a psychological anomaly.

With all the money I was dumping trying to defend myself from a baseless accusation of car theft, I wondered what Joaquin told McBride about the car and how he was paying him. Joaquin had a tendency of making even the most professional people do things that they wouldn't otherwise do for anyone else.

As soon as I received the letter, I sent it to my attorney. Gideon responded to McBride, instructing him that any further communication would need to go between attorneys. McBride already knew that I had an attorney, but he'd chosen to send the letter to my personal email.

I was relieved that the car seemed more important to

Joaquin than Prince. Maybe this meant he'd leave us alone. I tried to keep that thought prominent in my head, but I knew in my heart he would eventually come after us. He saw me and Prince as his possessions and I worried about what his anger toward me would mean for Prince. I felt incredible sadness for Prince. His father didn't care about him, and this was heartbreaking.

I looked at Prince's sweet face and wondered how anyone could avoid falling completely in love with him. Prince slept most of the time at that age, but when his eyes were open, they seemed as though they gave way to the gates of the universe. He had chocolate-chip-colored eyes that were so dark they reflected light and seemed to glow. Prince got his eye color from Joaquin, but the difference between their eyes was drastic. Where Joaquin's eyes appeared soulless and blank, Prince's eyes shined with innocence and joy. The image of his tiny eyes looking up at me in those early days will be burned into my memory forever.

While Joaquin hadn't responded to my custody papers, I couldn't shake the unsettling feeling that I had to learn whatever I could about Joaquin if I was to be prepared to prove in court what I knew to be true.

Gideon suggested I hire a private investigator. After Gideon paid his friend $500 to run a Google search on Joaquin, which revealed nothing more than I'd found myself, I decided to take the job to a professional who could offer a more thorough investigation. I hired Simon Clint, a private investigator in Northern Virginia, who'd worked in the prison system. Simon was a wonderful man. Many people were willing to take my money during this time and run in the opposite direction. Simon kept it real with me from the beginning. He never oversold his services, and he prepared me for the personality type that I was dealing with. Simon had seen this before, as the prisons are filled with people who had severe personality disorders.

Instead of relying on open source, Simon hit the pavement and interviewed potential witnesses. Simon had a gift of getting people to tell him just about anything. He interviewed Sheryl Mason (Sammy's grandmother, the mother of Shawn Mason), Crystal Toussant (Joaquin's ex-girlfriend), and officer Sgt. Christine Perry, all of whom ended up providing testimony during the trial.

I'll never forget the day Simon called me to inform me that he'd completed his investigation. I was in the car driving to dinner with Prince and my parents.

"Hera, I've completed my initial report and want to share some things with you," he said, with a hesitancy in his voice that I hadn't heard previously.

"Of course, I can chat now if that works," I responded, eager to hear what he found.

"Are you sitting down somewhere . . . safe," Simon's voice trailed off before finishing his question.

I told him I was driving, but that I could pull over. I was so excited that he'd found something. After searching online, and being frustrated when I came up completely empty, I was relieved that I would finally know something about the father of my child.

My relief quickly turned to terror as I listened to Simon explain his findings. As I sat in the parking lot in front of a shopping center in Maryland, I was frozen with fear and panic. What I learned was so much worse than I could've ever imagined.

Simon ran a thorough investigation, including location and background, asset, social security, criminal and civil court records, and employment reviews. He interviewed two witnesses, one person two reported to be a victim, and three of Joaquin's previous neighbors. His report uncovered evidence that Joaquin had been the subject of multiple criminal investigations, including murder—violent assault—and business fraud. Several witnesses agreed to speak to Simon, but insisted they remain anonymous, for fear Joaquin would physically harm them for talking about what they'd witnessed.

Sheryl Mason

One of the first interviews Simon conducted was with Sheryl. Fearing for her safety, Sheryl didn't speak with Simon until Sargent Christine Perry verified that he was a safe person to speak with. Sheryl provided us with information on what Joaquin was like before I knew him, and how he behaved during the custody trial she'd gone through with him years earlier.

During their interview, Sheryl told Simon that her daughter, Shawn, met Joaquin in 1996 when Shawn was only 15 years old. While Joaquin claimed he was also a teenager, Sheryl later learned that he was 24 years old.

In the fall of 1999, Shawn Mason had a child with Joaquin. According to Sheryl, Joaquin was verbally and sexually abusive toward her daughter, forcing her to take nude pictures. Shawn filed an emergency custody order against Joaquin in late 2002, citing that Joaquin made false police reports against her to separate her from the son that they shared. Months after Joaquin changed his name from John Anthony Ramirez to Joaquin Shadow Rams. In the spring of 2003, Shawn was murdered—on the eve her murder, she and Joaquin were set to go to trial regarding custody of their son Sammy. Almost immediately after her murder, Joaquin tried to claim that Shawn's life insurance policy (that she'd assigned her son as beneficiary of) was for him.

After Shawn's murder, Sheryl and Shawn's father gained custody of their grandson Sammy, but after police failed to formally charge Joaquin for Shawn's murder—he regained custody a year later.

Sheryl told Simon that she was convinced that Joaquin killed her daughter, as during the investigation Joaquin told the police that she'd been shot—about an hour before the police determined the cause of death. Without being a forensic pathologist and performing the autopsy himself, everyone wondered how Joaquin was the first to identify how Shawn died. To police arriving on the scene, the wound she had was *not* an obvious gunshot wound.

Sheryl had to endure the murder of her daughter and was then forced to watch the man she believed killed her daughter raise her grandson. After Sheryl spoke to Simon, he connected the two of us by phone. From the moment I heard Sheryl's voice, I felt like I'd known her my entire life. Her voice had a warm quality about it that put me at ease. She also projected a deep pain, which I assumed was the result of her losing her daughter so tragically. Sheryl was gracious enough to give me copies of all the files from her custody case with Joaquin. She also subsequently agreed to testify during my custody case, noting that she wanted to do anything she could to stop Joaquin from hurting someone else.

Crystal Toussant

Crystal Toussant left Joaquin in early 2009, a few months after his mother Alma Collins died. She reported that Joaquin started physically abusing her shortly before she left him. Crystal' statements were the most disturbing of the bunch, as she reported having been forced to have sex with multiple men. She also reported that Joaquin had held her at gun point, on occasion, as a form of intimidation.

Shortly before Crystal left Joaquin, she found his mother (Alma Collins) dead in Joaquin's home. Crystal believed that Joaquin killed his own mother, given that she was found with blood coming out of her nose and lying on a plastic bag. Joaquin obtained several hundred thousand dollars in life insurance benefits after his mother's death, which was likely what he was living off when we first met.

When Crystal finally left Joaquin, he sought revenge on her by posting sex videos of her on a revenge porn site that he created. He also sent text messages and emails of her nude pictures to her family and her boss. Though she reported this illegal behavior to police, he was never convicted of this crime. Crystal reported that by the time the police subpoenaed the phone records that would prove he'd sent nude pictures of her to people, it was beyond the limit of time that the phone company retained the records.

After reviewing Crystal' interview with Robert, my attorneys later decided to debrief her further. In addition to the disturbing details that she told Robert, she also reported that Joaquin was physically and emotionally abusive toward his older son. On one occasion, Crystal reported that Joaquin had thrown his son into a wall during an argument. His son cut his head on the crown molding. Instead of taking him to the hospital, Joaquin put liquid adhesive in the child's head because he was worried that he would get in trouble for hitting him if he took the child to the hospital.

With regards to the murder of Shawn Mason, Crystal reported that she was with Joaquin the night that he found Shawn. They arrived at Shawn's apartment to return his son after a visit. Joaquin told Crystal that since Shawn didn't answer her door, he busted the window to go and see if she was all right. He found her dead on the floor of her condominium.

Crystal said that just before Shawn's death, Joaquin told her that he hacked into Shawn's email and was enraged about what he read. He then asked Crystal if she knew of anyone who could "take care of her" for him. While Crystal said Joaquin's comment after reading the email was suspicious considering the murder, she believed him at the time when he promised her that he had nothing to do with Shawn's murder.

Additional Witnesses— Neighbors

In addition to interviewing Sheryl and Crystal, Simon went to Joaquin's previous neighborhood where we'd lived together, to speak with his neighbors. Most of the neighbors refused to provide their names, stating that they were afraid that Joaquin would retaliate against them. Many of them noted that the entire neighborhood was afraid of him, and that Joaquin made it clear that he always carried a gun. Several neighbors were able to verify that Joaquin had prostituted Crystal Toussant and others, noting that they saw loads of women coming and going from the house all throughout the day.

One neighbor claimed that Joaquin's mother Alma was frightened of Joaquin. Alma would visit this neighbor and vent to her, crying about the awful abuse she suffered at the hands of her son. This neighbor insisted that Alma didn't kill herself, and that she believed Joaquin killed her because of how much he hated his mother.

When asked why the neighbors never attempted to report their concerns to police, or speak with me once I moved in, one reported that Joaquin would walk up and down the street while I was at work waving around his gun. Neighbors were terrified that he would retaliate against them should they attempt to warn me in any way. I tried to be friendly with all my neighbors, but most of them either ran in the opposite direction or said hello before turning to run back into their homes.

Simon's report was terrifying. I started to wonder what else Joaquin was capable of doing and couldn't imagine how I'd handle ever having to turn Prince over for a visit with his father.

Chapter 10

State-Sanctioned Terrorism

According to records I obtained from the Virginia Police Department in response to a Freedom of Information Act (FOIA) request, Joaquin had Shawn arrested multiple times. Joaquin successfully had Shawn arrested, after he accused her of hitting him and was able to obtain a protection order against her. After that, he reported she'd violated the order (though she hadn't) and an Officer Jameson arrested Shawn. Surprisingly, the police documents report that Joaquin was with Officer Jameson when he arrested Shawn.

Every time Joaquin got in trouble, he'd tell which ever officer arrived on the scene that he was a friend of Officer Jameson. He name-dropped Jameson the night I called the police on him. I remember the officer who arrived was skeptical that Joaquin knew Jameson, but after a phone call to whom I can only assume was Jameson or someone connected to him—the tone of the entire night changed, and I saw the officer at the scene chumming it up with Joaquin as though they were old friends.

October 12, 2011, the day after my 31ˢᵗ birthday, I turned myself in to the County Police Department in Virginia in response to the warrant that'd been filed in the weeks after I fled Joaquin. I was innocent and had I *not* cooperated with the police several months earlier, I wouldn't be sitting in a police station accused of this crime.

I felt like I was being punished for following the rules and that the police were now an extension of Joaquin himself-terrorizing me on his behalf. The similarities between what Joaquin did to Shawn, in hopes for a custody advantage, were terrifying. I felt like I was watching history repeating itself and had no defenses against an entire system that seemed to be working on behalf of my abuser.

As I watched Detective Timothy Jones scribble unintelligible chicken scratch on the warrant paperwork, I still wasn't sure what I was being charged for. Since the police arrested my sister, due to their belief that she falsely reported a rape, I wondered if they'd also assumed I had falsely reported something that night.

'Shit, what did I do?' I thought, still running that night through my head as though it might offer up clues as to why I was sitting in this police station.

Since my attorney Gideon instructed me not to say a word, I sat there biting my tongue. I grew angrier at Gideon by the second. He sat there speaking in a sweet tone, while I wanted to kick Jones in the nuts. I'd expected him to advocate for me and didn't realize that this would be a meeting where we'd exchange uncomfortable, awkward, and disingenuous pleasantries.

'Why isn't he asking this officer why we're here?' I thought.

It appeared Jones believed I knew why I was being arrested, because he made no attempt to explain. Was this normal? Did people often get arrested and have no clue what they'd done to break the law?

I called the police the night I left Joaquin because I was scared. Up until that point, I believed that the police would help me if I was ever in danger. A belief system that I had spent almost 31 years cultivating was shattered within the course of 24 hours. Not only was I terrified that Joaquin would find and kill me, but potentially more terrifying was the knowledge that there would be no part of law enforcement that would lift a finger to stop this from happening. Not only would they not help me, but they were also helping the abusive (suspected serial killer) that I was desperately trying to escape.

My entire life I'd been careful about my reputation. I didn't drink in high school, never touched a cigarette, and would never have considered trying drugs. Working in National Security made me proud. My ability to obtain one of the highest clearances in the US Government was something I wore like a badge of honor for all my hard work. I'd been a good girl—the best girl. I held onto the idea that my life-long honesty would protect me if I ever needed it. I could always rely on my integrity and my strong reputation. But in this small, corrupt Virginia town, my history was meaningless. I didn't know anyone, and Joaquin seemed connected to everyone in power.

I looked down, to avoid meeting Jones's gaze, just in time to watch his swollen fingers scribble "Black" inside the racial identification box on the form. I swallowed hard, and my brow furrowed angrily. My face began to overheat, and I felt like the walls were closing in around me. I wanted to get out of this office. Had I felt as though I had the power to leave, I would have gotten up and run out of there.

Had this been what this was all about? Did he look at Joaquin and just see a White man, and because I look Black, he assumed I must've been the person less credible? This thought also seemed insane, but I was at the point where I was entertaining any explanation of why this was happening.

Months earlier I'd smiled at this same officer, trying to make him feel better about the horrible story I felt forced to report. I'd coped the only way I knew how. My kindness in that moment seemed to betray me now. I'd tried to be tough, and brave, so that he would be able to do his job and arrest my abuser. Now, I didn't smile or speak to him at all. I sat as still as possible, rage welling up.

It didn't matter that I'd never been arrested, that I had a security clearance, and that I went to work every day to protect *all* Americans. None of that mattered here. What did matter was only his version of the truth. No matter how false and asinine the charges, he could do whatever he wanted. I was completely powerless. They were forcing me to fight them in court, and they'd have the pockets of the taxpayers on their side.

'Obstruction of Justice', I've since heard from family and friends who are police officers in different jurisdictions, is a common charge police officers use when they want to arrest someone and don't necessarily have anything solid to charge them with. I didn't know that at the time, nor can I be sure about their true motives behind my arrest, but I can say that at the time it felt as though I was being targeted. And my extreme lack of knowledge about this system fueled my anger and confusion. Joaquin wasn't classically educated, but he seemed to have enough knowledge of our busted system to exploit it for his needs—or it sincerely felt that way to me. And every time one of the Virginia police officers acted in a way that felt like an extension of Joaquin, I'd remember the times when Joaquin made sure everyone knew he had "friends" on the force.

I've never met Jameson. He never once came to the house during the year I lived with Joaquin. But I heard his name on several occasions. Specifically seared into my memory were the times he name dropped "police friends" when he was arrested for abusing Sammy and the night I fled his house with Prince.

"I come from a long line of police officers—seven generations in my family," Joaquin would frequently boast when encountering a police officer.

He'd gush about how much respect he had for the profession. Joaquin kept cool and collected no matter how ridiculous the fib. And he had elaborate stories about playing golf with his buddy Jameson—a decorated officer who's since retired.

I stared intently at Jones. He continued to scribble away, with a smirk that appeared irksomely gleeful.

'I am a good girl,' I kept thinking to myself.

Repeating this in my head was my attempt to comfort myself and calm the pounding. I bit my lip, as I felt tears well up in my eyes. I didn't want to give Jones the satisfaction of seeing me cry.

"Hey, good luck. I wish there was something I could do for you," Jones said, as I took the warrant and started for the door.

The smirk, that he appeared to be trying to hide, widened as he spoke. This revealed pieces of what I assumed were his breakfast still stuck in his teeth. Him wishing me luck, and saying that he wished he could help me, was insulting. I knew he wasn't pulling for me to come through this untarnished. There actually *was* something he could do—he'd been the arresting officer. It was fully within his power to drop the charges.

The depth to which he tried to distance himself from his own actions was astonishing. Throughout the years, I've noticed a tendency from law enforcement authorities to say things that they'd likely never say to someone they knew had deep knowledge of how these things worked. Most of us don't grow up learning about criminal and civil procedure, or what to do should we find ourselves relying on police intervention—or wrapped up in a police interrogation. And for people like me, it's not until tragedy strikes that we're forced to get the education we wish we'd known *before* the trauma.

My father has always said, "better to be thought of as a fool than open your mouth and remove all doubt."

If only Jones had received that same guidance. But I knew enough then to know that I couldn't pop off on Jones. My rational side didn't allow me to speak the high volume of curse words that were flooding my mind. Instead, I rushed out of that station as fast as I could to avoid severing my tongue that was being clutched in a death grip by my teeth.

It felt like Officer Jones started a war. This whole thing felt like a show and that he wasn't coming after just me; he was coming after my livelihood—and therefore, I felt like the was coming after my son too.

Lip bleeding, and soul crushed, I walked out of the station with a copy of a warrant. I no longer believed in the American Justice System. Along with my faith went my sense of safety. I wasn't sure which was worse in the long run, but at that moment I needed protection. I was terrified of Joaquin. I knew he wasn't going to just let me leave, but I wasn't sure what his end game was either.

I regretted going to the police for help. I wished I'd just run off in the middle of the night, vanished into obscurity, and left before Prince was born. Though I hadn't heard from Joaquin in months, I believed him when he said he would come after us.

Gideon failed me that day. We missed out on the opportunity to ask questions because he simply sat there like a scared deer in headlights the entire time. I paid him 250 dollars an hour to escort me to the station and sit there like he'd lost his ability to speak.

I felt like an outsider watching my own life unfold. I spent days closing bank accounts that Joaquin had access to and changing all my personal documents to reflect my new residence. Establishing that Maryland had jurisdiction in my court case wasn't straight forward because technically it takes six months to establish residency. Prince wasn't even close to six months old, so he hadn't lived anywhere long enough to establish clear residency.

While Gideon insisted that our best chance to fight Joaquin was in Maryland, Gideon's timid behavior in the police station didn't inspire confidence that he could handle this case.

"Gideon, I need to hire a Virginia attorney for the criminal case," I said over the phone.

"Yeah, uh oh, we're still good with the custody case, right? I mean, I agree for the criminal stuff. I can see why you might need someone local for that," Gideon responded, sheepishly.

After firing Gideon for the criminal case, I hired Noah Levin. Noah was notoriously fierce, and expensive. I knew affording to pay him would mean that I'd be eating ramen noodles, living with my parents, and racking up credit card bills. I also knew that if I lost my clearance, due to the judge not understanding the insanity of this charge, I'd be unable to provide my son with any sort of financial security.

It's possible that Noah's harsh personality was one of the reasons he was successful, or maybe being a defense attorney had hardened him. I wondered if Noah's fierce demeanor and wicked tongue would get the prosecutor to drop the case.

Shortly after hiring him, Noah convinced me to pay a professional polygrapher. I'd been through a polygraph before, and I knew they were never pleasant. I was 24 years old when I had my first polygraph. It was a requirement to become a Case Officer at CIA and we had to endure the most extensive type of polygraph. My first polygraph lasted four hours. I left having confessed things even as small as inadvertently removing a company pen from the office. I argued with my first polygrapher because he didn't believe I'd never even stolen a candy bar from the corner store as a child.

I had deep seated Catholic guilt, the aftermath of years attending catholic school. Catholic guilt is basically a fully developed and overly functioning conscience. Being strapped to a chair, while a stranger speaks to you in an accusatory tone, is torturous. Even answering questions for things that I knew I didn't do made me anxious, simply because I felt like I was being accused of it.

I was so desperate to clear my name, that I agreed that this would be a good investment. Surely once I passed the polygraph they would believe me, right? I'm not sure why I still believed I was dealing with rational and logical opponents.

To Noah's credit, he was the first attorney capable of getting Josiah Henson, the prosecuting attorney, to explain what the state was charging me for. The police believed that my sister and I were colluding against Joaquin, to get him arrested for a crime they believed he didn't commit. Joaquin told the police he didn't rape my sister and insisted he could prove it because he surreptitiously filmed the encounter. When the police couldn't find the evidence Joaquin claimed was on my camera, they agreed with Joaquin that I must've erased it to obstruct the investigation.

"If I had even seen the video, I would've raced to the police station. Because, to me, the video would've proved rape," I said, disgusted at the accusation.

"Calm down, Hera," Noah said, rolling his eyes with a patronizing tone.

"This charge is bullshit, just like the charge against your sister," Noah continued.

I was silent on the phone for several seconds, trying to catch my breath.

"Call your polygrapher. This is going to be simple. Just ask me if I even knew this video existed," I said, confident of my innocence.

Though I didn't know the arresting officers, I felt a sense of betrayal from them. The CIA isn't a law enforcement agency, but I *also* took an oath to protect and serve—just like they did. I trained alongside FBI agents and perhaps that gave me a false sense of solidarity with law enforcement officials. Never in my wildest nightmares would I have thought a law enforcement official would side with Joaquin over me.

A former FBI polygrapher, Noah's "go to guy", gave me a polygraph in February of 2012. He spent decades working for the FBI and took his professional reputation very seriously. Nobody who knew me was surprised when I passed the polygraph. Through hours of relentless questions, I proved that I had no knowledge of the video the police were accusing me of erasing. I breathed a sigh of relief when the polygraph was done.

Though Noah never admitted it, I wonder if he didn't believe me when I first came to him for help. His demeanor seemed to change after I took the polygraph, as though he didn't realize I had been telling the truth.

"I am used to representing a lot of guilty people," he said.

After this comment, I wondered if hiring an expensive attorney made me look guilty. I wondered if I'd ever be able to figure out this strange justice system. Possibly sensing my distress, Noah assured me that he would present this evidence to the state. Even Noah assumed this would end this charade.

A few days after Noah sent the polygraph results, Josiah wrote back rejecting the validity of the exam. He cited that he didn't believe in private exams. He then went on to insult the polygrapher, stating that he was a hired gun, and the results were worthless. I immediately offered to take the police polygraph, to remove what they believed was a bias. Of course, likely because Josiah wasn't interested in uncovering the truth, he refused to allow me to take their polygraph.

After the polygraph strategy failed, Noah met with Detective Jones and Mr. Henson at the Commonwealth Attorney's Office to view evidence and discuss the case. During this discussion, it was clear that Gideons on hadn't shared my polygraph results with the police. Josiah went on to further insult the 35-year FBI veteran polygrapher by stating that he was essentially hired to lie for Noah. When Noah clarified by asking if Josiah was calling the polygrapher a "whore," Josiah replied quite clearly that this was exactly what he was saying.

Josiah didn't appear interested in anything that could possibly go against his theory that I had somehow staged that entire night just to set Joaquin up for rape. On March 21, the day after this negative meeting, Noah wrote a letter to Josiah attempting to state his position, given that he was unable to do so in person:

"Josiah, I will tell you that I have rarely had such a meeting as that which took place between us and Detective Jones on March 20, 2012. The meeting was not an exchange of information, ideas or even advocacy on behalf of our positions, but rather an insulting cross examination by you, over-speaking me, interrupting attempted explanations and discussions, yelling and an indifference to the truth of what took place here versus further asserting the case is not going to be dropped and that is that. I was shocked and dismayed at how the meeting went. Further, it is incredible to me that you had not discussed with Detective Jones the polygraph results and my position on behalf of Ms. McLeod."

Despite numerous requests to the Virginia attorneys to provide discovery, they continued to withhold information.

After months of withholding information that I was legally entitled to, Noah sent one of his attorneys to the courthouse to face Josiah in person. The attorney tried to hand deliver the paperwork officially requesting discovery, but Josiah refused to sign the order and the attorney reported back that he was shocked at how angry Josiah became over a routine procedural request.

"Noah is a jackass and I'm sick of it," Josiah said as he walked away.

Noah and Josiah's regular bickering, most of which I viewed via forwarded emails, was clouding this entire situation—and I worried that the bickering back and forth was making this worse for me. I felt like my civil liberties were being stomped all over by a giant elephant that always seemed to be present during negotiations with Virginia prosecutors. And again, it didn't seem to matter that we were legally entitled to discovery because we just wouldn't be getting any. And despite not being able to provide any basis for my arrest to allow my attorneys to prepare for trial, Josiah continued to insist I plead guilty to a crime I didn't commit.

I continued to be thankful that during this process I no longer paid Virginia taxes. But as the case droned on for nearly a year, full of theatrical performances by grown men who should've known better, Virginia taxpayers were paying the price.

Though Noah was my second criminal attorney, it was clear after all the bickering between the two that hiring him was *also* a bad decision. I spent ten thousand dollars during the few months Noah represented me before I removed him from my case.

I tried to take some comfort in the fact that for ten thou-

sand, at least I finally knew what I was being accused of—
Obstruction of Justice. A charge that seemed wildly ironic
given how hard I'd been trying to assist in Justice finally
being carried out here.

Chapter 11

Antebellum

After my unceremonious arrest, and what seemed like months of back-and-forth battles with the police department and the District Attorney's office, it was time to begin the proceedings for the custody case. The first step was the scheduling hearing, which Gideon believed Joaquin wouldn't bother attending.

While a hearing meant to simply schedule the steps prior to trial might seem completely innocuous, even the thought of seeing Joaquin again made my heart race with fear. In the years since, I've learned that many abusers use court to legally abuse their ex-partners. Joaquin was no different—he knew exactly how to twist the system for his benefit and had experience using it to torture his victims.

"Joaquin doesn't just let people go," I told Gideon anxiously.

It'd been three months since I'd left Joaquin—and I still couldn't let it go. I felt like a monster was lurking around every corner and my hyper-vigilance was making me feel like I was going crazy. It didn't help that my attorney was acting like Joaquin was just a normal dude and that I didn't have anything to worry about.

"Hera, it's been months. He isn't coming back. Just relax," Gideon said, trying to reassure me.

"Gideon, didn't you see the PI report?" I responded, wondering why he was so cavalier.

I woke up on my birthday that year hopeful. I held Prince in my arms and was thankful that we'd escaped Joaquin. I tried to stay positive throughout the day, even though I couldn't shake the feeling that this wasn't going to be over so easily. Just as I was leaving the house to go to dinner with my parents, I received a call from Gideon.

"Hera don't freak out," Gideon's voice trailed off, clearly nervous about sharing.

I don't know why anyone bothers with this sort of opening. It's like starting with "no offense" before saying something completely ratchet. I was already freaking out before he uttered the news.

"We just received a response from Joaquin's attorney today," Gideon continued, his voice shaking.

He was wrong. Joaquin hadn't let us go—he was just waiting for the right moment to terrorize. He waited for that day because he knew it would hurt. The fact that he'd waited months, to respond on my birthday, also sent me a signal that he didn't care about Prince. Had he cared, it wouldn't have taken months.

"Hello, hello?" Gideon must have assumed there was a

bad connection because there was silence on my end of the phone.

"I'm here," I responded, trying to practice the breathing exercises my therapist gave me.

This was the giant shoe I'd expected would drop.

Mark McBride, Joaquin's attorney in Virginia, wasn't barred to practice in Maryland. So, Joaquin hired Chastity Carter for the custody case. A month prior to his response to my filing, Joaquin filed for custody in Virginia. I missed the first court date in Virginia because Joaquin never bothered to send a subpoena.

When I initially saw Chastity Carter, I remember feeling a sense of relief. McBride's connection with the Virginia authorities never made me feel as though I was on equal footing—but in Maryland, Joaquin didn't have the same types of connections. This was a naïve assumption, as Chastity quickly felt like an extension of Joaquin and family court is a breeding ground for emotional terror. Chastity came into the courtroom like a bulldozer that was ready to plow down anyone standing in front of her.

As she walked to the defendant's table, she had to turn to the side to squeeze through the narrow pathway toward her seat. I never saw her smile, except for when she was looking into Joaquin's eyes or rubbing his back. During the first few hearings, the two of them seemed to have a quick rapport—Joaquin whispering into her ear and her giggling in response.

While McBride's connections scared me, he was relatively non-threatening in most other ways. In contrast, I found Chastity's behavior triggering. When she's speak about me in court, I felt like I was being transported back to middle school, forced to endure the psychological torture of a mean girl. Every time she looked in my direction, I felt like she was glaring at me in a way that felt personal—even though we didn't know each other personally. Maybe intimidation of this nature was strategy, and it certainly was somewhat effective.

Whether attorneys intend this to be the case, they often become extensions of the abuser for abuse survivors. While I understand that they're being paid to defend their client, this often comes in the form of personal attacks against someone their client has abused. One of the things I advocate for is taking the profit out of family court. I know family court attorneys would hate to hear this, but there is something deeply flawed about a system that biases in favor of the party who can pay the most for their representation.

Without mention of why it'd taken Joaquin three months to even ask about his son, his attorneys insisted that Joaquin should have full physical and legal custody of Prince. Joaquin claimed that I forcibly removed Prince from his home at gunpoint. It must've slipped his mind that he'd been the one wielding the gun that night. Joaquin also claimed that my 59-year-old mother assaulted him the night I left.

I couldn't figure out what aspect of this story was stranger—the fabrication that his child's grandmother assaulted him, or the fact that he didn't feel shame in claiming that a woman almost 20 years his senior could kick his ass.

"I wish I *had* given him a black eye that night. In fact, give me a bat right now and I will show him just how it would look if I had hit him," my mom joked, utterly gleeful by the image of her beating Joaquin up that night.

While I can certainly understand the hilarity in this assertion ten years removed from this experience, at the time it was extremely disturbing the lengths Joaquin was willing to go to make it look as though I was the villain in his story. I've learned this is a common tactic of abusers—to concoct stories they know the court is unlikely to vet to fill the case with smoke. Doing this distracts from the problematic details surrounding them by making it look like both parents are just fighting with each other. The fantastical allegations cast doubt on the veracity of anything that either side claims, and many judges get fatigued by it and don't bother trying to assess which side is more credible.

Years after this incident, Sheryl Mason told me that Joaquin used that same image to accuse Shawn of hitting him.

Continuing to read Joaquin's assertions made me feel physically ill. It was also the first taste I got of how terrible this court case would be. Joaquin could say anything about me in open court, without any proof, and it wouldn't matter.

Joaquin was a criminal who didn't care about perjuring himself, and it didn't seem to matter that none of these claims could be proven. It appeared Joaquin's strategy was to throw as much horse crap at the judge to see if any of it would stick.

Joaquin's responses to my case continued, as he asserted that Prince shouldn't live with me because he believed that I was "a liar, thief, and criminal with no redeeming qualities whatsoever."

One of the first things that my attorneys told me was how dangerous it would be to make baseless accusations against the other party. If I'd come into court calling Joaquin a liar, thief, and a criminal without any proof, I would've been playing right into the hands of his attorney. I would've been labelled as a scorned woman who was just angry that her fiancé cheated.

As Joaquin's responses to my case rolled in, I learned that he and Sammy moved out of the house I'd been paying for and in with Ronan and Roxy Bailey. Joaquin suggested that Prince live with him and his new chain-smoking house-mates, sharing a room with Sammy.

Ronan and Roxy's relationship with Joaquin continued to confuse me. Remembering how they'd only come around to ask Joaquin to repay them money he'd borrowed, I won-dered what sort of arrangement would allow them to now be providing housing for him and Sammy.

Ronan, pale and skinny, with thin, white hair, bore a striking resemblance to the famous serial killer Robert Durst. He smelled so strongly of cigarette smoke and bad body odor that his smell often wafted in the room before he entered. Ronan always had a curmudgeonly scowl on his face. Even before leaving Joaquin, every conversation I had with Ronan made me feel like I needed to take a shower after. He had a way of looking at women as though he was undressing them with his eyes.

His wife, Roxy, claimed to be blind. She walked around with big, dark sunglasses and was most often seen holding onto Ronan in public. I caught her in court several times walking around solo and looking out the window when she thought nobody was watching. As soon as it was time to go before a judge, however, she always fell into the character of a blind woman. In the court documents, Joaquin claimed that Ronan and Roxy were Prince's grandparents. A move I suspected was an attempt to even the playing field given that I was living with Prince's actual grandparents.

Carter's court filing also suggested that Prince should

spend as little time with me as possible. To this day, I'm baffled how any attorney could let this type of language seep into the court record. The only explanation I have is that Joaquin wasn't paying enough for his team to edit, or fact check his claims.

The gross amounts of paperwork that came through to my attorneys from his contributed to the legal abuse. Every shred of paper represented cold, hard cash that I'd need to pay for legal review.

Joaquin believed that my contact with Prince would be "detrimental to his upbringing." While at this time Joaquin had no legal means of income, he suggested that if given custody of Prince he would find a nice townhouse in Virginia where he could keep Prince away from me and my family. He believed *we* were of "questionable moral character."

Joaquin believed that he, however, was an "honorable man and [had] a proven record of being a responsible single parent."

To prove that he was a responsible man, he claimed that he had a Defense Department security clearance. Joaquin was unable to even obtain a passport, given that he was living with a fraudulent birth certificate from a state he wasn't even born in. If Joaquin *had* tried to apply for passport, he'd have been in violation of federal law. If he'd applied for a security clearance, he'd face up to ten years in prison for presenting the government with false identification.

One of the common complaints that I hear from court officials is that the "he said, she said" game is exhausting. While custody evaluations are often a part of the process, conducted by social workers, these can give the courts a false sense of accusation verification. In many states, there aren't standard trainings required for social workers as it relates to domestic violence, child abuse, or high conflict custody cases. They're often under-resourced and have limited access to what they'd need to properly investigate both parties.

For example, in the state of Maryland custody evaluators cannot travel outside of state for home visits and don't have access to child protective service records outside of state. So, Joaquin could say anything he wanted about his living conditions and deny past, documented child abuse and there was no mechanism within the court to prove him wrong.

Joaquin accused me of everything he embodied himself. To make himself look better, he tried to cloak himself in bits and pieces of my background. His mother was dead, likely by his own hands, and the rest of his family believed he killed her. So, he invented a family, just has he'd done with me when he presented the Flores family, by presenting fake grandparents.

Ironically, the county police accused me of making up lies to gain a custody advantage. It was their belief that I talked my sister into reporting a rape, to put Joaquin in jail. In Joaquin's response to my suit, he tried to use the charges against me to prove to the court that I was an unfit parent. The very thing that the police had accused me of trying to do, Joaquin was *actually* doing. And as I read the documents, it became clear why Henson was stalling my case without providing a shred of data—Joaquin needed to keep my case alive until the custody hearing.

The first time I saw Joaquin after the night I left was in the courtroom for our first scheduling hearing in November of 2011. I held my breath as we walked through the large glass doors of the courthouse, my mother to my right and Gideon to my left. My breasts were engorged, which only served as a painful reminder that I had to leave my son with a babysitter so that I could protect him from his father. Gideon and my mother surrounded me as though they were forming a human shield. After the information the PI collected, I was more afraid of Joaquin that day than the day I left him.

This first hearing was the first and last time I allowed Gideon to step foot in the courtroom as my representation. After Gideon's timid silence in the police station a month earlier, when I went in to respond to my warrant, I'd already lost a significant amount of trust in him. The only reason he started on the custody case was because I didn't have anyone else to replace him in time for the hearing. Like my relationship with Joaquin, I stayed too long in my professional relationship with Gideon. I kept giving him chances, and by the time I realized he wasn't going to work out, I was stuck with him through this initial hearing.

I had to keep reminding myself to breathe. My mother also appeared pained at the idea of having to face Joaquin in court. Despite the strength it required to watch her daughter suffer, she came with me to every single hearing and trial. And while she stood at only 5 foot 5 inches, a couple inches shorter than me, having her there felt more important than having my attorney.

Just after going through security, I looked at Gideon for any sign of assurance. I wanted so badly for him to tell me this would be okay, but there was nothing about his demeanor that assured me. One of the mistakes that I made early on during the legal trauma was expecting my attorneys to act as a therapist would. I wasted so much money talking through the issues with them when I should've saved most of that for my therapist. When I talk to parents who are in family court, I always recommend a good therapist and remind them that if they expect their attorney to fill that role—they will be disappointed and have less money in their pocket.

Gideon was sweating profusely, his shirt already soaked with perspiration. Papers were falling out of his binder and his coffee was spilling all over his wrinkled, sweat dampened suit.

"Shit, what the hell is wrong with him?" I asked my mother.

We hadn't even made it to the courtroom, and I felt like things were already falling apart. We were rushing to get to the courtroom in time, and while I'd been confident months prior—I didn't walk into the courtroom that day feeling as though we had this under control.

"Don't worry Hera, it's going to be okay," my mother assured me, her eyes darting between Gideon and I with concern.

By the time we reached the courtroom, I relaxed a bit. This couldn't be worse than the moments that preceded this hearing: not worse than Joaquin attacking my sister, than having to leave our home with the clothing on our backs in the middle of the night, and not worse than looking down the barrel of a gun as I walked out of the prison that Joaquin had once passed off as our home.

Determined to avoid eye contact, I looked at the floor as we walked to our seats. Even before I sat down, Joaquin's attorney flounced over to me and shoved a piece of paper in my face. I was finally being served for the counter case that Joaquin filed in Virginia months after mine.

As I started to read the paperwork, I looked up and caught a glimpse of Joaquin, standing in the corner against the opposite wall. He was dancing around nervously, as though he had just been bitten in the crotch by a pack of fire ants. A wave of nausea came over me. He was paler than I'd last seen him and the dark rings under his eyes had deepened. His suit was about three sizes too large, which reminded me of how ridiculously he'd always dressed. Now that I was no longer infatuated and under his spell, he looked like a depressed, sleep deprived clown.

I wondered how I could've ever have found him physically attractive. Maybe now I was seeing him for who he had always been, without the rose-colored glasses.

The judge requested we meet face to face, immediately after the hearing, to work out a visitation arrangement in the months leading up to the trial. I was going to have to sit across from this man who just a few short months earlier raped my sister and threatened to kill me. I had no idea that this was an optional request, as any agreement made that day wouldn't have been court ordered. Gideon went along with it and didn't inform me that the judge's request was merely a suggestion.

After the hearing was over, my attorney and I headed up to the scheduling room. It took place in a room that was barely large enough for a small wooden roundtable. I couldn't help but to focus on the roundtable. I didn't want to collaborate or compromise, and I wondered how it would be possible for me to sit there and pretend as though I intended to allow some sort of visitation. Chastity's bust entered the room before anyone else from Joaquin's team. She squeezed her way past me, shoving my chair into the table and nearly knocking the wind out of me. As Joaquin sat down across from me, I tried to focus on everything else except for his face. As soon as all parties were seated, Chastity led the meeting with how she believed visitation would go.

"There is no way I am letting Prince visit with him without supervision," I quickly interrupted her.

I wanted her to know that despite her larger-than-life presence, I wasn't intimidated by her. Chastity acted as though she didn't hear me, and Joaquin used this opportunity as if he were on a stage performing.

"I'm terrified of Hera and her family so the visits need to be in Virginia," he said, glancing over at Chastity as though he needed her to physically protect him from me.

Virginia was his haven because he could legally carry a weapon there and he had police willing to do his bidding. Chastity droned on, reading from her notes, and acting as if she were running the show.

When it became clear that Gideon was being bulldozed by Chastity, I stood up and asked, "So as a point of clarification, is this decision and any agreement that results bound by any sort of court order?"

Gideon piped up and mentioned that this meeting was optional, to which I responded by walking out of the room. I wasn't going to sit there and let Joaquin act like the victim after all he'd done, and I wasn't going to put my son in harm's way without being forced by the court to do so.

This was my first act of defiance against a system that didn't appear designed to protect my son.

After leaving the room, I turned to Gideon and told him he was fired. I asked him to gather the case records to turn them over to my new attorneys—the law offices of Borger and Kaplan. In the week it took Gideon to turn over the records, he burned through $12,500 which he claimed included previous charges of $30 every time he'd answered the phone, $70 per email, and $600 for phone calls he'd taken with Commonwealth Attorney Henson regarding the criminal case.

If you pay a lawyer a large retainer, and fire them before they've depleted it, beware that they will find ways to take as much as they can before turning over the case. To avoid this, it's best to interview the attorney prior to committing to ensure that the person has a clear understanding of the area of law. It's also helpful to ensure mutual understanding of fees and accounting to avoid being taken advantage of by morally corrupt attorneys.

On October 24, 2011, in an email Gideon wrote to my new attorneys, he wrote, "I am not sure what the leftover retainer will be, but [Hera] moved home and earns over 90k per year so in addition to the retainer, she can pay attorney fees."

I don't think Gideon ever intended for me to see that email, as he didn't include me as a recipient. I later found the email while independently searching through my case documents in my new attorney's office.

One of the reforms I advocate for in family court is taking the money out of the hands of private attorneys. While I was fortunate enough to have a decent salary at the time, many families cannot afford representation. Providing the option of public attorneys would remove the wage wars from these cases where protective parents go bankrupt trying to protect their children.

Starting over with new lawyers required me to tell my painful story all over again. The first time I told the story, I always sensed as though the person on the receiving end would wonder whether such a ridiculous chain of events happened. I was exhausted by having to continue to prove my credibility. After several hours debriefing me, they assured me that they'd been in court with Chastity Carter before, and Mr. Borger was personal friends with Judge Jude (the judge who'd been assigned to the case).

Though my new attorneys assured me that they had the case under control, I couldn't stop searching for more information on Joaquin. I knew there had to be more to find. I also wanted to remove myself from "he said, she said" by providing proof beyond my word.

I was still naive about this process and believed that if I showed the court what I found, it would matter.

Chapter 12

Terrorist Negotiations

"Why are you trying to rationalize crazy, Hera," my psychologist said, gazing intently at me from over the rim of his glasses.

He always knew exactly how to talk me off the ledge when I started down the rabbit hole of crazy. He told me to think of a psychopath like an empty shell without a soul, and to stop trying to project how I felt about relationships onto this empty shell. I've since given this same advice to other parents in the thick of family court madness.

It's a hard lesson to learn because as people we try to understand others based on our experiences and understanding of the world. While I believe most people are capable of empathy and emotions, psychopaths are not—and trying to understand their behavior with your own lens of emotion is going to cause confusion.

While I knew this was a futile waste of time, I still found myself trying to understand why Joaquin acted the way he did. Trying to understand him gave me the false sense that maybe I would be able to predict his next move. I thought this was the only way I'd be able to keep us safe. And a part of me kept hoping that the man I first met was real, somehow trapped inside this horrible shell, even though the rational part of me knew that version was only a mask.

My psychologist was a tall man, roughly in his early sixties. He was slightly gnarly looking with disheveled gray hair. I imagined that he was a great father to his daughter, and he was the type of man I hoped I'd be healthy enough to choose someday. He was a forensic psychologist who studied psychopaths, but he was far from one himself. He helped me understand the obvious signs I'd been blind to, so that I wouldn't repeat the behavior that caused me to fall for Joaquin.

He also helped me learn to cope with the trauma so that I could be the best version of myself possible. It's extremely hard to do this when you're still actively being terrorized, but seeing my psychologist weekly at least helped me maintain a job and parent my son during the worst of it.

Going through this type of trauma and refusing to see a therapist is like breaking your leg and then, years later, wondering why you can't walk correctly. Yet in the decade since my own trauma, I've met so many people resistant to therapy. Seeing a therapist doesn't make you crazy, but refusing to see one when you need to—might.

"This is going to sound crazy," I said the first day I walked into my psychologist's office, dawning an awkward smile.

I hated telling anyone about the Joaquin saga because I

was deeply self-conscious that the person on the receiving end would make judgments about me. They'd wonder why I hadn't responded to the red flags and assume there was something deeply wrong with me for letting myself be targeted by this type of monster.

My therapist was a contractor with several U.S. Intelligence agencies, as well as several police departments in the D.C. area. He later told me that our somewhat parallel professional experiences spooked him when we first met. My story was so wild that he wondered how much of it was true. He thought he was being set up, and that I was a test from one of the agencies he worked for. He later asked around town about Joaquin to confirm the claims I made about Joaquin's criminal past. I wasn't surprised when he admitted that my story checked out, but I think he was surprised when he realized it was true.

Most people during that time, who heard my story for the first time, immediately jumped to the conclusion that I was unstable. The story was so scary that I can understand how it was probably easier to believe I made the entire thing up. But I appreciate that my therapist didn't share his skepticism with me until he could assure me, he believed me.

Despite the extreme circumstances that broke apart my relationship with Joaquin, nearly every person in the court system wanted to fit our case into a neat, little average box. I was often met with an overwhelming presumption that I was making up claims of abuse to gain a custody advantage. The system is designed to get parents to come to a swift agreement that will keep them out of the court system, thereby making it cheaper for taxpayers. Assuming I was making things up, and that I'd eventually resign myself to co-parenting with someone I merely disliked, was much easier than to entertain that co-parenting just wasn't possible.

The sooner the courts acknowledge that there are some parents who might never be fit to have unsupervised visitation with their child, the safer many children will be. And while I understand some parents lose parental rights, it often only occurs after the child has endured irreparable damage.

My therapist was the only person outside of my family who seemed to understand the danger Joaquin posed to Prince. After our first few meetings, he explained the Hare checklist for psychopathy. As I looked at the checklist, I realized that Joaquin displayed every flag for a textbook psychopath. Though I acknowledge this should've scared me—I felt overwhelming relief in finally having a classification.

The Hare Psychopathy Checklist that my therapist handed me listed all twenty traits assessed by the PCL-R score. In the short time I dated Joaquin, 17 months, he exhibited every single one of the traits. I read down the list and highlighted a few traits, with examples for the therapist.

1. **Glib and superficial charm:** Joaquin was incredibly charming. It was a trait he turned on full steam when he targeted his victims. He'd effectively charmed me, the women before me, and it appeared as though he'd also charmed police officers and professionals inside the court system. His stories were often unbelievable, but he had an artful way of making complete strangers want to listen and get to know him.

2. **Grandiose (exaggeratedly high) estimation of self:** Joaquin thought he was a talented singer, though he couldn't hold a tune. He also believed he was

the most attractive man alive, though many would argue that was only true in his head. He often commented about how he believed women were checking him out because of his stunning good looks. One time, he claimed a 12-year-old girl was checking him out at the movie theater. People certainly looked at him in public, but this likely had more to do with his oversized clothes and vampire like hairdo than good looks.

3. **Need for stimulation** (an excessive need for novel, thrilling, and exciting stimulation): I spent two American Independence Days with Joaquin. Joaquin had a sick fascination with fireworks. He insisted we go out of state in the weeks prior to our first July 4th together so that he could purchase large fireworks that were illegal in Virginia. He set these dangerous explosives off in his backyard, which was only a few hundred feet from four of his neighbors. While I acknowledge that putting off fireworks is common, he was reckless about them in a way that seemed intended to scare everyone nearby.

4. **Pathological lying:** This was potentially the most obvious trait on this checklist. As I read this trait, I paused. I looked up from the paper.

"I'm not sure Joaquin can tell the truth from the lies. His stories are so twisted that I wonder if he even knows the truth from what he's invented in his head," I said, burying my head in my hands.

Remembering how much of Joaquin's life was complete

fiction made me incredibly ashamed. I felt embarrassed about how gullible I was for believing him, even though there wasn't any hard evidence to back up his unrealistic claims. And it didn't matter whether Joaquin was sitting across from you at a restaurant or on the witness stand in open court—lies would fly off his tongue in rapid succession like a machine gun indiscriminately firing down range.

5. **Cunning and manipulative:** Joaquin was a skilled manipulator. The first two private investigators I hired (one that Gideon hired for a Google search and the one I'd hired) never found a shred of evidence that would indicate that Joaquin ever held an honest job. Instead, he manipulated the women in his life into supporting him. At one point, he convinced several friends and business partners to put money into a business account. After they invested their money, Joaquin drained the account and used it to put a down payment on his house (this was a detail uncovered during the private investigation).

6. **Parasitic lifestyle:** Joaquin was living off death benefits, the financial assistance of his girlfriends, stolen money from business partners, and his mother his entire adult life. During his deposition, he was unable to identify one job he held or a time in his life when he made an honest living. By the time I met him, every cent of money he had was a result of life insurance and social security death benefits he was collecting from Shawn (his son's mother) and Alma (his mother).

7. **Lack of realistic long-term goals:** In addition to his fictitious music career, Joaquin held the belief that one day he'd be wealthy after winning the lottery. He actively planned how he'd spend money and would get unreasonably upset each time he didn't win the jackpot. It was as though he believed it was some sort of prophesy that he'd win. At one point, the only money Joaquin had coming in each month was from his son's social security death benefit. This money, the result of Shawn's death, was only around a thousand dollars a month. Instead of using that money for clothing and food, Joaquin spent hundreds of dollars each month on lottery scratch-off tickets.

8. **Failure to accept responsibility for own actions:**

Joaquin always said, "For every action, there is a reaction."

This was absurd considering how hard it was for Joaquin to take responsibility for his own actions. He looked for anything or anyone he could grasp onto, so he had something to blame for his lack of success. Something bad would happen, but instead of owning up to his actions he would claim that he must have been a terrible person in a past life. He simply couldn't bring himself to see that it was his action in *this* life that led to his circumstances.

9. **Criminal versatility:** I'm sure that Joaquin's criminal life didn't begin in the early 2000s with the murder of Shawn Mason. I'll likely never know the extent of all of Joaquin's crimes, but I know that he has been arrested for fraud, murder

(twice), illegal distribution of pornography, and child abuse. He's been accused of rape at least twice (according to accounts from his own family).

I had to put down the paper. I had a rush of emotions that I felt ill equip to handle at the time. I hated crying, and I loathed crying in front of other people. Crying in front of my therapist made me feel as though I was being torn into two separate pieces. One piece was completely overcome with sadness, while the other was trying to manage my doctor's emotional response to my visible pain.

I fought tears, but the therapist's pained look caused me to give into the emotional flood.

"Why are you crying?" he asked frankly.

I felt shamed, and stupid. Now that the fog of infatuation lifted, I saw Joaquin for the monster he was. It was terrifying and deeply embarrassing.

By the time I was sobbing on my therapist's office couch, I'd been enduring Joaquin's legal abuse for almost seven months. Though it seemed as though the family court case had already lasted years, we'd yet to have an actual custody trial.

"This case will settle out of court," the therapist said confidently.

Though he seemed spot-on with his assessment of Joaquin as a psychopath, I wasn't confident we'd reach a settlement. A settlement meant we'd need to negotiate, reaching some sort of agreement that we were both willing to accept. I had enough information about Joaquin to know that the settlement process would be like negotiating with a terrorist. He wanted unsupervised access and I was unwilling to willingly accept that as a term of any agreement.

But still playing by the rules and trusting that the justice system would protect my son, I dutifully went through the motions of settlement. The first step was to sit down with the court appointed social worker for an interview. My lawyers, clearly worried about my ability to handle myself in an interview, sat me down for a coaching session.

"Only respond to what she asks you, Hera," Mr. Borger warned.

Kaplan, my other attorney, explained further that I shouldn't offer concerns until the social worked asked. Instead, he advised to focus on highlighting positive things about myself. And when she asked about concerns, I should only offer information that could be validated through one of the witnesses we'd call.

The first bits of advice seemed reasonable. Then, they started telling me things that sounded like crazy talk.

"You should put up a picture of Joaquin in your house, so it shows that you intend on fostering a healthy relationship between Prince and his father," Borger suggested.

I immediately regretted taking a sip of coffee before Borger spoke. I nearly choked on it as I looked up from the cup. I was *not* going to put a picture of my abuser, and the man who just a few months earlier threatened to kill me, in my son's nursery. I couldn't even do this for the show because I knew it would be disingenuous and would make me look like I was putting on a show.

While I completely understand the sentiment, this recommmendation felt very much like it came from a checklist. I don't think putting a picture of the other parent in your home is a true indication of your intention to foster a rela-

tionship. And I don't think it's at all reasonable to ask a
survivor of domestic violence to do this. If my son were old
enough to decorate his room and wanted to hang a picture
of him with his father, I wouldn't take it down. But I pride
myself on being authentic and putting up a picture would've
been inauthentic.

I *didn't* intend on fostering the type of relationship the
courts expected between Prince and Joaquin. I knew Joaquin
was dangerous, and it was against every maternal instinct in
my body to intentionally put my son in danger. And while I
planned to let my son discover that his father wasn't healthy,
in a safe supervised environment, I wasn't going to encour-
age unfettered access to a criminal either.

I believe that each parent is responsible for fostering
their own relationship with their child. While parents often
don't realize the damage that speaking negatively about their
co-parent can cause to the psychological well-being of their
child, I also don't think it's reasonable to expect one parent
to take full responsibility of the relationship. Both parents
must put in the work and children are naturally predisposed
to love their parents.

While I'm not an attorney, my recommendation for
parents going through this is to be graceful, authentic, and
respectful. It is possible to show understanding and a will-
ingness to allow your child to have a relationship with the
other parent, without ignoring danger. I wish that Prince
had been able to learn on his own who his father was, in a
setting that ensured his physical and emotional safety. So,
if you are concerned that your co-parent is unsafe, I recommend getting yourself to the point where you can both
acknowledge your child's right to know the parent—while
also insisting that safety be the primary focus. There are

parents who've been able to successfully form healthy relationships with their children while in a supervised setting.

Before the settlement hearing, Joaquin and I both met with the custody evaluator. Custody evaluators work for the court and are supposed to be a neutral party to investigate both parents for their fitness as parents, their relationship with the child, and their ability to co-parent. At the end of their investigation, they submit a report to the judge for consideration. My attorneys informed me that judges in Maryland often relied heavily on what the evaluator suggested, so this was an important stage in the overall custody case.

The meeting with our evaluator felt extremely formal. The evaluator was a soft-spoken, petite Black woman. She didn't crack a smile during the interview and seemed as though she was all business, all the time. I respected this because it showed me that she took her job seriously, knowing how important she was to this process. She vigorously took notes, and it appeared as though she was careful not to openly react to anything I told her. Though I can imagine this annoyed some people, I was confident because I knew I had witnesses who'd corroborate my reports. I respected that she couldn't be swayed simply by meeting me because I needed her to treat Joaquin the same.

Before even asking me what I thought of Joaquin as a father, the evaluator asked me questions about myself. I went through my entire resume with her, as though I was in a job interview. I explained where I'd worked, what I enjoyed doing in my free time, and talked about my relationship with Prince. When it came time to discuss the concerns I had about Joaquin, I came armed with documents. As I pulled out my binder of evidence, I saw her eyebrow raise at the amount of information I brought to her to back up my concerns. I was eager to share with her why I was asking that the court require Joaquin to have a supervisor on each visit.

Though the report from Simon Clint's private investigation was not admissible in court, I was allowed to show the evaluator the report. I explained to her that after learning that Joaquin assaulted my sister, I hired an investigator. The report served as a good organization tool with summaries of what she'd hear from witnesses.

If you are concerned about your co-parent, I highly recommend spending the money on a proper investigator. While you cannot present the findings in open court, having this helped me provide the court with witnesses outside of myself and my family. It breaks my heart when I hear from a parent who reports abuse and is the only witness to back up that claim. If no other human on the planet can testify to the abuse, there is a high likelihood that the court will not believe it happened.

Shortly after her interview with Joaquin, we met the evaluator at my parent's house for a home visit. I showed her all the things we'd done to make it a safe home for Prince. And I told her I worried she wouldn't be able to visit Joaquin's residence because they didn't visit homes outside of the state.

"Not being able to view his living conditions isn't my only concern about him," she responded.

I breathed a sigh of relief. Her words meant that he hadn't been able to charm her. And that she got it.

The settlement hearing was in February 2012, seven months after I left Joaquin. In a move that my attorneys said was uncommon, the evaluator requested police escort and that Joaquin not be allowed in the courtroom when she gave her recommendation. Her preference was to present her findings to the judge and our attorneys in the judge's chambers.

My attorneys believed that the evaluator's concern would pressure Joaquin's attorney into settling based on the recommendations of her report.

As I waited in the hallway, I noticed Joaquin brought his older son's therapist with him to court that day. This was the same therapist whose court report got the state to drop the child abuse charges against Joaquin a year prior. Given that she was Sammy's therapist, and not Joaquin's, I was surprised to see her there. We weren't there to present any testimony, so I wondered why she was there.

"Is she rubbing his back," I asked my mom, gagging at the sight of the two of them together on the bench.

My mom shook her head and her face twisted in disgust as she turned away from them.

"God—this system is so busted," I sighed, remembering all that Sammy endured without any relief.

The Evaluation

During the evaluator's investigation, she learned disturbing information about Joaquin from witness testimony. Instead of solely relying on the information I provided from the PI report, she interviewed Sgt. Perry, Crystal Toussant, and Sheryl Mason herself. They all assured her that what Simon wrote in his report was the truth. One detail that Crystal hadn't shared with Simon, that she shared with the evaluator, was that Joaquin told her that the only way she would leave him would be "through the window or in a body bag."

In addition to providing the evaluator with witness testimony, I shared Alma Collins's autopsy with her. Simon
obtained the report from a family member who was afraid
to be identified as an official witness. The report stated that
she died from "lack of oxygen to the brain." The autopsy
report also noted that she was "found lying unresponsive
on her bed with a plastic bag about her head." Her toxi-
cology report was negative, proving she was free of drugs
that could've made her pass out. It didn't seem possible for
someone to be able to suffocate themselves with a plastic
bag. Not unless that person first overdosed on something
that would cause them to pass out before the suffocation
occurred.

Despite the near medical impossibility of Alma killing
herself via plastic bag, the police ruled Alma's death a suicide.
A suicide note was found in the home but witnesses close to
Alma have claimed the note wasn't in her handwriting. I
don't know if the police ever conducted a handwriting anal-
ysis on the note for authenticity prior to closing the case.

As the evaluator collected her evidence, Joaquin fought
hard to silence previous victims. He tried to deny living with
Crystal for any length of time, despite court documents from
his custody case with Sheryl in 2005 when he admitted she'd
helped him raise Sammy and was financially supporting
them both.

Joaquin's account of the night I left him was also bizarre
and completely different from what I remembered. Just as
he'd done in his discovery response, he pulled out that old
photo of his face bruised—again trying to claim that my
mother attacked him. Luckily, the evaluator wasn't convinced by the photo. She asked him why he hadn't filed his
own report that night, especially if his face was as injured as

the photo appeared. And if he was so injured, how come the officers who arrived that night didn't see signs of a physical altercation on his face?

The evaluator noted that Joaquin had several inconsistencies in his story, including his claims of having been attacked. All of the inconsistencies led her to conclude that he wasn't an honest reporter.

The report recommended that I maintain primary legal and physical custody. The evaluator believed my safety concerns were justifiable, and that the visitation Joaquin would have with Prince should be supervised. She also recommended that Joaquin obtain a psychological evaluation and follow all treatment recommendations generated from the findings.

If Joaquin had accepted the custody evaluator's recommendations, we could've settled the case that day and saved thousands of dollars in legal fees. Instead, Joaquin's attorney suggested we "compromise" with unsupervised visitation instead of his initial request for full custody. I suppose asking for the moon, even if you know it's more than you'll likely receive, is a good tactic. Because when you come back with another over the top recommendation, given the circumstances, it will appear as a reasonable compromise.

As the ridiculous negotiations began, I imagined a street haggler—starting out saying that the fake designer bag he was selling was real and therefore worth thousands. And when an inspector pointed out that the designer label had a misspelling, he backed off and agreed to accept just under a thousand. Unsupervised visitations were still a rip off to Prince's safety and I wasn't buying it.

Chapter 13

Trials and Tribulations

It took roughly a week, and thousands in fees, for our attorneys to realize that this case wasn't going to settle out of court. Despite everyone telling me this would settle before we went to trial, I always knew it wouldn't. I didn't know how Joaquin was paying his legal fees, given that he still didn't have any overt sources of income beyond the death benefits, but he always had expensive attorneys in his corner.

But despite heading into trial, I was still feeling confident. In addition to solid character witnesses, several of Joaquin's victims agreed to testify against him. To my surprise, even Sgt. Perry agreed to testify. This meant crossing state lines, which she wasn't legally obligated to do.

The trial, a month after the failed settlement hearing, was set to last two days. I presented the first day, and the second day was reserved for Joaquin. The moment I stepped foot inside the large double doors of the courtroom, I felt as though I was being stripped naked and repeatedly beaten with a baseball bat. The room was void of any vivid color, with dull brown seats and white walls. A coldness was in the air, as though it was set to freeze out all feeling and emotion.

Judge Justin Jude, a middle-aged white man, entered the courtroom. He looked like he was scowling, and this immediately made me feel uncomfortable. We'd barely started, and his expressive face made it appear as though he'd rather be anywhere but in this courtroom.

"This is an unusual case in that there is a history here which is very disturbing, and the last chapter has probably not yet been actually written," Mr. Borger stated.

Borger was a brilliant man, but he didn't have the gift of brevity in communication. Though he'd stopped arguing cases years earlier, something about my case made Borger want to re-enter the courtroom. Though I can appreciate that my case evoked passion in my attorney, I'd have preferred Frank as the litigator. I preferred Frank's style in the courtroom because he knew when to keep it clear and brief. Borger would go on and on down verbose rabbit holes full of jargon that wasn't always easy to follow. But I wasn't confident enough to fully advocate for myself. I kept my preference to myself, which now seems silly given the fact that I was paying them for their services.

In the years since my case, I've told parents that they should feel confident in their representation. You're the customer and have the right to stop paying for an attorney who isn't representing you the way you want to be represented. It's like agreeing to go into open-heart surgery with a surgeon whose exhibiting hand tremors and being too nervous to opt for a replacement. While that might seem like an over the top comparison, you could have a completely competent attorney (as mine were) and if they don't make you feel safe and heard—they aren't the right ones for you.

Borger continued by describing Joaquin like a runaway train, leaving death and destruction in his wake. He stumbled through his opening statement. I understood the picture that Borger was trying to paint for the court, but I wasn't sure that his delivery was intelligible enough to engage Judge Jude.

Chastity started right into her case trying to discredit any evidence against Joaquin: "Your honor, um, we are here on a bunch of snuck. This is a 'where there is smoke there is fire' argument, but that is not how a court works. We need to look at actual facts."

Chastity never defined the word snuck, which continued to distract me throughout parts of the day as I wondered if the judge understood her.

"The actual substance of this case involved two parties, who were together . . . they were engaged . . . the plaintiff sent the defendant numerous cards telling him he was a great father . . . for months and months. She got pregnant, she had a baby, and Mr. Rams had sex with her little sister two weeks after the baby was born. That was pretty awful. I don't think you will hear any excuses from him. That was a pretty horrible decision," Chastity continued, her tone making me feel as though it was laced with judgement and accusation against me.

I felt my face get hot. Anger boiled inside of me. Joaquin was troubled, and terrifying, and the way Chastity summarized our relationship made me feel as though she was suggesting I was a scorned woman, and my concerns were trivial and fueled by jealousy. When I knew this wasn't the case. I hoped that Joaquin would meet someone new so that he'd move on from me and Prince. And if he *just* cheat-ed—I wouldn't be fighting so hard to keep him from unsu-pervised access.

In the years I've spent listening to other cases, I've learned that it's a common tactic to make women who allege abuse seem petty or vengeful. Doing this deflects from issue, hijacks the discourse, and helps make it appear more of a "he said, she said" than issues based in evidence and fact.

"What we are supposed to be looking at is two people who had a baby and don't get along—what do we do now?" Chastity said.

'Well, isn't that framing of what happened conveniently thin,' I thought, rolling my eyes.

There was more here than just two people who didn't get along. Whether I liked Joaquin as a human was irrelevant. What the court should always consider is whether each parent is fit to have access to their child.

The trial started with testimony from the court evaluator. As she approached the stand, I could feel terror and anxiety as though it was floating through the air. Her eyes darted around the courtroom from the witness stand to the judge, to Joaquin's attorney—and to the door. She didn't look directly at Joaquin once. Voice shaking, she explained the process she went through to conduct her investigation: a home visit, interviews with both parties, professional collateral, police officers, and other witnesses provided by both parties.

As soon as the evaluator started speaking, Chastity began a string of objections which ultimately led to her arguing that there was a foundation problem with the evaluator's report. Judge Jude glanced at Chastity with a baffled look, his nose scrunched up like he was being forced to smell a dead animal's carcass.

"She is the court evaluator that just conducted a full evaluation. What is the foundation objection after she has conducted a whole evaluation," Judge Jude asked, seemingly irritated with the consistent interruptions.

Chastity shifted in place and asked the evaluator to testify to the facts that drew her recommendations.

This testimony was painful with the evaluator stumbling through her notes. She tripped on her words and with every objection, it just got worse. As Chastity continued her objections, the evaluator began to waver on her convictions and by the end it was no longer clear what the evaluator was recommending.

The scene felt like high-powered smoke machines were being directly pointed at the judge. It was important to Joaquin's defense that the judge view the evaluator as not credible because her report highlighted safety concerns.

As soon as she was done with her testimony, the evaluator left the stand and quickly exited the courtroom. I was relieved when she left because I felt for her. She did an excellent job in her report and shouldn't have had to ensure attacks on her work product in open court.

Every time Joaquin's attorneys presented something that I knew to be untrue, I elbowed Frank in the side. I'd have elbowed Borger, but he was on the other side of Frank from where I was sitting. My attorneys knew she was presenting false information, but they believed continuing to challenge her would irritate the court more than it would help. This might've been true, but I didn't appreciate these untruths going unchallenged in the public record.

More than a decade removed, I understand that my attorneys knew what they were doing—but there on a human level I think the court should understand the psychological torture that comes with allowing things like this to stand. It felt like death by a million paper cuts on my character, baseless accusation after baseless accusation. And just once, I wanted my attorneys to point out that much of what was being said was simply cruel. Joaquin was unable to present one person from my past or shred of evidence to back up his claims.

Sgt. Perry was the next witness to testify. She confidently walked to the stand, and I imagined her dressed in armor and ready for battle.

"He had motive, opportunity, and was at the scene of the crime when Shawn was found," Sgt. Perry stated frankly, referring to Joaquin as the prime suspect in Shawn Mason's murder.

Borger's direct examination of Sgt. Perry was brief. He wanted to show the court that Virginia police believed Joaquin murdered his older son's mother. And potentially more impacting was the fact that she was so passionately against Joaquin having access to a child that she was willing to drive outside her district to report her concerns.

On cross-examination, Chastity questioned Sgt. Perry about whether Joaquin had ever been convicted of any crimes in the Commonwealth of Virginia. Though he had yet to be convicted at the time, Sgt. Perry was able to testify about Joaquin's extensive criminal history. Just as Sgt. Perry began to explain Joaquin's history of multiple arrests, Chastity interrupted her and stated her belief that previous arrests were irrelevant to Prince's safety.

When he wasn't serving in Family Court, Judge Jude specialized in criminal court. Without any convictions, it's possible he assumed that the Commonwealth of Virginia had no evidence that Joaquin killed Shawn. One of the flaws I point out in the family court system when I advocate for reform is how detrimental it can be for courts to force judge rotations in and out of civil court. The legal threshold for criminal court is much higher than civil court. In family court, to protect a child, the judge only needs believe past abuse likely occurred and is likely to continue occurring. And for Jude to have considered Shawn's case as it related to the danger Joaquin posed to Prince, he'd only have to believe Joaquin likely killed her—not beyond a reasonable doubt.

Sgt. Perry also brought proof that Joaquin was arrested for abusing his older son Sammy. Because Sgt. Perry wasn't the arresting officer in that case, Judge Jude didn't allow that part of her testimony. And because Child Protective Services isn't required to share case information outside of the state, Joaquin was allowed to wipe that part of his history from the court record. Because Joaquin took a plea deal, to avoid conviction, we couldn't even obtain the arrest information via the Freedom of Information Act (FOIA).

After the evaluator and Sgt. Perry testified, Borger called my character witnesses. While I have many friends and even ex-boyfriends who were willing to testify on my behalf, it made sense to call two of my family members. I come from an extremely close, Irish Catholic family on my mother's side. My mother and I raised Prince together, and my aunts were all like bonus mothers to me growing up. These women have known me since I was born, and they're some of my fiercest advocates. Presenting them would show that Prince was going to be raised by an intelligent, professional, and morally strong community.

I knew it wouldn't have helped Prince to jump out of my

seat and scream at Chastity, but I had the urge several times when she was cross-examining my mother. Though physical assault was never an acceptable response in my community, when someone attacked our family verbal assault was fair game. And while I know this is a common tactic to be somewhat aggressive on cross-examination, it felt like an attack to me. Instead, I bit my tongue and tried hard to appear as though her behavior didn't bother me.

"When you decided to have Prince baptized, did anyone think to invite Mr. Rams?" Chastity asked, in a tone that seemed admonishing with a scowl on her face.

"You mean when my *daughter* decided to have him baptized? No, why would she have invited someone who threatened her," my mother retorted.

Despite Chastity's aggressive line of questioning, my mother remained calm. I knew this took superhuman strength from her, and I saw her face get red as she held back venomous words. It made me smile to know that she was likely thinking the exact same thing I was in that moment.

Throughout the day, Chastity took a line of questioning that is common from defense attorneys—pointing toward the protective parent as an "alienator". Parental alienation is a baseless accusation commonly used by abusers, attempting to gaslight the protective parent. Chastity was trying to make the case that my negative feelings toward Joaquin would eventually spill over to Prince and ruin a chance at a healthy relationship with his father.

Regardless of whether concerns about the other parent are warranted, the attorney presenting the parental alienation argument tries to make it appear as though limiting access to the non-custodial parent is equal to physical child abuse. In this case, I had to tread carefully. I *did* want to exclude Joaquin from Prince's life. It wasn't because I hated Joaquin, though I truly did hate him. I wanted to exclude Joaquin from Prince's life because I cared more about my son's survival than whether he had a relationship with his biological father. Since I knew the court wasn't going to immediately understand that my concerns were warranted, I was careful not to take this sort of bait.

When it was my time to testify, I felt prepared for what would happen, as I'd seen the other witness testimony before me. Luckily, Borger started out somewhat light by having me explain my career and educational background. I felt like a very public job interview, except that my abuser was in the front row staring at me.

"I have a Bachelor of Arts in Political Communications with a minor in Electronic Media from George Washington University. I graduated cum laude with a 3.5 GPA. I then received my Master of Arts in Special Education from Loyola Marymount, and graduated with a 3.9 GPA," I carefully explained, walking through my credentials as though it mattered.

On the stand, I thought about how I'd attempted to give my credentials to the County Police Department the night I fled Joaquin. It seemed laughable that I thought doing this would somehow wipe away my Blackness.

Even though I was experienced in talking about my achievements, my voice was shaking. I hated the idea that I had to prove to the court that I was a good mother by offering up my professional credentials. Did where I went to school even count as a notch that could prove how good of a mom I would be? It was pretentious, but I followed the rules of the game anyway.

For so long, I relied on my accomplishments and my

strong reputation in my community. In my personal and professional life, amongst those who knew me, I didn't have to prove I was trustworthy. I'd done this my entire life through hard work. I earned every morsel of respect from my friends, family, and colleagues. But in this court, it was like walking into a new country, not able to speak the local language. I wondered if the judge was listening to what I was saying or if he was more interested in my non-verbal language.

Talking about the abuse I'd ensured in our relationship was hard, but I thought the judge needed to hear what that time was like—perhaps to better understand why I was so afraid of Prince being alone with his father. Possibly even more difficult than my testimony about how Joaquin treated me, was recounting how he'd treated his older son. I felt incredibly guilty for protecting Joaquin by staying silent during that time.

"I still don't know a lot about the man who is sitting over there, because everything he told me . . . well, I've since learned it was a lie," I testified.

"I'm not proud of the fact that I stayed with Joaquin, despite the obvious red flags I saw over the course of our relationship. I stayed for my son, and I hoped that the monster I kept seeing was not the real Joaquin. I kept hoping that things would get better, when they'd never get better— because Joaquin was really the monster and not the man he was pretending to be when I met him."

Tears of shame streamed down my face. I was embarrassed to admit that I didn't really know the father of my child. I was ashamed that I brought my son into such a dangerous situation. Working with my therapist I'd come a long way emotionally from the night the Virginia County police officers interrogated me. At that time, I was almost incapable of showing them a normal emotional response to the trauma that I experienced. In addition to being in shock, I was trained from a young age to avoid public displays of emotion. While I was still careful to not let my emotions get the best of me, rendering me incapable of continuing, I allowed my true feelings to show on the outside in a way I hadn't been able previously.

After a tear-filled direct examination, Chastity questioned me about holiday cards I'd written Joaquin while we were still together. To her, my words to Joaquin during that time proved that I was now lying about the abuse. I understand that to someone who's never been in an abusive relationship, a written card might appear as a sign of a happy relationship. But I knew the motivation behind those cards had more to do with my futile attempts to calm the beastly side of Joaquin—because stroking his ego was one of the ways he'd back off from terrifying levels of anger.

I'd like to believe that most people have seen friends posting on social media about how amazing things are in their relationship, days before announcing their separation. There was a time when I did love Joaquin, the man I believed him to be, and I wanted to do or say anything to bring back that man I'd first met.

When things got scary, I'd do anything to try to stop the rages and get Joaquin to a better place. Sometimes, this meant writing to him about how much I cared about him. It turned my stomach to now be sitting on the witness stand having these very letters thrown in my face. Because they brought me back to the exact moments when I'd written them and how truly painful that time was.

It was hard to testify about Joaquin, and why I stayed, having the knowledge I obtained after leaving him. The court seemed to have trouble believing that such an accomplished woman could've been so fooled by this unaccomplished man. I worried that the court also wondered whether I knew that he was bad from the beginning, and that maybe this meant I was bad too.

It didn't surprise me that these letters entered the trial because taken at face value, without context, they were incongruent with my testimony. Remembering how excited Joaquin was each time I wrote one, made me feel like a fool. Having them thrown back at me made me feel as though he'd been planning for the day when he'd weaponize them.

Even though I was prepared to testify, my voice still shook violently during parts of my testimony. Describing things like the night he threatened to kill me on my way out of the house, and the frightening rages I witnessed while living with him, brought me back to the most traumatic time in my life thus far. I described to the court how I changed my routine after leaving Joaquin: I drove a car he wouldn't notice and lived with my parents out of fear that Joaquin was going to come after us.

Cross examination felt like an attempt to provoke me so that I'd shout out and scream, appearing like a crazy and scorned ex-lover. Like the goal was to see me break in open court, so my breakdown could be used as proof that I was somehow not fit to parent. I knew this, but it didn't make enduring the questioning any easier. During my cross-examination, Joaquin sat with his arms crossed dawning a villainous and satisfied smirk on his face. It felt like this was the show he'd been waiting for, and he got sick satisfaction out of seeing me in pain.

I stepped down from the stand, feeling as though I'd just been in a fight. Just about every question Chastity asked triggered my PTSD, and several times I had to grab my hands to try to keep them from shaking. Every time I felt like I was going to break down, I tried to think about Prince. My therapist recommended that when I felt a panic attack coming on, I should imagine myself on a sunny beach with delicious drink in my hand.

Instead, I always imagined myself rocking Prince to sleep while nursing him. He was my happy place—with his soulful brown eyes and giggle that always melted my heart. As I sat back down next to my attorneys, I closed my eyes and took several deep breaths.

To finish off the day, Borger presented two witnesses from Joaquin's past—Crystal Toussant and Sheryl Mason. Both testified to the things they told my private investigator, Simon. Since my attorneys couldn't present Simon's report, the two of them agreed to testify.

"When I left, I had to leave Sammy behind," Crystal said.

"I couldn't save him from the abuse, and I feel terrible about what he must be living through without me there to protect him. If I now can save another child, I am going to do it."

Crystal and I aren't similar in most ways, but when she said this, I understood because it was a guilt I also shared. I'm not sure whether Crystal has always been on the right side of history, but I appreciated that she came to do the right thing for Prince.

"Did you have any concerns regarding how [Joaquin] acted as a parent," Borger asked.

"He was a very stern parent and strict with him. Whenever he got in trouble with school, he would spank him with a belt and sometimes he'd punch him in the chest," Crystal responded.

Then, it was Chastity's turn.

"You're very *angry* at Mr. Rams, is that correct," Chastity asked Crystal.

Without even a second thought, Crystal immediately responded that she was not angry. This answer drew surprised reactions from several in the courtroom, including Chastity.

"Not angry, but I *am* afraid of him," Crystal clarified.

She responded in a cool, calm, and collected voice. It appeared the years she spent recovering from Joaquin's abuse had given her a perspective that I hoped to obtain one day. I envied her ability to speak frankly about how she felt. She appeared as though she'd made some level of peace with the terror she lived through and had actively gotten her life together despite the trauma.

Crystal's testimony was chilling, and when she walked off the stand, I imagined her dropping the mic before stepping down. She even seemed a bit taller when she left the courtroom that day. Though she came to court that day for Prince, and for Sammy, getting the chance to finally testify against Joaquin perhaps offered some type of closure. She'd accused Joaquin of many things, but none of them ever stuck (which was a common theme for many of his victims). There is power in telling your truth in public, and I hope doing that gave her some power back over her own story.

When Sheryl approached the stand, I was in awe of her strength. For ten years, she was forced to watch her grandson be raised by the man she believed killed her daughter. During biweekly visitation exchanges, she had to force a smile for the sake of her grandson. Something I'm not sure I'd be strong enough to do.

"In the few days before your daughter's murder, was there anything going on between her and Joaquin?" Borger asked Sheryl.

"They were in a custody hearing, yes. Shawn filed for emergency custody of my grandson. The hearing was to take place the day after she was murdered," Sheryl stated unflinchingly, glancing toward the judge.

Sheryl continued her haunting testimony by explaining to the court that, shortly before her murder, her daughter tried to obtain a protective order against Joaquin but was unsuccessful. Shawn was murdered on the eve of a custody hearing with Joaquin.

Testimony ended that day with my attorneys feeling confident that we'd made a strong case for supervised visitation. But despite their confidence there was a nagging sense of doubt given what I'd experienced in Virginia with the authorities. Joaquin always seemed to slither out of trouble no matter how egregious the offense.

And from the independent research I'd done into the family court system, I knew that the bar would be set low for him to get visitation. We lived in a climate where if a parent wanted to see their child, the court would do whatever possible to make that happen—regardless of history of abuse.

I wasn't worried that I was going to lose sole legal and physical custody of Prince. It seemed clear to me that even a one-eyed baboon could see that Joaquin wasn't the more suitable parent, but even unsupervised visits would be dangerous. And despite the show my attorneys put on in the courtroom, I wasn't convinced even they truly believed he was as dangerous as I knew him to be.

Chapter 14

Smoke and Clouds

The first day in court was an emotional marathon, leaving me exhausted by day two. I worried about whether my constant state of anxiety was negatively impacting Prince. He was like a sponge, and he watched me intently when we were together. Whenever I'd get upset about something, he could be on the other side of the room but would come crawling toward me to give me a hug. He kept me grounded, but I didn't want Prince to have to worry about his mother. He was barely mobile and already seemed to be soaking up the family drama.

Now it was Joaquin's turn to present. While I knew his case was weak, I braced myself for what he'd attempt to throw at the way in hopes some of it would stick.

'You just need to survive this day, Hera,' I told myself that morning.

After Joaquin presented his case, the judge would issue his order. I was still reeling from what happened with the police in Virginia, and I felt like the justice system had nearly beaten all hope out of me. But I felt like I had no choice but to try and make the system work and tried to hold out some level of hope that Judge Jude would do the right thing. I wasn't yet able to accept the idea that he'd leave Prince without protection.

On what I hoped would be our final day in court, I walked in with my entire Irish Catholic tribe. My mother's side of the family rolled in deep, with my three aunts, three uncles, several cousins, and a couple of people from my father's side as well. Joaquin came to court with Sammy's therapist as his sole character witness.

My side of the courtroom was overpowering, filling every seat in my section. Looking back on this, it might not have been a good idea to bring all of them. I wonder if the judge saw it as a form of intimidation instead of simply a show of support for their loved one. When together, we've never been a quiet bunch and while I'd been trained to temper my emotions, my extended family could sometimes be the exact opposite. If they felt like one of us was under attack, it was as though all of us were to them.

As soon as I sat down, I looked over at Sammy's therapist—Dr. Becky. As soon as she met my gaze, she looked down at her toes immediately.

Borger vigorously objected to the testimony of Dr. Becky, stating that their office was sandbagged. Chastity hadn't included the therapist in her witness list, and after all that transpired this felt intentional—whether purposeful or not. Chastity and Borger erupted into a verbal spat reminiscent of a middle school playground argument, angering the judge.

"I know that you are both lawyers, and I know that you have been trained in courtroom demeanor, and I know what schools you both went to and what training you have had. I think you both know that responses back and forth to each other . . . I don't know if you do that in other judge's courtrooms, but that is not how you conduct yourself in a courtroom and it *sure* isn't how you are going to conduct yourselves in *my* courtroom," Judge Jude reprimanded.

'Good lord,' I thought to myself.

Things felt like they were getting out of hand, and I was exhausted by how much like theater this all felt. Given how serious this was to me, it was upsetting to see two attorneys going at each other in this way, at a time like this.

Borger continued, now that Chastity was no longer interrupting him. Borger explained to the judge that Chastity had submitted an extensive witness list, which is proper procedure; however, the *one* witness she chose to call was curiously missing from that list. Borger also questioned the substance of Dr. Becky's testimony and noted that there hadn't been a proper waiver from the child who she'd been hired to evaluate. Typically, to obtain a waiver, Sammy would've had to have been appointed a Guardian Ad Litem. Chastity had five months to announce her witnesses, and Borger correctly pointed out that this shouldn't have been allowed.

As they bickered, I thought, 'but who's gonna check her boo? Jude certainly isn't.'

The trial seemed like a series of calculated risks when it came to breaking civil procedure. For example, if your only witness was excluded from the witness list—and you knew that not allowing the testimony would just require everyone to come to court another day—you might go for it and hope that the judge allowed it in favor of expediency.

I felt ambushed, as my attorneys likely did too, and perhaps that was by design. If we'd known Sammy's therapist would testify, we'd have conducted a deposition. This would've allowed me to poke holes in her testimony and provide evidence where she wasn't being truthful. Chastity issued a timely subpoena to the therapist, indicating that she knew in advance her intention of presenting her as a witness.

Judge Jude reprimanded Chastity, acknowledging that this seemed like an attempt to sneak the therapist through the back door. Disappointingly, though, he allowed it—noting that he was able to use his discretion and allow the witness anyway.

I sank a bit lower in my chair. This wasn't right, and it left me wondering if the rules only applied to me. Joaquin was able to skip the required co-parenting class, but I had to attend. If I brought in a witness last minute, would the judge have used his discretion to allow me to get away with this too?

Borger made excellent points about the testimony infringing on the right to exclude privileged information as it related to a diagnosis. While this therapist never treated me, I'd spoken to her about my concerns about Joaquin in confidence. But that day, I wondered if she didn't remember our conversations or perhaps, she just chose to only share the things that she believed made Joaquin appear like an upstanding man.

I felt betrayed by her testimony, especially since I'd once looked to her as someone who might be able to help our family in a time of extra strife and trauma.

As soon as Dr. Becky started speaking, even just to state

her name, I had to close my eyes to avoid looking at her. She sounded completely different from how she sounded outside of court. When I knew her, she was not a soft-spoken person. She never seemed to have a hard time speaking up in her office when handing down some advice on how Joaquin should handle his son. On the stand, I could barely hear her without straining my ears.

Dr. Becky testified in open court that she believed the CPS investigation was unfounded. I knew this was not true because I'd seen the report myself. The sole reason she was hired was because the report was *founded*, which led to the police formally charging Joaquin. Part of the plea deal was that Joaquin needed to hire a therapist for his son and adhere to her recommendations.

'Hera, get your jaw off the floor—fix your face,' I coached myself silently.

Jude was watching me closely, and he reacted to my facial expression with a grimace of disapproval. I've never been good at fixing my face, especially in the presence of complete tomfoolery like this.

When it was Borger's turn, he didn't disappoint. He tore the therapist apart on the stand like he was a rabid dog who'd just caught his dinner. He asked her if she'd ever met Crystal. The therapist admitted she hadn't met Crystal but rattled off a story that Joaquin had told her about their relationship.

"I believe she lived in the home, and I believe she slept on the floor," she said, as though forcing your partner—or housemate—to sleep on the floor was perfectly sane behavior.

During her testimony, I felt like I was in the twilight

zone where odd behavior was explained away as though it was perfectly normal.

Borger continued by questioning in rapid-fire succession, naming off all the things he wanted the therapist to explain:

- The creation of sexually explicit videos while his minor son was in the next room.
- The glue Joaquin used to close a wound he'd caused on his son's head.
- How Joaquin hadn't earned a dime and had solely lived off death benefits.

Dr. Becky stumbled over her words as she testified that she believed Joaquin worked at a Smoothie Business. But Borger had her cornered and was ready to go in for the kill. His face exploded with glee because he knew there was no logical explanation the therapist would be able to provide to explain away previous testimony. And he knew Joaquin was unable to provide evidence that he worked at the smoothie place.

To my surprise, Dr. Becky avoided the direct questions and instead testified to her belief that Joaquin was a famous singer.

"Are you aware that he's claimed to perform with Beyonce, Snoop Dog? You said he was a good father. I want to know if you know how he supported his son," Borger asked pointedly, a smirk still lingering on the corner of his mouth.

"I know about some concerts he had done, and I know because of his son. As you are aware, this is about what is in the best interest of his son that I am here," she responded defensively.

I watched as Dr. Becky's demeaner changed on the stand

as Borger cornered her with his words. She began to raise her voice, the timid version fading away more rapidly with each question.

"We're actually here to discuss what's in the best interest of Prince, just so the record is clear," Judge Jude interrupted Dr. Becky.

Dr. Becky told the court that she understood, from conversations with Sammy, that I also attended concerts where Joaquin performed. I raised an eyebrow, looking right at her—challenging her with my non-verbal language. I remembered the conversations I had with Dr. Becky, sharing my concerns about how I'd never seen a shred of evidence that Joaquin was a famous musician. And in open court, she was acting as though I'd said the opposite. It also didn't feel right that she was disclosing anything Sammy said to her, given that he hadn't given her permission to talk about him.

"Would it be of concern to you if you learned that Joaquin hadn't earned a penny in the last ten years? How would that factor at all into your opinion of him," Borger questioned.

"There are a lot of people who don't work, sir," she responded.

Her testimony then erupted into an argument between her and Borger. Dr. Becky started cutting off every question, making it hard to make any progress. I think this is what is referred to as a "hostile witness."

"Ma'am, you have rendered an opinion. If you could just stop talking and listen to the question. How about listening for a second. I would imagine that given your expertise, you ought to be able to do that. The question is that you have offered an opinion that you think that the defendant is a fit and proper person to have custody of this child, is that correct?" Judge Jude rolled his eyes as he interjected.

"Yes," Dr. Becky responded affirmatively.

"Upon what are you basing that opinion," Jude asked with an irritated tone to his voice.

"Not based on money, sir," she defended, shifting in her seat and puffing out her chest.

"So, you don't know where he works or what his past employment has been, is that correct," Jude asked, his tone now seeming irritated.

"Except for that he was in the music industry," she responded.

Judge Jude continued taking over the cross-examination until he uncovered that Dr. Becky didn't really know much about Joaquin at all. She'd solely relied on what he'd told her without any ability to vet the credibility of his statements.

"Does it concern you in any way, that Sammy's mother was shot brutally in the head on the day before a custody case with Mr. Rams?" Borger moved on, going for the jugular.

"I don't believe it was the day before a custody case. It does not for me," Dr. Becky stated.

"What goes into your reasoning for disregarding this as a concern," Borger questioned, leaning in closer to the witness stand.

"Well, because he wasn't charged and there was nothing that was actually documented about it, or I haven't seen anything documented about it," she said, voice trailing off at the end.

She then admitted that she hadn't been aware there was a custody conflict going on.

"Let's move on to something that's relevant, and not something that happened nine years ago," Jude interrupted.

My heart felt as though it dropped into the pit of my stomach. Why didn't the judge think a murder that was associated with Joaquin was relevant? If he didn't, then so many things I'd been afraid of—weren't a concern for him.

Judge Jude so easily dismissed what I believed was an important detail—the haunting coincidence that Shawn was killed the night before Joaquin had to face her in court.

If he wasn't factoring this in, he was willing to discount a large point of evidence to the danger this man posed to Prince.

Dr. Becky's testimony ultimately didn't do Joaquin any favors. Between Borger and Judge Judge's questioning, it wasn't clear why she'd come. But what was uncomfortably clear was that Joaquin was unable to call one single character witness who'd had a relationship with him outside of one where he was a customer.

If Dr. Becky had simply received a subpoena, and testified honestly, I could forgive her. But after openly lying about what I'd told her in open court, it felt like she was an extension of Joaquin himself.

Joaquin's testimony was up next and watching it was like viewing a horror film unfold. The strangest thing about it was that his own attorney's line of questioning made him look like he didn't remember basic details about himself. Chastity began out of the gate asking Joaquin to state his birthday.

"6/12/77," Joaquin responded, confidently.

"And why do you believe that to be your birthday," Chastity asked.

"I was given a birth certificate with that number, which my true date of birth is 6/12/72," he replied.

Joaquin went on to reply that he'd received this birth certificate from Richmond. What he didn't mention, however, was that he was born in New York.

'Why did he receive a birth certificate from Virginia if he was born in New York,' I thought, still trying to rationalize what was clearly crazy.

Chastity also didn't ask him why he'd been using this incorrect birth certificate to obtain government documents like a driver's license and concealed weapons permit. Perhaps because asking him this would be prompting him to admit that he'd committed a felony in open court. He was, however, admitting on the stand that he'd committed fraud. I was confused by this strategy from his defense team.

"And how old does that make you today," Chastity asked.

Joaquin responded, "30."

"How old are you really today," Chastity asked.

"38," Joaquin said, with a strange smile on his face.

I buried my face in my hands and began to rub my temples. I was embarrassed for my son that this man was his father.

As Chastity continued direct examination, my brain was still stuck on this strange exchange of numbers that had just occurred. The math wasn't mathing:

- The trial took place in March 2012, which meant that if Joaquin was born in June 1972, he would've been 39, not 38.
- If he'd been born in 1977, as his fraud-

ulently obtained birth certificate stated,
he'd have been 35 and not 30.

'Is anyone else in this courtroom seeing this,' I thought, looking around the room wondering why nobody else seemed confused.

What I realized in this moment was that when Joaquin spoke confidently, people just accepted what he said as truth—even when the facts showed that he didn't seem to even remember how old he was. It was like his hubris had a way of hypnotizing people into acceptance, no matter how wild the details.

Joaquin moved on to talking about being a musician. Joaquin was never able to produce a shred of actual evidence that would support his claim to have performed in concert, but under oath he stuck to his story by saying that he'd performed in concert with Beyonce, Destiny's Child, Snoop Dogg, and Mya. As Joaquin went on and on about his music, he sounded bat-shit crazy.

At one point, Chastity even tried to discredit Crystal Toussant's testimony by having Joaquin deny they were ever in a relationship.

"Okay. Actually, before we go forward, let's go backward. Prior to meeting Ms. McLeod, were you involved with Crystal Toussant," Chastity asked.

Joaquin quickly denied ever having been in a relationship with Crystal and noted that they'd simply been friends. Joaquin went on to claim that Crystal simply stayed in his house "from time to time." He made Crystal out to be a troubled woman who'd been the mastermind behind his involvement in the pornography.

Joaquin's description of his relationship with Crystal

was an example of Joaquin's inability to remember what he'd previously testified to under oath. Official court records from his 2005 custody case for his older son completely contradict his more recent description of his involvement with Crystal. Back in 2005, he described Crystal as someone who was living with him full time, and intimately involved with raising his older son. Joaquin testified previously that Crystal picked his older son up at school, bathed him, and helped financially take care of him and his son. In fact, while Joaquin vehemently denied that Crystal ever helped him financially, he claimed in 2005 that her income contributed the most to the total income in their household.

Joaquin continued his testimony by trying to paint himself as the victim. He claimed that Officer Jones instructed him to stay away from my family, for his own safety. He then struggled through a discussion of his finances, claiming that his government contracts for his personal business dried up in 2005. Offering that he'd applied for a job at the smoothie place contradicted testimony that he was a successful musician.

As more questions came about his financial history, he pulled out the crocodile tears. Joaquin began to cry about how much he missed Prince, trying to paint me as a villain who was just upset that he cheated on me.

Borger began his cross-examination by exposing that Joaquin hadn't bothered to attend the court mandated co-parenting class. Then Borger called attention to the giant elephant that has been camping out in the middle of the courtroom.

"Are there any human beings on the planet Earth that you believe are of the opinion—other than that you have a professional, some professional connection with, such as the doctor—who have some real knowledge of your life and who believe that you are a fit parent? Is there anybody in the world that you are aware of who thinks that," Borger asked, in his long-winded and dramatic style.

Joaquin shifted in his seat before responding, "My family."

Joaquin had to know this wasn't true. But he also knew that the court wouldn't contact his family to determine why they weren't there to support him. This was a lie that nobody would be able to verify without finding these people and instantly teleporting them to court. I wondered if there'd ever be a situation in which I couldn't get one member of my family to vouch for me as a parent. Though I finally saw him as a monster, a small part of me was sad for him. He was so incapable of forming meaningful relationships that even his own family wouldn't stand up for him.

"Okay. Well, where are they," Borger asked.

Visibly nervous, Joaquin started to banter about how he wasn't originally from Virginia and his family couldn't be at the trial because they were not in town. Borger continued to push Joaquin by asking why he had listed a bunch of people in his pre-trial documents who didn't show up to testify. Joaquin seemed to have an excuse for everyone. His friend Eduardo was in the hospital after foot surgery, and his housemates were caught up due to medical issues as well.

Borger knew, as I did, why no one showed up for Joaquin that day. Nobody showed up because Joaquin wasn't the good guy that he wanted the court to believe he was. Joaquin's real family believed he'd killed his own mother. So, if any of them showed up, it wouldn't have been to sing their praises.

"When was the last time you didn't live off your mother,

a girlfriend, or the proceeds of life insurance," Borger asked casually, as though he hadn't just dropped a bomb.

Chastity objected, and the judge overruled it.

"I didn't live off a girlfriend. So, I lived with my mom, and she helped support me," Joaquin responded defensively.

But his attempt to defend himself proved Borger's point and backed him further into the corner.

"So, when was the last time that you supported yourself, if you ever did," Borger continued to push Joaquin.

He seemed careful not to come across as aggressive because this topic was embarrassing and coming off too aggressive would've backfired. And he didn't need to be combative because Joaquin was proving his points effortlessly.

"I supported myself from, I was involved in a car accident in 2002, and I was awarded a settlement," Joaquin said, his eyes shifting and darting nervously around the courtroom.

I couldn't figure out if he knew this made him look bad, and was embarrassed, or if he thought living off insurance was a respectable way to earn a living.

Borger continued trying to get a shred of truth out of Joaquin, essentially proving to the court that Joaquin had been surviving off death benefits, his mother, girlfriends, and now his friends Ronan and Roxy. But this was like trying to get juice from a rock. They bickered back and forth, arguing about the definition of "earning" and whether life insurance qualified as earned income until it was time for lunch.

My tribe of supporters and I went across the street to have lunch. As my family joked about how ridiculous Joaquin's testimony was, I felt terrible. I kept thinking about how terribly he'd presented and wondered how I missed all these obvious red flags. How could I have been so blind?

Nothing he said made sense, but when we were together, I wanted so badly to believe him. I remembered hanging onto his every word and thinking that his stories were fascinating. Now, he just seemed disturbed.

'Had he been always this way and perhaps I just saw what I wanted to see,' I wondered.

I wanted the day to be over. I was exhausted, humiliated, and terrified. No matter what happened at the end of this day, Joaquin would surely have access to Prince. I couldn't stand the thought of Joaquin touching Prince, let alone spending hours with him. I prayed through the entire court recess for something I knew would never happen. I prayed that the judge could see what I saw, and I prayed he'd save my son.

After Joaquin put on what was possibly the biggest stage production of his life, it was Judge Jude's turn to issue his order. He issued his order right after lunch.

"Well, now it's my turn," Jude said, with a stern look on his face that made me feel like I was back in middle school about to be reprimanded.

"I've sat here patiently and listened to one of the reasons I . . . this is not the part of the job I enjoy doing. It's part of the job I prefer not to do. I'm very honest with my position. I'm in Family Law because I have to be. It's a required 18-month rotation. I don't like it. And if I could choose not to do it, I would not do it. And it's for these kinds of cases."

These statements infuriated me and lit a fire inside of me that burns to this day. *Nobody* enjoys being in family court. It's a place most people find themselves in when they're out of options. Parents are forced to put the lives of their children at the mercy of the courts, and the least we can ask for is a modicum on respect and kindness during this extremely stressful process. As he continued talking, I had to force myself to not obsess over how his words made me feel, to try and listen.

"Let me begin by saying I don't care what the two of you do in your lives, what each of you do, what choices you make, what decisions you make, what you do behind closed doors, I could care less. That's your decision to make. I don't have any involvement in that. I don't have any authority to address it. It's about this young child. That's what drives my decision solely, exclusively, only this young child. And I approach that as if this child were mine, what would I want," he said staring at both of us, leaving me feeling like the gum he'd just picked off his shoes.

I didn't believe that Jude based his decision on what he'd do if Prince were his own child. His callous words made me feel like he based his decision on what he felt *my* child deserved. If this were his child, he wouldn't have rolled his eyes—appeared to dose off during the trial—and he'd have fought for access to the child abuse records that Sgt. Perry tried to bring into court. He'd have exercised his judicial discretion for that, just as he'd done to allow Dr. Becky to walk in the back door to testify as a surprise.

"Let me tell you what I conclude this case is not about," he continued, "and this has been referenced in the opening, it's a lot of smoke. The difficulty is with all that smoke I can't see clearly."

I assumed from this statement that he was talking about the testimony that I'd presented regarding all the danger surrounding Joaquin. Both my attorneys and I hoped that Jude would see that behind every billow of smoke there's a fire looming. Unfortunately, Jude just saw the smoke and it was too hard for him to see through it.

"It's not about a homicide investigation. I don't know anything about the homicide investigation," he said.

Jude continued to express his confusion about how Joaquin was living by exclaiming, ". . . Evidence he lived off of the insurance proceeds from that deceased mother that maybe that was the basis for the homicide, except there's no evidence to support that."

At this moment, I wanted to run up to the bench and shake him. Joaquin admitted to having no means of support. Joaquin also admitted that he'd received life insurance from his mother and death benefits from Shawn. What evidence did Jude expect to see? It was clear that Joaquin was only able to survive off the brutal deaths—which happened to all be connected to him.

"What this case *is* about," he lectured, "is two people that met each other online. Isn't that wonderful," he asked with rhetorical sarcasm.

I felt my face getting hot, and I could almost feel the steam coming out of my ears. This statement sounded eerily like Chastity's opening statement. It felt like he'd boiled all my trauma down to a trivial disagreement between ex-lovers.

Perhaps in Jude's day, people met their significant others at the local general store or in church. That's not how things typically worked in 2012, but there was nobody giving Jude this type of education.

"A young lady who comes from a different walk of life and a young man who comes from a completely different walk of life, and the two have nothing in common whatsoever. The sad part is they now have something in common. It's called a child. And that's never going to change."

With these last statements, it was clear that he wasn't

thinking of Prince as he would his own son. He was thinking of Prince being the product of a relationship he felt
should never have existed. While I certainly wish I'd never
met Joaquin, Prince was a blessing. Jude should never have
referred to my son in open court as something that was
"unfortunate."

"This is not a CINA action," Jude said.

"This is not a Child in Need of Assistance . . . Ms.
Tassant [which wasn't actually her name], who likes to get
undressed and go on websites and perform whatever the
heck she does, that's a great witness," he said sarcastically.

Jude concluded that because Crystal Toussant was in a
ten-year relationship with Joaquin and was once a stripper,
he wasn't going to believe that she'd been a victim of Rams'
abuse. While it was clear from the testimony and documented evidence that Joaquin allowed Crystal to help him
raise Sammy, this decision didn't appear to show poorly on
Joaquin's judgment. Jude only showed distain for Crystal
and ignored Joaquin's involvement in this distasteful lifestyle.

After Jude made it clear that he had completely dis-
counted the testimony of one of my key witnesses, he turned
to Joaquin.

"When you go on the [internet], Mr. Rams, you don't
find he was the opening act for Destiny's Child. You find
that he runs a porn site. That's not the kind of environment
that I want a child to be raised in. Where's the child going to
live, if I were to go the opposite extreme and award custody
to you? Well, he's going to live with these people, whatever
their names, that aren't here, that are sick, couldn't come
here today. You're going to live with them. Somebody's
renting your house. But you don't work. You supposedly

have a job starting sometime in April. I don't have a single scintilla of evidence reflecting anything about Mr. Rams' employment—nothing."

'So maybe he was listening a little,' I thought, trying to remain as optimistic as possible.

Jude then showed what appeared to be a slight understanding that Rams might not be operating with all the tools of a sane person when he said, "I don't care who you've played with or who you've played for or whether you're just singing a lonely tune."

Jude turned back toward me and said, "That does not mean that Ms. McLeod comes in necessarily with clean hands either . . . what attracted the two of you together on the internet, God knows. I have no idea, nor do I really care. But whatever it was, that fairy dust has long since dissipated. And the result is Prince McLeod Rams."

After these words, it felt as if Jude was doing the same thing to me that he'd done to Crystal. Because Crystal was associated with Joaquin, she was automatically seen as a whore. Because I'd been involved with a man that he deemed to be vile (rightfully so), he felt as though I was vile too and deserved to be punished. What was interesting was that as vile as he considered Joaquin to be, he made sure to set up a simple checklist for him to be able to gain unsupervised access to Prince. Jude looked at Crystal, who had effectively turned her life around and was now working with Special Needs children and believed that she wasn't a credible witness.

Joaquin just had to prove to the judge that he could be on acceptable behavior for three months, and then he could have unrestricted access to an innocent child. Forget about all the danger that'd occurred around this man and his extreme pattern of callous behavior. Joaquin, in Jude's eyes, was redeemable and deserved a chance to have a "relationship" with Prince. If Joaquin checked the boxes, it was as though that would prove that Prince would be the *one* person he wouldn't hurt.

Jude concluded that day by awarding me sole legal custody and primary physical custody of Prince. Joaquin was awarded supervised visitation for three hours a week (which we both had to pay for) for three months. At the end of three months, the court instructed Joaquin to return with a psychological evaluation by a psychologist of his choosing. He was also instructed to begin paying child support and bring witnesses to the next trial who could vouch for his legitimacy (i.e., living arrangement, work, etc.).

My attorneys walked out of the courtroom feeling as though they'd just won. I didn't share their joy. Joaquin was a master at finding fake family and the court didn't seem interested in hard evidence and vetting lofty claims.

"Go out and celebrate. This court order proves that you own your child, "Borger said gleefully.

I didn't want to *own* Prince. I wanted to be his mother, and I wanted him to have a fair shot at living.

Chapter 15

Jumping Out of Moving Cars

The first time I jumped out of a moving car, I was trying to survive. The second time, I was trying to kill myself.

It'd been three and a half years since I'd jumped out of that cab in Brazil. Before I entered the custody war and inherited the legal abuse that came along with it, I was never suicidal. With obvious threats to my safety, I always acted quickly and without trepidation. If someone even looked at me the wrong way while I was in operations mode, I wouldn't think twice about running in the opposite direction. Given my background and previous training, it might seem strange that I was unable to recognize that I was in danger for so long. If Joaquin had tried to kidnap me on our first date, this would've been a much shorter story.

The year I spent with Joaquin changed me. The psychological abuse I endured made me question myself in ways I never had before. Every time I would have negative reactions to things he said, he'd craftily hijack the course of the conversation to a degree where I'd question whether my reaction was fair. Before Joaquin attacked my sister, I never recognized that I was living in a red zone. I falsely believed that being home on American soil gave me the luxury of letting my guard down.

In the months leading up to Prince's first birthday, I felt as though I was on the verge of a mental breakdown. Lack of sleep, a constant flow of legal and personal attacks, and the fear that I wouldn't be able to protect my son wore me down daily. Nearly every night, I had nightmares that Joaquin would come for us, and my mind was constantly spinning, trying to stay one step ahead of him.

We had court two days before Prince's birthday. While anxious, I was somewhat hopeful leading up to this hearing. I knew that Joaquin hadn't complied with the judge's order to get a job, and the supervised visits hadn't gone well either. Prince screamed through most of them, and Joaquin cancelled several others at the last minute.

As part of the court order, a retired police officer (whom I'll call "the supervisor") was named as the person who would supervise the visits. She'd recently retired from a Maryland Police Department. I was initially encouraged by her experience as an officer. My initial trust in her showed that I still wasn't ready to give up completely on inherent belief that the police would protect us. I wanted to believe that my experiences with the County Police were an anomaly. Because any belief to the contrary would've added to the dangerously acute fear I walked around with daily.

My initial confidence eventually turned to skepticism. The supervisor spent several hours a week with Joaquin, and I worried she was falling for his charm too.

In the years since my case, I've learned more about the area of supervised visitation and the biggest issue with this recommendation is that she shouldn't have been recommended solely based on her previous career. Instead, we should've been referred to a supervised visitation center or at the very least a solo professional who'd undergone some training in the profession.

If she was trained in supervised visitation, perhaps she'd have felt comfortable documenting her observations without omission. While she expressed concerns, she seemed to have trouble identifying the behavior she'd observed during the visit that concerned her. Training would've helped her understand her obligations to the court in this role, which weren't the same as a police officer.

During supervised visits, the court relied on her to evaluate the visits. In her capacity as a supervisor, she *was* authorized to make commentary about how Joaquin behaved around Prince. Reporting things like Joaquin's inability to console his son when Prince was crying and reaching for a hug—paying more attention to the supervisor than his son—or returning Prince with a soaking wet diaper after a visit where he refused to change him—were all things the supervisor should report to the court.

On the day we came back to court, essentially for Joaquin to prove whether he'd complied with the judge's order, things weren't going well for me. I'd started carrying a gun, but forgot it was in my purse that morning. In a complete pretrial daze, I was steps away from the security desk when I realized I'd forgotten to remove the weapon.

Running back and forth to the car was exhausting, and I showed up to court drenched in sweat and out of breath. My attorney looked at me, and without a word raised his eyebrow as though to ask if I was ready for this. I sat down at the lawyer's table without saying a word.

Chastity appeared gleeful that morning, like she couldn't wait to show off how wonderful Joaquin had been in the previous months. She focused her argument that day on the fact that Joaquin had complied with the judge's order—he'd checked the boxes.

During the previous trial, the judge asked Joaquin to remove the revenge pornography website that he'd created on his ex-girlfriend Crystal Toussant, pay child support, show up to supervised visits, and get a psychological examination. To prove his compliance about the pornography, he printed out an HTML screen shot that showed a 505 error. This basically means the page didn't load, but it didn't prove that what he showed the court was the website the judge referred to. Since the website wasn't pulled up during court, Joaquin could've easily doctored the paperwork to make it appear as though the website was removed. Later, we learned that he never removed the website.

One of the family court reforms I recommend is having an investigative body to independently verify claims. While removing the site wouldn't ensure Joaquin was a safe parent, having a third party verify his claim would've at least showed the judge that Joaquin hadn't bothered to comply with this simple request.

Joaquin paid child support once, and then never again. Showing one receipt was enough to check the box. He showed up to 75% of the visits and didn't hit Prince while supervised. The supervisor documented that Joaquin showed up to the visits, which led the court to assume they'd been a success. And since the court allowed Joaquin to choose his own psychologist, Joaquin picked a school psychologist who wasn't licensed to conduct a psychological examination on an adult. This school psychologist testified in open court that she was a clinical psychologist, and the court never verified her credentials.

An abusive psychopath will always be able to produce a witness who claims to be an expert, and if the court doesn't insist on standards with psychological professionals they might as well not bother ordering these types of tests. Had the court furnished a list of vetted professionals, they could've at least ensured the examiner was licensed to examine adults.

As Chastity presented the evidence to the court of the boxes Joaquin checked, she told the court that it was her belief that it was a tragedy that Prince hadn't been able to have the "positive" influence that his father could provide. I was nauseous and actively tried to avoid vomiting all over the table.

My mind wandered as Chastity spoke, thinking about all the times Joaquin flew into rages. I thought about how terrified I was that I'd step on one of Joaquin's psychological landmines. I was gutted at the thought that Prince would someday have to face him without my protection. As soon as the thought crept into my mind, I choked back tears. Judge Jude watched me intently as Chastity spoke, as though he was studying my reaction.

I stared back at him unflinching. Unlike my reaction in the police station, I didn't smile. I wasn't interested in making the judge feel better about his decision if it meant that he was going to put my son in danger. I didn't try to hide my fear this time.

Joaquin checked the boxes nearly enough to satisfy the judge, but there was one lingering question. The judge expressed concern over Joaquin's psychological state during the previous hearing. Chastity presented an exam, but the exam revealed that Joaquin lied to the therapist with respect to having been previously examined. He told her that he'd never had a psychological exam, when in fact he had. During the custody trial for Sammy, the court asked him to submit to a psychological exam just like they had this time. Luckily, my lawyers had this information and Chastity didn't.

Chastity didn't initially call the therapist who conducted the exam as a witness. As a result, the judge decided that he'd postpone his order until the therapist was able to present her findings. My attorneys were also ordered to give Chastity a copy of the previous psychological report that we obtained from Sheryl Mason.

Though the judge hadn't yet ruled to lift the supervised visitation, my attorneys were certain that as soon as the therapist testified a few weeks later, the supervision would be lifted. As terrifying as it was to expose Prince to visits that were supervised, I couldn't bear the idea of what would happen to him if there was no one watching. My mind kept going to the worst-case scenarios, and no matter how much I tried to think of a way out, I knew that there was nothing I could do within the law to protect my son.

I felt myself start to panic, and I started looking for a way out of the courtroom. My entire body felt like it was on fire, and I felt like my throat was closing. With the way Jude watched my every move, I couldn't risk him witnessing a panic attack that could put my fitness as a parent into question.

Just when I thought this could be over, Chastity raised another issue, insisting its resolution before we could leave for the day.

"Your honor," she started, "I would like to talk about splitting time on Prince's birthday."

My eyes shot up from the desk. There was no way I was going to allow this, as I'd already planned to take Prince to the beach for his birthday. Joaquin mentioned nothing about splitting the day and saving this request until we were in court was calculated to evoke a reaction and make me look unreasonable for non-compliance.

Borger, at my insistence, informed the judge of my plans, and questioned why he was bringing this up now. Chastity pressed on, suggested that I allow, and pay, for Joaquin to have an extra visit. She also suggested that I do something special for him by planning a party at a notoriously loud, dirty children's play area so that Joaquin could celebrate with his son. I shook my head vigorously.

As I mentioned, I firmly believe that each parent is responsible for their own relationship with their child. Had Joaquin planned something special, given notice, and paid for the activity—it would've shown positive intent. Instead, he waited until the last minute and insisted I pay for him to have an experience with his son. In the warped view of people who prescribe to parental alienation, my refusal to allow myself to be financially abused played into their narrative that I wasn't supporting his right to parent.

It was in that moment that I realized that as much as I didn't know who Joaquin really was, he also didn't know me. He probably remembered me as just an empath, always bending over backward to meet his needs. I was a shell of myself when I was with him. I allowed his desires to trump my own, and I completely lost my voice and identity. Sitting there next to my attorneys, giving Chastity the side eye, I wasn't that woman anymore.

My lawyers pushed back enough against the birthday madness. My insistence that it not happen, however, likely burned political capital with the judge. I knew that in this situation, playing nice was expected. And playing nice meant being a doormat, rolling out the red carpet, and pretending to not be afraid that your son's father would kill him. And I knew denying this request could make me look unreasonable. But I needed to be able to provide my son a peaceful birthday, and splitting the day with a man I knew was dangerous didn't seem like the move here.

I walked out of the courtroom feeling as though I was walking outside of my own body. Like I was watching a scene from someone else's movie. My lawyers were somber, like they were also aware the mood changed. We all felt the judge's mood shift that day. They spoke to me as we walked back to their office, but I didn't hear a word they said. Like I'd been transported to the classroom in the Charlie Brown cartoons with the unintelligible teacher.

I felt as though something wasn't right with me, like I was about to break. I didn't know who to warn, or whether I really wanted to warn anyone. My mental state was hanging on by a thread, and my mind and body seemed to be shutting down. It took effort to breathe, so much so that listening to my attorneys wasn't possible.

Later that day, as we prepared to drive to the beach, I plotted how I could remove myself from this equation of life.

I'd reached my breaking point. And my thoughts weren't at all based in logic.

At first, I wondered if I could take Prince and run. Maybe I could take him across the Canadian border. Maybe we could move to Mexico and finally be free. I knew these thoughts were crazy, because these actions would've put me on the FBI wanted list for child abduction. I wouldn't be able to disappear because the government would come after me, and we didn't have enough money to effectively hide. Every bit of savings I had already been spent trying to fight Joaquin the legal way.

I sat silently in the car as my mother was lamenting about the day, and Prince was sleeping in his car seat next to me. Every possible scenario I could think of wasn't a good one. In every scenario, Joaquin was still coming after us. In every single scenario someone wouldn't survive. Then, I finally completely broke down. The lack of sleep, the constant mind racing, and the terror final got the best of me.

'Maybe if I remove myself from this equation, Joaquin will stop fighting,' I thought.

"Please, take care of Prince. Please keep him safe," I cried, barely audible.

I grasped my hand around the door handle of the car, closed my eyes, and jumped out into oncoming traffic. I can only describe this moment as an out-of-body experience because I'm a survivalist—but that day I was *not* myself. Trauma response is a very real thing and can fundamentally change how you behave during a stage of acute trauma. Unfortunately, many people within the court system don't understand it when they see it. In court, I was the one who was starting to spiral out—while Joaquin was able to present as cool, calm, and collected. If the judge wasn't paying attention to the flawed logic in his words, and only focused on our body language—he was bound to get it wrong.

The decision I made that day surprises me to this day and serves as a reminder to show others living through trauma extreme grace. That day I believed, if only for one instant, that if I died then perhaps Joaquin wouldn't have anyone to harass and would leave Prince alone. If given the choice between my death and my son's, I'd choose for me to be the one who died.

I was incredibly lucky that I wasn't hit by another car that day. After jumping out of the car, I just started walking. I wanted out of that life. I had severe Post Traumatic Stress Disorder (PTSD). Regardless of how many times my therapist told me not to let Joaquin drag me down a rabbit hole of crazy, this day was the straw that broke the camel's back—and the rabbit was dragging me down the hole.

I wandered around for hours as my family tried to find me. Eventually, my mother saw me walking down the street close to our house. She drove up next to me and pleaded with me to get in the car.

"Prince is hungry, Hera. You're the only person who can nurse him, and that is what he wants."

I was walking on a main street that didn't have a sidewalk. My mother then rolled down the back window so that I could see Prince. As soon as Prince saw me, he smiled and got excited to see me. He lifted his little toddler finger and pointed at me—reinforcing that it was me he wanted. He couldn't have possibly fully realized what was going on, but this kid had an incredible knack for filling even the darkest moments with sunshine and dragging me from the depths of despair.

His eyes shined as he looked at me and held out his arms.

He needed me, and I'd been selfish to think I could just leave him because I was tired of fighting. Surviving hadn't been enough—Prince deserved a fighter. He deserved a mother who would be his rock in the hard times, and someone who was willing to swim through burning flames to protect him.

'What am I doing?' I thought.

There was no way I could leave my son. I got back in the car, hugged Prince, and went home. I immediately called my therapist to discuss what happened and ask for advice on how to cope with the events of the day.

Despite the high drama of the day, and my clearly fragile state, my mother insisted we keep our plans for Prince's birthday. We took Prince to the beach to celebrate his first birthday. It was an amazing weekend. Prince played in the sand, dipped his feet into the cold water, and we all spent the weekend spoiling him—me, my father, my mother, and my sister. For an entire afternoon, Prince rode on my father's shoulders as we all walked on the boardwalk overlooking the beach. Everywhere Prince pointed, my father would take him. Prince was with his family that weekend, and I am so grateful I was able to give him such an amazing day.

Chapter 16

Danger Assessment

On July 12, 2012, two weeks after the previous court date, Joaquin checked the final box for the court by bringing in the School Psychologist who conducted his psychological evaluation to testify. She testified to her belief that Joaquin wasn't a danger to Prince and that he was simply suffering from a "mild case of depression."

In family court cases, where at least one party in the case has been accused of child abuse of violence against anyone, the court should conduct a Lethality (or "danger") Assessment. The state of Maryland has a Lethality Assessment Program (LAP), which is a multi-pronged intervention program that consists of an evidence-based tool called the Lethality Screen. This screen helps field practitioners more clearly assess a victim's risk of intimate partner homicide, which proactively connects victims to community-based domestic violence services. The LAP addresses questions such as whether a parent has a history of threatening others with weapons, verbal threats to harm the co-parent or child, and a previous history of physical violence or controlling behavior.

The Lethality Assessment is validated and one of the most widely used, reliable instruments on lethality for adult women; however, it hasn't been validated to measure the risk to children. While opponents might dismiss its use in family court as a result, I argue that the same criteria to measure a whether a perpetrator is dangerous to another adult would also make that person dangerous to a child.

Even if the child isn't old enough to have an established relationship with the offending parent, as was the case for my 15-month-old son Prince, that parent's history of violence should factor into whether unsupervised access is safe for that child.

Unfortunately, lethality assessments aren't commonly leveraged in Maryland family court. So, when my therapist suggested one, in hopes that it would force the court to reconsider the risk, my attorneys asked him to testify.

He was a forensic psychologist with a doctorate degree and had given this type of assessment in the past; however, the fact that he was *also* my therapist didn't help his testimony. He had to acknowledge that he hadn't tested Joaquin and could only base his assessment on the facts presented to him, including the two previous psychological assessments, Joaquin's court testimony, the evaluator's report, and other witness testimony in the court record.

"I'm not going to ask you to do a diagnosis of him, but I'm going to ask you, really, really a hypothetical basis, in effect, based on all the information, assuming the information you've read and it as a professional, hypothetically, do you have concerns about the subject's involvement, the subject having unsupervised possession and control of this 1-year-old child," Borger asked in his long winded, and roundabout way.

Borger knew he needed to be careful with my therapist as a witness, given that he hadn't tested Joaquin. Chastity jumped out of her seat to object, but Judge Jude over-ruled her, waving his fingers in the air as though he was swatting away an annoying fly. Jude seemed interested in what the doctor had to say, given that he was the only forensic psychologist who had his attention on this case.

After patiently waiting for Chastity to return to her seat, my therapist responded and carefully outlined his concerns:

"Well, if you go back through the four reports the following kind of information is of great concern to me as a psychologist with a, you know, a part-time forensic practice.

There's a report that [Joaquin] pulled a gun in anger in a domestic argument with Crystal. That hasn't been addressed in the current psychological exam, nor has he had a chance to explain it. He reportedly physically, was physically and emotionally abusive towards his son and Crystal in the evaluator's report, according to Sergeant Perry and others.

The evaluator reported that Joaquin participates in photographing nude models in a room next to his son; that concerns me. There's a report that he may have been an early victim of sexual abuse, that concerns me. I would like, if I were going to interview him, I would want to talk to him about that before I would get comfortable with that.

There's a report from Sergeant Perry in the evaluator's report that he's been arrested for embezzlement, denial of visitation, posting compromising videos without knowledge or consent, secret videotaping, and has no means of support other than living off other and insurance payments. So, I'd want to ask him about that.

There's another report where he failed to seek medical care for his older son's head injury, which it's unclear how that evolved, but it could have been in a confrontation with him, and rather than take him to the OR, he used adhesive to bind the wound. And then, there's a report that when he found his mother unconscious that rather than call 9-1-1, he called Mr. Bailey.

An earlier forensic report says Joaquin, sometimes, is vulnerable to confusing his interests and the child's interests, and I think those two episodes support that."

From the edge of her seat, Chastity once again bounced up to object. Judge Jude responded to her by noting that he understood that my therapist's testimony was his opinion. She flopped back into her seat with a scowl on her face.

Once the circus calmed, the doctor continued, "The evaluator, after her interviews, suggested that Ms. McLeod's safety concerns were legitimate and there were reports in that earlier, in the evaluator's summary that unsupervised visits may allow him to create unfounded charges against others. So, without witnesses present, he may create situations to manipulate others."

The doctor went on to explain how some of Joaquin's actions should be considered dangerous, as they related to the Association for Threat Assessment Professionals' criteria for risk of dangerousness. The doctor noted that Joaquin's history of weapon use associated with emotion should've been explored. It was curious that the court didn't bother exploring Joaquin's reasons for having a conceal carry permit, whether that permit had ever been revoked, what kind of weapons training he had, and how the weapon was stored in the home.

At this point, Mr. Borger asked the doctor what he made of the fact that Joaquin reported that he graduated from high school in 1996. Given that he was 40 years old at the time of the testimony, that would've had him graduating from high school at the age of 24.

"The first thing you do with a subject is you make a chronology starting at birth. You start at year zero . . . She certainly did not miss the fact, after reading the previous psychological report that the subject is not a reliable reporter of information."

Borger continued his line of questioning by pointing out that both psychologists reported that Joaquin exhibited a pattern of social, emotional maladjustment which is exasperated by stress. He asked the doctor if he agreed with this assessment.

"That is the classic definition of a personality disorder. So, a personality disorder is something in which the subject has a biased view of incoming information, and his interpretation of incoming information is biased and it results in problems in the area of love and work. Problems with relationships, problems maintaining employment, problems getting along with others. The subject is like a bull in the china shop when it comes to getting along with others, maintaining jobs, maintaining relationships."

"How does that impact your suggestion earlier that you have concerns about the safety of the child in his unsupervised possession," asked Mr. Borger.

Chastity made audible attempts to interrupt, huffing and puffing loudly. I imagined the courtroom as a theater, where there was a fox standing right in front of the judge—threatening to blow down a little pig's house in the middle of the courtroom. These were the types of thoughts I had throughout the trial that served as a mental escape. I'd think about all the things that seemed ridiculous about this process, letting my imagination dance around to avoid paying full attention to the horror show playing out in real life.

My therapist turned toward Chastity and patiently waited for her to quiet before continuing, "Well, I listed a number of areas, but I think the primary concern is that Mr. Rams will confuse his interests with the interests of the child. In the reports, the failure to take the kid with the split head to the OR because he might be accused of child abuse—things like that are of concern."

After Mr. Borger was finished with his line of questioning, Chastity questions whether the doctor could render an informed opinion since he was *my* therapist. This was an ironic objection given that Joaquin's sole character witness was his son's therapist.

The doctor, a clear pro at this, didn't try to deny his bias in the situation and noted to the judge his recommendation that a proper lethality assessment occur given what was presented in court.

After the psychologists testified, my attorneys called me to the stand. They hadn't prepared me to testify that day, and I was a wreck. Over a decade later, I can firmly say this was a mistake. The doctor's testimony was triggering, and not being emotionally prepared to testify was dangerous given the acute trauma reaction I was having in that moment.

Even before the judge made his decision officially, I worried that he would give Joaquin unsupervised access. If the judge respected both therapists, they would basically cancel each other out. Joaquin checked all the boxes, and it didn't matter that they were just barely checked. It also didn't matter that some facts wouldn't stand up under a thin amount of investigation, because the court would never check his evidence.

For our court system, indefinite supervised visitation isn't a sustainable situation, and the goal that day was to get us out of court as soon as possible—and to avoid us returning for a custody reevaluation. When I walked up to the front of the court to testify, I felt my legs shaking. I tried sending non-verbal cues to my attorneys, so they'd realize the fragile state I was in. I shook my head as my eyes darted back and forth between them on my way to the stand.

Borger asked me a question. Even though I saw his lips moving, I couldn't hear what he'd asked. I broke down on the stand in a humiliating puddle of tears.

"He's so little. He isn't even old enough to be speaking. Please, please protect him. If something happens, he can't even tell me. Please don't allow Prince to get hurt."

My normal behavior would've been to act like I had in the police station the night I escaped Joaquin—and smile while a piece of myself died inside. I was so afraid for my son that I was unable to focus on coming across as calm and articulate. It was the first time my true emotion came through, and I was worried Judge Jude wouldn't appreciate this show of raw emotion. The floodgates opened, and I was unable to close them.

This also made me angry at myself. I was breaking the cardinal rule in the McLeod family. We were supposed to "hold fast" and show no emotion. We were not supposed to show weakness, and I was emotionally bleeding all over the witness chair. This emotion would've potentially been better in front of the police, but it didn't help me in Family Court. In Family Court, my tears made me look unstable. And as many traumatized mothers do—it made me look hysterical.

Judge Jude ordered that Joaquin would have unsupervised visits with Prince for seven hours, every other Saturday and for two hours on Wednesdays during the weeks he didn't have a Saturday visit. Joaquin never took advantage of Wednesday visits. I retained primary physical and legal custody of Prince, which my attorneys said I should have considered a "win."

"I didn't 'win' anything," I cried after leaving the court.

My attorneys told me I was being over dramatic. I wondered how after all they knew of Joaquin, they could still think my fear was merely melodrama. I guessed that to them this was a job, and maybe remaining emotionally disconnected was some sort of defense. But I wondered whether this all came at a cost to their humanity.

Though the visits were to be unsupervised, we were ordered to participate in the safe exchange program. Each visit, we both paid the previous supervisor to drive Prince from one police station to another so that we'd have no contact with each other. Though most of the witness testimony reported that Joaquin was a danger, Joaquin didn't have a problem with the safe exchanges because he reported to the court that he was afraid my family would harm him.

It felt as though several witnesses saw a criminal punch a stranger in the face, and the criminal then turned around in court and asked the judge to give him a protective order against the person he'd just assaulted.

Every time I had to drop off Prince, I felt as though I was saying goodbye to him forever. I'd watch him leave and imagine my little boy toddling over landmines, while I was being physically restrained (by a court order), forced to simply pray he wouldn't step on one of the mines that day.

For the seven hours the visit took place, I tried to distract myself and just pray I would see my son again, and that he would be OK. The first visit, Prince came back hungry, tired, and soaking wet. Despite my anger at the state Prince was in when he returned, I was so relieved that he came back to me alive.

On the second unsupervised visit, just moments before I was scheduled to pick Prince up, the supervisor called to let me know that Joaquin took Prince to the hospital. Before she could explain what happened, I slammed my foot on the gas and speed out of the parking lot where I was waiting. I'm thankful that I didn't pass any police officers that day, as I wouldn't have stopped to explain why I was driving as though I was running away from the devil.

I arrived at the hospital completely frantic. Angry that I wasn't called sooner, and even angrier when the doctors treated me as though Joaquin slandered me before my arrival.

"I already told the child's father about what happened," the doctor said, rolling his eyes when I asked him to tell me what happened.

He acted as though asking what tests they'd run was an inconvenience.

"Your son had a febrile seizure. They are completely benign, and he is going to be fine," the doctor explained, pushing me toward the door.

While I was surprised that Prince had his first seizure with Joaquin, since he'd spent most of his life with me, it was possible the fever alone caused the seizure. I had them as a child, and I knew they were genetic. I also knew that febrile seizures weren't something a parent should worry would irreparably damage their child.

Pushing past the doctor, I ran toward the hallway where they told me Prince was waiting. My mother arrived before I did, and she was holding him when I approached. At the time we received the call that Prince was in the hospital, she was closer. With his usual demeanor, Prince lit up as soon as he saw me. I pointed at him, and he lifted his little finger and pointed back. It was how we greeted each other, and every time I pointed at him, he would cackle with laughter. He was my person, and I was his.

Tears welled up in my eyes, but I fought against them. I knew Prince must've been scared, and I needed for him to know he was okay now because he'd be coming home.

Joaquin's behavior was frightening. He lied to the doctors and pretended as though Prince lived with him full time. When doctors asked Joaquin what Prince had eaten, how he had slept, and other information required to diagnose and treat him, Joaquin lied. Instead of admitting that he didn't have custody of his son, he chose to instead lie and deny my existence.

I worried about Joaquin's ability to be an honest reporter in a medical emergency. Monday morning, two days after the hospital incident, I stormed into my attorney's office with Prince in a stroller.

"We need to file an emergency order immediately," I said, without a proper greeting.

This would keep my son in his home state (and out of Joaquin's home). After an emotional weekend, I couldn't stop my mind from racing and worrying about something happening to Prince that couldn't be reversed.

"Well, I don't see what the problem is. Joaquin took

him to the hospital when there was something wrong. That shows he did the right thing." Borger was trying to manage my emotions.

My anxiety only grew stronger the more he spoke. I wanted him to shut up. I was tired of his smug, misogynistic attitude.

'Why don't they get it?' I thought.

I felt like I was speaking another language, and they understood only half of what I said.

"Hera, you need to start focusing on what Joaquin can provide your son," Borger said with a cocky smirk, as though he knew he was about to tell a bad joke.

"What is that?" I asked, slowly blinking while staring at him.

"Well, he is *really* good at manipulation. This could be a good skill for your son," Borger continued smugly, giggling to himself.

I started to cry, picked up my purse, and began wheeling my son out of the office. After spending $150,000 in a little over a year, I was completely out of money and knew there was nothing these attorneys would be willing to do at this point. I already owed them about $5,000 from the last court date.

On my way out, Borger yelled, "If you don't stop fighting Joaquin, you are going to lose your son!"

I'm not sure it would've been possible for me to not be emotional during that time, but I wish I'd written down my specific concerns before approaching my attorneys. As the war drew on, my mental state remained fragile. While this would have been a good opportunity to show that Joaquin had trouble putting his son's needs before his own, all my attorneys saw that day as a woman enraged.

Instead of making the connection they should've made, they thought I was only upset that Joaquin hadn't told the hospital that I had primary custody. Borger words were insensitive that day but was right about one thing. If I'd continued trying to block Joaquin from having access to Prince, I probably would've eventually lost custody of my son. Over the years, I've met dozens of protective parents who have solid proof that their co-parent is abusive and because they continue to fight to protect their children—they're the ones who end up losing custody. Courts in America don't care about the safety of children. They only care about shared parental access and if you are against that, even for valid reasons, in many cases it could be what causes the child's abusive parent to have full custody.

My lawyers knew that Judge Jude wouldn't be impressed if I'd questioned his final order by filing an appeal. There's a fair chance that appealing Jude's decision would have given Joaquin's attorney ammunition to launch a successful parental alienation attack against me.

My attorneys wanted to claim victory and close the case, but I knew this was far from being over.

Chapter 17

Casualty of War

For nearly an hour almost every night, I watched Prince sleep. Often, after I would put him down, he'd open one eye just to make sure I was still there. Just as I would try to back out of the room, he'd sit up and give me a huge smile to entice me to stay in the room. It worked every single time.

In the weeks after the judge lifted supervised visits, I worried that every day would be our last together. And besides my immediate family, more and more people though I was overreacting and needed to stop obsessing about Joaquin and Prince's safety.

I worried about Prince nearly every minute of every day. I searched the internet, called attorneys, sought answers from my therapist, all to protect Prince. The thought of Prince alone with Joaquin would send me into a panic attack. Most interactions I had with the supervisor had a similar effect. I began to associate her with Joaquin. Every time she'd call or text, I knew it was about Joaquin and it was usually about something that would upset me.

So, when my phone rang while I was driving home from work one day, and I saw the supervisor's name pop up, I hesitated before answering.

Did I really want to take this call while driving? Despite my better judgment, I answered because not answering—and subsequently not knowing what she wanted—would've eaten away at me all the way home had I waited.

Diane started the conversation per usual, asking me how I was and how Prince was doing.

"What's going on?" I asked impatiently, not at all interested in small talk with a woman who'd allow herself to become an extension of Joaquin.

"I've been working on a case in Maryland that has me thinking," her voice trailed off, leaving me to wonder what had her thinking.

I allowed the awkward silence to fill the phone as the supervisor mustered the courage to tell me what she'd called about.

After a few long seconds, she continued, "well, do you think Joaquin would take out an insurance policy on Prince?"

My hands gripped the steering wheel with so much force my knuckles turned purple. Taking a deep breath was a necessary next step because I knew screaming at the supervisor wouldn't be productive.

"What caused you to think this and why are you telling me," I asked

I was worried that he was going to hurt Prince, and all the information I'd gathered during my own investigations showed he had a penchant for living off life insurance death benefits. But other than what I'd already done—presented the information in court—I was at a loss.

"Well, he just seems like the type, and I keep wondering why he wants Prince," she said casually, as though she hadn't just suggested Joaquin was premeditating the murder of my son.

Her statements made it appear as though she saw behavior from Joaquin that showed his motive was not simply that he loved his son. While I knew Joaquin was incapable of loving anyone, I needed for the supervisor to be an honest reporter with the court. The judge didn't believe me, but I hoped he would believe her.

Despite what she told me that day, the supervisor never uttered these concerns during her court testimony. When I asked her why she kept quiet about these things, she later admitted that she believed she could "manage" Joaquin. What this told me was that her desire to keep getting paid outweighed her duty to protect Prince. She was smart enough to realize that if she'd documented what she'd observed that concerned her, Chastity would've insisted we find a replacement supervisor.

After the supervisor suggested that Joaquin's motive for trying to obtain access to Prince might be life insurance, my mother and I started searching for ways we could uncover this sort of information. I learned that even if Joaquin had taken a policy out on *me*, I wouldn't have a right to that information. And unless we knew the exact company and details about the policy, we also couldn't get information on whether he had a policy on Prince.

My trust for Joaquin continued to deteriorate after the

supervisor's comment. I became obsessed with trying to figure out his end game.

On the Thursday before the fourth visit, Prince was running a fever. Every time he had a fever, after that first seizure in Joaquin's care, he had a seizure. This time was no different, and despite all of Prince's doctors telling me they were benign, each one scared the hell out of me.

As soon as Prince started seizing, I called the ambulance. Per usual, as soon as the EMT arrived, Prince was fine—smiling and babbling at everyone. After checking him out, they suggested I take him to the doctor in the morning instead of taking him to the hospital. The next visit with Joaquin was a couple days away, and I hoped that Prince's doctor would suggest he stay home on Saturday. I was desperate for Prince to be able to avoid the visits.

Prince and I arrived at the doctor's office that Friday morning before it opened. Prince was his usual bouncy self, pressing the elevator buttons and running to push open doors just to see what was on the other side. He beamed at the doctors with a huge smile and continued bouncing through the office playing with every toy he could get his hands on.

During the exam, I told the doctor about the febrile seizure that occurred the night before and noted that I wanted them to check and make sure he was okay. Part of me wondered if they'd think I was over paranoid, as it was clear that Prince was healthy and had completely forgotten about being sick. I told the doctor that Joaquin had a court ordered visit the next day and asked him if I should cancel the visit until I was sure he was past the fever. I knew Prince was perfectly fine, but I was looking for any excuse I could get to cancel. The next thing the doctor said, I will never forget:

"Febrile seizures are a benign condition. They don't kill people. Are you just looking for an excuse to cancel the visit with his father? His father should be able to handle the fever just like you can."

I understand that the doctor was just being pragmatic. He didn't know Joaquin and didn't fully understand why I was trying to block the visits. To him, I probably just looked like a scorned woman who wanted to block her ex simply because I disliked him. I had five minutes with this doctor, and I didn't think there was any way of explaining the whole story to him without sounding crazy.

I worked overtime on Friday night, the eve of the fourth visit. The annual Halloween event was happening at the zoo in a week, and I was trying to earn enough comp time to bring Prince to the event for Halloween. In addition to the comp time, I was trying to save money to hire another attorney who'd agree to help me appear the judge's decision. I got stuck at work longer that night because someone reported a mysterious package in the parking lot. Staring out the large windows, I fought back the tears thinking about the time I was missing with Prince.

When I finally got home that night, two hours later than I expected, Prince greeted me with what I liked to call the "Mama Dance." He stood at a glass door that separated the garage area from the main house, waiting for me to arrive. As soon as I came through the garage door, his entire face lit up. He lifted his arms in the air, wiggled his little butt, and pointed at me. All the anger I harbored at my job, for getting stuck there late, melted away when I saw Prince dancing. I ran through the door, lifted him into my arms, and kissed him all over the face. He giggled and leaned into my hug.

Given his low-grade fever, I texted supervisor to tell her that I worried he was not over what he had that was causing the fevers. I asked her if we could reschedule. She told me that I'd need doctors' proof to cancel the visit, and that if I didn't agree to her terms for another date, she'd have to tell Joaquin that I refused to comply with the order. I took this as a clear threat that she'd go straight to Joaquin and give him the ammunition he needed to fight me in court. Prince wasn't sick enough to get a doctor's note. I collapsed under the pressure and told her that I'd send him on the visit if he woke up without a fever.

Prince slept in and woke up with a huge smile on his face. He threw blocks at the dogs, hugged me, hugged my mother, and ate his baby yogurt. He didn't have a fever, so I made the decision to take him to the visit. I was going to confront the supervisor this time about how Prince came home in the same diaper we sent him in. It was the first time I ever dropped him off for a visit with his father. My mother dropped him off on the previous visits. She wanted to shield me from as much of the drama as she could, and we both wanted to limit the messages from Joaquin that supervisor would pass each time we met face to face.

Just before the visit, I took Prince into a local grocery store. I wanted to get more snacks to pack Prince for his trip, and I wanted to give him a chance to run around and play for a bit before the visit. Prince loved to be independent. He hit the ground running and wanted to talk to everyone in the store, though nobody understood his special language. He ran for the balloons and pointed at all the lights. I chased him for a bit and watched him laugh as we played tag. Prince tried to convince me to buy him a balloon, and I assured him that I'd bring him one when the visit was over.

When it was time for the visit, my friend Brian and I took Prince to the police station. We were a bit early, so I changed his diaper and let him play with the steering wheel of the car. He wanted to press all the buttons. He wasn't very verbal yet, only saying a few intelligible words. This didn't stop him from chatting as though he knew exactly what he was saying. Prince flashed an enormous, toothy smile at us. He was expecting a response to his Prince jabber. I grabbed him close to me and kissed his forehead.

"It's going to be OK, baby. Mama loves you SO much. Have a good day, baby, and mama will see you tonight," I whispered softly in his ear.

It was time to say goodbye. I looked at Prince, lifted him out of the car, and hugged him close to me. When I put him in the supervisor's car, Prince looked as though he was worried. I kissed his forehead and told him how much I loved him.

"I love you GeGe Bean," I said to him. This was one of my many nicknames for him.

I was nervous all day and anxiously awaited the time when I could return to the Police Station and pick up Prince. I thought about how he would smile, reach for me, and how I would breathe a sigh of relief knowing that we got through another week. Working again to earn more comp time, I received a phone call from my mother telling me that Prince was at the hospital again, and that I needed to call the supervisor.

I dropped everything and ran out of the office. I worked on the opposite side of the CIA compound from where my car was parked. That day I ran the fastest mile of my life.

Running through the empty halls, my footsteps echoing as my feet stomped across the marble floors, horrible thoughts flashed through my mind.

'I shouldn't have sent him. I should've run. I should've just kept him with me,' I thought, jumping into my car, and speeding out of the gates of the compound.

"OK, so Prince must have had another seizure, and he must have just been taken to the hospital. He is fine just like last time," I tried to remain calm, speaking audibly to myself as I drove.

I wasn't even sure which hospital I was driving to, so I just started driving toward Virginia.

Then, a police officer called me. He didn't give me any medical information, other than that Prince was being flown to a different hospital. It was weird that nobody was talking to me while I was driving. Why weren't they telling me what happened? Why did a police officer call me?

When I arrived at the hospital, I waited a torturous three hours. I met with a social worker and a police officer all before I even knew what happened to my baby and why we were all there. As the hours passed, I felt myself dying inside. Something didn't seem right. I knew this couldn't be good—we were in the pediatric ICU. Prince had never gone there before.

After hours of waiting and pacing the hallway of the pediatric ICU (just a few halls from where I gave birth to Prince just 15 months prior), I was finally led back to see him. As I looked through the glass to the room, my heart broke into a million pieces. I saw my baby laying on the bed, unconscious and hooked up to a dozen tubes and monitors. I entered the room and touched his forehead—he was cold as ice. Before that moment, I didn't know hair could feel that cold. As I ran my fingers through his curls, I knew my worst nightmare had come true.

As soon as the doctor saw me touch Prince, she grabbed my arm and told me she needed to talk to me.

"Prince suffered cardiac arrest. We don't know at this time what happened, but when he arrived at the hospital his heart wasn't beating, and they were administering CPR. He isn't responsive to the medication, he is on a ventilator, and the prognosis is poor. He will likely die—and he will likely die soon. If he doesn't die, he will have significant neurological deficits," the doctor said in an extremely deadpan voice, devoid of emotion.

I was in shock. I stood there, with my father by my side, and I couldn't cry. Hoping that I'd wake up from this nightmare, or that I'd heard the doctor wrong, I walked over to Prince and held his hand. Before I knew it, a nurse was trying to shove a chair under me as I fell to the ground.

My world was slipping away. Prince was gone, and I was staring at his empty body. It was clear to me that his soul already passed on. My heart ached worse at the knowledge that I wasn't there when this happened. I wished I could have been with him. Maybe then I could've protected him.

The doctors didn't know what happened, but I knew from the moment I saw Prince's lifeless body. His father killed him. He killed him just like he killed the others before him, Shawn, and Alma. Joaquin carried out my biggest fear. The thing my own attorneys believed I was crazy for worrying about, and the concern that just a day prior I couldn't verbalize to Prince's doctor.

The next few hours seemed like a blur. Twelve family members crowded into the room with us and prayed with me as I held onto Prince.

I sang to him and cried, "please don't leave me baby—Mama loves you SO much."

He didn't respond to my voice and his lifeless body was completely motionless and cold.

Moments later, the nurses shuffled everyone out and told me that they needed to speak with me alone. As soon as everyone was out of the room, they said that "the father" arrived, and they had to let him see Prince. I couldn't believe this was happening—on Prince's death bed, Joaquin still wouldn't leave us alone.

I started to scream at them and tell them I had sole legal custody and that I didn't want my baby to have to be with his murderer. They told me that they didn't care about custody and that I needed to understand that it was best for Prince to allow his father to see him. I held onto Prince and shielded him with my body while I cried.

Joaquin came into the room twice and made a huge scene. Whenever Joaquin got upset, he reminded me of a monkey the way he waved his arms and rocked back and forth. The hospital staff was getting ready to have "visitation hours" ordered, where we would have to take shifts, when I decided it was time to finally put my foot down.

"I know my rights! Give us some peace!" I shouted, feeling as though I had absolutely nothing to lose at this point.

I called my attorney and told him to talk to the staff and explain how they were breaking the law. At one point that evening, hospital staff threatened to take me to the psych ward if I didn't stop screaming at them and blocking Joaquin's visit. By then, the entire Irish side of my family was split between the hospital room and the waiting area—each ready for battle in the protection of the family. If they took me out of the room, they'd have to fight all of us.

My cousins stood at the door, waiting for Joaquin and ready for a fight if necessary. After hours of distress and combativeness, the hospital staff finally backed off and instructed Joaquin to leave the hospital.

I was furious at myself for trusting the system. And while Joaquin was responsible for his action in killing Prince, I was gutted by the reality that an entire system enabled him—court officials, police officers, and attorneys. Joaquin had effectively manipulated our justice system to carry out a reign of terror on an entire community. But my deepest pain and anger rested on myself for not being the advocate my son needed and not understanding the system to stop this from happening.

I sat with Prince for 48 hours as his body shut down. Doctors informed us that Prince's death was now a criminal investigation. I was advised that if I could wait out the 48 hours for them to confirm brain death, they'd be able to get a more accurate read on cause of death without legal distractions. So, I waited. As my son's body shut down, the smell was indescribably awful. His body looked less his own with each hour that passed. Fury boiled inside of me, and I could feel myself transforming into someone who was merely a shell of the pushover I once was.

Finally, after 48 hours, Prince was pronounced dead. The nurses handed me his lifeless body, removed the medical collar from his neck, and unplugged him from life support. He officially died in my arms, bleeding out all over me. Part of me died with him that night. I knew there was no way I could un-live that moment, no matter how much I wished I could.

"You are my sunshine . . . my only sunshine . . . you make me happy when skies are grey . . . you'll never know dear . . . how much I love you . . . please don't take my sunshine away," I sang to him between sobs, as his heart stopped beating.

There are no words that can describe how horrible it felt every moment of every hour in the days and months after my son was killed. I was a zombie moving through life without my heart. Something magical happens when you become a mother. You always know where your children are, and your thoughts are always somehow with them. This instinct didn't go away just because he was gone.

In the days after he died, I kept looking for him. I'd instinctively search the backseat of my car when things were too quiet, and then suddenly panic, remembering what happened. I couldn't eat because my son would never again eat. And I couldn't go to sleep because I'd have nightmares of what he looked like when he was dying. As bad as sleeping was, waking up was worse because each time I'd hope his death had just been a nightmare.

Chapter 18

Rest in Peace

"Hera, I'm sorry . . . we need to have the funeral at night,' the priest at our church, said over the phone.

Our church was attached to an elementary school, tragically close to where we'd been in family court. Since Joaquin still hadn't been arrested, the school worried it wasn't safe to have the funeral while the children were in school.

In the months leading up to Prince's murder, I confided in our priest. He knew my story, struggles, and he was great at listening and offering solid advice. He also knew Prince, remembering him as the toddler who loved to fill the silence in church. As soon as the priest had the slightest pause in his sermon, Prince would shout from the balcony. I generally brought Prince to the balcony to watch the service because there he could walk around the pews without disturbing others.

I understood the school's concern. Given the obvious security threat Joaquin posed, I wanted the priest to understand that I agreed with the parents. I never wanted another parent to endure this type of tragic loss, and I didn't want Prince's funeral to put another parent in the position where they had to worry about the safety of their child.

"I understand, Father. Having it at night will be fine," I said quietly.

I didn't want the priest to worry that he was offending me or feel as though any of this was his fault. Truthfully, I didn't care when the funeral occurred. I was still in shock that I had to plan my own son's funeral.

I didn't get out of bed for days, except putting on the only black dress I owned and attending the funeral—four days after I last held Prince in the hospital. As my parents and I pulled up to the funeral home, I hugged one of Prince's favorite stuffed animals and held onto his favorite book, "Oh Baby, Go Baby," by Dr. Seuss.

My eyes darted around, trying to find any distraction I could that would keep me from crying. My entire extended family would be at the funeral home, and I didn't want them to hover over me. Private grieving wasn't an option with a family as close as mine. I knew they'd all be grieving alongside me. But a large part of me wanted to just crawl into a hole by myself and mourn alone, without what felt like the entire world watching.

Suddenly, a strange but welcome distraction came in the form of a skimpy, inappropriate dress. A young woman stood in front of the funeral home wearing an electric blue, skintight dress with cut-outs on the sides.

'Who brought the hooker?' I thought, laughing a bit to myself.

When I looked at the man on Ms. Blue dress' arm, I realized that the woman I thought was a hooker was one of my cousin's girlfriends. Did she have *nothing* else to wear? Did he neglect to tell her that this was a funeral and not a New Year's Eve party? I shook my head, thankful at the temporary distraction.

Before the rest of the family viewed Prince, I asked if I could have a moment alone with him. When the funeral director opened the casket, I gasped. Prince didn't look like himself. He looked like a pale, plastic doll-like version of himself. I could see the cuts on his hairline where incisions were made from the autopsy, and his lips looked a strange bluish color.

"My poor little guy." I said this under my breath, and to myself.

The funeral director left the room, and I read to Prince for the last time. I put his favorite stuffed bear beside him, and I told him that I'd never stop being his mother.

"I won't stop fighting, Prince. I will not stop fighting for justice, and I'll never let any of the people who had a hand in putting you here forget what they have done." I was assuring him, and I was also assuring myself.

To keep living, I knew I had a job to do. Staying silent wouldn't honor him. And jumping in the casket with him would mean he wouldn't be living in my heart anymore either.

My family members all started coming into the room. They each placed a note for Prince in his casket. I never cried so much in my life. I wondered if there was ever a point where the body would be incapable of additional tears. If so, I was probably reaching that point. I felt several emotions that evening—pain, sadness, rage, and helplessness were among them. I hated sadness and helplessness the most. But Rage made me feel as though I could fight anyone, and I felt ready to fight.

My brother, two years older than me, was wearing jeans and a torn shirt. When he heard that Prince was in the hospital, he jumped in the car with his wife and two young boys without even taking a moment to pack a bag. My father loaned him a jacket, but it hung on him like a dress as he was at least 100 pounds lighter than my father. As I watched my brother talking with my father, I worried they were plotting ways to make it so Joaquin disappeared into the night. My brother's eyes were blood shot, having likely not slept well since meeting us in the hospital.

My attorneys, Borger and Frank, showed up at the funeral. I didn't invite them and was immediately angry that they were there.

"You were right." It was the first thing that Borger said to me.

"Oh okay, well maybe we can just go grab his body out of the casket and bring him back to court," I responded with angry sarcasm.

My eyebrows furrowed, and I shot him a look that seemed to startle him. I took a deep breath and walked away from him before the conversation had a chance to deteriorate. I'm not sure what sort of reaction they expected from me given the circumstances and the tone of our last conversation.

Tons of people showed up for Prince's funeral: my large family, coworkers, Prince's nanny and her family, daycare workers, friends, members of the church community, Sgt. Perry, Sheryl Mason and her family, attorneys, the supervisor, and a host of other people I didn't recognize. I appreciated all these people—even the ones I didn't know. The service was just as Prince would have wanted it. We played the upbeat song that he danced to at his baptism, and my favorite hymn—"Jerusalem."

"Bring me my bow of burning gold! Bring me my arrows of desire! Bring me my spear! O clouds, unfold! Bring me my chariot of fire!"

I knew the lyrics of "Jerusalem" weren't written for a grieving mother who was plotting ways to seek justice for her son, but that night I felt as though they were.

We buried Prince the next day. My cousin's volunteer firefighter unit showed up with the antique fire truck to escort the hearse that carried Prince's body. It was a parade that I hoped Prince was able to view from heaven. So many people loved him, and I hoped he knew the incredible impact he made on the world in only fifteen short months.

Just as the small service was ending, the cemetery staff began motioning for the crowd to leave, so they could finish the burial. I grabbed a fistful of dirt and walked over to the gaping hole in the ground where my son's tiny coffin was lowered. Every time I looked at the small, white coffin it felt as though I was walking through someone else's life. Maybe that was a defense mechanism. If I felt like I was going through the motions as someone else, I could tuck away the horrible reality that I was living.

The dirt was cold, and full of hard rocks. It hurt my hands to grab at the cold ground, but I was determined to take as much of it as I could. I stopped the men with the shovels as they prompted us to leave the site. They seemed eager to finish the job, and maybe they worried that seeing my son buried would be too disturbing. I was going to be the one to bury my son. That seemed like the right thing to do for him.

Each step I took seemed as though I was walking a million miles, and I felt as though I was taking this journey alone. So many people there loved Prince, but I was the only one who'd been truly responsible for him. Family members moved toward me as though trying to stop me. My face must have haunted them, because as soon as they met my gaze they quickly backed away. I continued to grab at the dirt and throw it on top of my son's small coffin. With each toss, my heart ached as though someone was stabbing me with a blunt object.

A mother is not supposed to bury her child. This was completely against the natural order of life. As I continued to throw the dirt on top of my son, my family and friends also began to dig at the dirt. One by one they joined me in burying my son.

Making the choice to throw dirt on my son's grave was a natural reaction for me. This was my way of getting through the situation. I needed to take control, and I needed closure. I needed to take care of my son, and I needed for people to understand that I could do it. Relying on others, and not effectively advocating for my family, had led me to this place. I was done waiting on the arc of justice to swing in the right direction. It was clear that I would need to help push it.

In the days that followed the funeral, I didn't get out of bed. I binge watched an entire series of a television show as I laid in bed, trying desperately to escape into someone else's world. I liked going to sleep because the dream world hadn't caught up with reality, but when I'd wake it was like being punched in the face repeatedly. Several mornings, I'd wake up and run into Prince's room—praying the entire thing had been just a nightmare. For a while, I wondered if it would be easier had I chosen to lie down next to Prince and die too.

Family and friends came to the house, and it seemed like there was constant conversation going on downstairs. It was the first time some of them had come to my parents' house, but I didn't care about being rude. I wanted everyone and everything to go away so that I could continue lying there. I was in the type of overwhelming emotional and physical pain that seemed to send an eerie numbness through my body. And I had no capacity left to host anyone.

If someone you care about experiences a tragic loss of someone close to them, consider sending food and giving them space—perhaps instead of flowers and hovering. While I couldn't eat the food, I was thankful that there was food in the house for all the people who came over. I appreciated that nobody in my family had to cook anything for days. A few months after Prince died, one of my college friends flew to DC from New Orleans and spent the week cooking delicious, flavor filled Cajun food. Shopping with her for esoteric spices was just the escape I needed. It was the first time I'd tasted anything since Prince died, and I appreciated that she just came to take care of me and didn't require anything from me.

The day I buried my son, a sense of fear was reignited in me. I felt like a child again, but this time I couldn't rely on my parents to protect me from the dangers of the world. Dawning a fake smile, and "being tough" so to put others at ease, wasn't going to get me through this funeral. It was also not going to get me out of bed in the morning, as I was forced to live without my son. I needed to start thinking about how I was going to make it on my own, without the incentive to save someone else—I needed to save myself.

Chapter 19

Motive

After several days in bed, my father came to speak to me. He told me a story about how several hundred years ago, a warring clan came to the village in Scotland where the MacLeod's lived. They burned the church down on Sunday with entire families inside, including children. The only people who were not killed were those who didn't happen to be in church that Sunday.

Though it was a little ironic that only those who didn't go to church were saved, the lesson wasn't about how I should stay away from church while in the rural Scottish village. It was a story about resilience, and the point was to understand that it is possible to both live and thrive despite unimaginable atrocity.

"If those people had just given up on life, and chosen to die with their loved ones, we wouldn't be here. Prince would want you to fight. He would want you to live," my father said, in his familiar stoic tone.

I smiled at my father's ironic choice to share an image of a burning church full of children with me at that time. Like his unconventional childhood lessons, he also had a gift for storytelling. Though he didn't elaborate on why he chose that story, I think it helped me remember that many people had lived through worse than what I'd experienced. I still had so much to be thankful for and allowing Joaquin to forever steal my joy wasn't going to happen.

I'm not sure if my father's story was complete bullshit or not, but it was what I needed to hear, nonetheless. Getting out of bed that day, about two weeks after the funeral, I knew what I had to do. For nearly the entire 15 months of Prince's life, I'd been at war. I'd collected information on Joaquin, and I'd be damned if I was going to let him get away with the murder of my son. The killing would stop here, and the police would need to deal with me.

I dug through closets, printed hundreds of pages of paperwork, and made photocopies of journals I'd written. Then, I drove the hour and a half to Virginia to visit Michelle Merritt who was the detective that was assigned to Prince's case. Given that numerous criminal accusations swirled around Joaquin previously, I was terrified that Joaquin would get away with murdering Prince.

While I waited to speak to Michelle, the Police Chief came out to the waiting room and asked if I wanted to meet with him. I had no idea who he was, and I hadn't requested a meeting with him. I wanted to see Michelle, because my main goal was to provide police with as much information as possible to help my son's case. Reluctantly, I agreed to meet with the chief, figuring perhaps it would help me understand why Joaquin hadn't been arrested yet.

"Why hasn't he been arrested?" I asked, looking him dead in the eye unflinching.

Prince was the first person close to me who'd been murdered. There wasn't any doubt in my mind as to who killed him, and after learning about the insurance policy, I assumed the police would feel the same way. I asked, expecting the police chief to completely agree with me, apologize, and cite some procedural problem that required them to wait just a bit longer before making an arrest.

"Well, because there is no crime yet. We must wait until the autopsy report comes back," he said defensively.

The chief's response caused my chest to hurt and panic to rise inside me.

'Oh God, it's happening again—they aren't going to do anything to stop him,' I thought.

His response felt insensitive and dismissive. It reminded me of the way the police treated me the night I left Joaquin and how confusing it felt to be asking the police for help and receiving this type of response.

During my training at the CIA, I was taught to be observant and gain as much information as we could about a person. Sometimes this included looking at what a person wore, how they walked, the car they drove, or any other clues that could lead us to learn their motivations. This was required in my line of work because we essentially had to find a way to talk someone into doing something we would never do ourselves—betray their country.

I beat myself up for not using the lessons I learned in training at the agency during my relationship with Joaquin, but I was determined not to make that mistake again. If I was going to advocate for my son, I needed to know the obstacles that stood in the way of justice.

I learned a lot from the chief's office. It felt more like a shrine to his achievements than a place where business occurred. Though I didn't know him personally, his office only served to bolster my negative opinion of him. It was cold, stale, and looked as though it was merely for show. I spotted a picture of his two children. Both were wearing preppy polo shirts and appeared as though they just stepped off a golf course.

"How would you feel if this happened to one of your kids?" I asked to try to appeal to him as a father.

"Well, this wouldn't happen to my kids, because they don't hang around with bad people," he answered immediately.

He was smug, and I couldn't figure out if he was intentionally making commentary about me or if he simply couldn't imagine something like this happening to his children. I hoped for his children that nothing like this would ever happen to them, but I knew that being a good person didn't entitle anyone to a natural psychopath repellent. I kept to myself that I attended a preppy New England board school and *still* ran into a psycho.

Months earlier, I likely would've started smiling at the chief and tried hard to put him at ease. I would've tried to convince him that I wasn't a bad person. I wasn't the same woman I had been months earlier. Yelling at him probably wasn't the best thing, and I wasn't considering my safety at this point, but damn did it feel amazing. I certainly wasn't going to sit there and try to prove that my credentials didn't match his judgement. Joaquin was still walking a free man two weeks after murdering an innocent child. He couldn't weasel his way out of this as he'd done with all the previous crimes.

"If you don't arrest him like you should, I'm not going to stay quiet about what happened here," I said, getting up and walking out before slamming his door behind me.

By the time my son died, I had enough documented proof of Joaquin's criminal history that the public would likely question why authorities hadn't arrested him prior to Prince's murder. And I knew enough about how our system worked to know that the media often played a critical role in checks and balances.

After leaving the chief's office, I walked over to Michelle's cubicle. I didn't need her to drop her work to talk to me. I came only to drop off all the information I'd collected on Joaquin during our custody case. In stark contrast to the chief's office, Michelle's cubicle was a mess. She had open files all over it, and handwritten notes everywhere. While some might view this as a disaster, I saw it as a clue that she worked hard.

Just before I dropped off my box of paperwork, which would surely clutter her cubicle more, I spotted a picture of a young child who looked about Prince's age.

"Is that your son," I asked, still looking into the child's eyes.

I didn't know anything about Michelle's personal life at this point but wanted to know if she had children of her own.

"No, that's a child from another case I'm working," she responded.

Michelle explained that the child died a couple months before Prince. She was also investigating his death. I later learned that Michelle had several children, one who was the exact same age as Prince. Even without the additional information about her own children, I could tell from her desk that she cared about children. The picture of that little boy on her desk told me everything I needed to know. Michelle soon added a picture of Prince to her desk, so that she could look at the two of them and remember who she was working for.

Michelle told me that Joaquin took out over $580,000 dollars in life insurance on Prince when he was only three months old. He was paying more than he earned in a month, and more than he'd been ordered to pay in child support, on insurance premiums. To obtain the policy without me knowing, he lied to the insurance agency claiming he had full custody of Prince and that I'd died in a tragic car accident. Prince was now the third person whose death Joaquin attempted to profit from.

I also learned that in the months that preceded my son's murder, Joaquin was running out of money quickly. The house he owned (presumably the only thing that couldn't be seized as part of the outstanding civil judgments against him) was going into foreclosure. The auction for his house was scheduled for November 2012, just weeks after Prince died. Joaquin had renters in his house and was collecting the rent without paying the mortgage. But once the house sold in November 2012, that source of money would dry up too.

As recently as July 2012, three months before Prince was killed, Joaquin was still attempting to petition the courts for access to Shawn Mason's life insurance policy instead of getting a legitimate job. As all the details clicked into place, it felt as though I'd been investigating my own son's murder before he died. I was angry that Joaquin seemed to get away with so much. And I wondered if Prince would still be alive had the Maryland court had access to some investigative function. Perhaps someone would've noticed the runaway train that was headed straight for Prince.

Chapter 20

Hell Hath, No Fury

A month after my son died, Eileen King (the founder of the Non-Profit Organization Child Justice) called The Washington Post about Prince's story. I met Eileen a few months before Prince died when I reached out to Child Justice about potentially helping with my appeal.

"He's going to kill him if I don't do something," I'd told Eileen over the phone.

Eileen told me my words haunted her, and she wondered why Prince's death hadn't even been announced in Virginia. It was like the local authorities didn't want anyone to know something happened.

Shortly after Eileen reached out to her contacts at The Washington Post about me, a reporter named JoAnn Armao called. At first, I could tell that she didn't entirely believe what I was telling her. Before Prince died, I'd never have spoken to the media for fear that the judge would have taken any negative exposure out on my son's case. This is how protective parents are often silenced—for fear that exposing the horrors will negatively impact the safety of their already vulnerable children.

Now that my son was dead, I suspected that the media might be my only chance to put pressure on both the police and the prosecutors to take Prince's murder seriously. If the public was watching them, they certainly couldn't get away with what they'd gotten away with before my son died.

"JoAnn, you should dig for yourself. Listen to the court case on CD, and read the reports for yourself," I said, confidently.

I knew that if she researched, she'd come to realize that what I was telling her was the truth. I wanted her to believe me because she vetted the information. I never asked her to take my word for any of it. I knew my story sounded crazy. Years prior, I wouldn't have believed it myself if I'd read about it in someone else's story.

JoAnn assured me that she'd be thorough and asked me to give her some time to review the case and make some calls. On Thanksgiving Day 2012, while making dinner for her family, JoAnn listened to the entire family court trial on CD. After the testimony for herself and digging around to verify my claims about Prince's death—she eventually believed me.

Though I knew the information about the insurance policies hadn't yet been made public, I made the decision to tell JoAnn. She needed to know why I believed so strongly that Joaquin premeditated the murder of Prince. I knew this information going public would anger authorities, but I didn't care. I needed them to do something they'd been unwilling to do in the two previous murders. Joaquin needed to be taken off the streets and I knew the only way that would happen is if they were pressured by the tax-paying citizens in their county.

Having one good police officer on the case wasn't enough. Shawn had a good one, but one police officer cannot force and entire system to fall in line and do the right thing. And I knew enough about Joaquin's history to know that there were some dirty cops who were likely waiting in the wings to pull strings and try to tank the case.

While I had no reason to trust JoAnn, I told her about the life insurance policies and asked her not to report about that detail until the police made it public. On November 26, 2012, The Washington Post ran the first article about Prince's case. Within minutes of the article coming out, it went viral. The Associated Press caught onto the story, and people started asking questions. Police and prosecutors started scrambling; they knew they didn't have time to sit on this case.

Every day, I called the District Attorney's office to ask if they were planning to make an arrest. I needed them to understand that I wasn't going to stop pushing them, and I wasn't going to stop talking to the press just because it made them uncomfortable.

"Why can't you arrest him for the crimes that you know he has committed, like perjury, obtaining a name change illegally, illegally obtaining a concealment license, etc.?" I pleaded with the District Attorney.

"Well, those crimes aren't hurting anyone," the DA replied.

"Oh, okay . . . so let me get this straight—your office didn't have a problem coming after my sister and me, but when this guy has committed several felony offenses that you can prove with a simple documentation check—you won't do it? Not to mention the fact that you know he has murdered several people!" I was now screaming over the phone, calling attention to myself from strangers who passed me in the street.

I hung up the phone before he could answer. My stomach was turning already, and I knew I couldn't handle the lame excuse he'd offer. Child Protective Services conducted its own investigation, independent of the police. They concluded that Joaquin caused Prince's death.

In December 2012, CPS finally removed Sammy from Joaquin's custody, but Joaquin still hadn't been arrested. Joaquin sat a free man for months after premeditating the murder of his own son. I'm thankful that he didn't flee the country. I think that shows how confident he was that the police in that small town would never arrest him, no matter what he did.

Pushing the story in the public domain forced the DA to pay attention. Now it wasn't just me pushing him, it was also the nagging public media knocking down his door for answers.

While the media kept the DA busy, I shifted my attention to Family Court. While I was certain Judge Jude heard what happened to Prince, it was important that he hear from me.

I wanted him out of Family Court because there is no room for burned-out judges when it comes to the safety of children. My first move toward pushing this change was to file a formal complaint with the Commission on Judicial Disabilities. In my complaint, I cited Judge Jude's public distain for Family Court. I explained to investigators that someone who admits that he's only serving in the role because he is forced to do a rotation, cannot be fit to determine the best interest of a child.

Judge Jude was reprimanded by the commission as the result of my complaint. In addition to my complaint, I sent a letter to Judge Jude in as many venues as I could think of, to ensure he read it: his home, his office at the courthouse, his office at the University where he taught, and via email. I also posted it online.

Dear Judge Jude,

You may not remember me, but I will remember you for the rest of my life. I am Prince's mother. The Prince who died on October 20, 2012. The Prince who died on just his fourth court-ordered unsupervised visit with his father.

In case you still don't remember me, I would like to take a moment to remind you. I was the woman who came into your courtroom in March 2012 (and again in July 2012) begging you to keep my son safe from his father. You heard testimony from several women Joaquin had abused. I told you about how I had fled Joaquin's house in July 2011 with my newborn son and the clothing on our backs— that was after Joaquin raped my 19–year-old sister. You heard testimony about all the people who died around Joaquin (including the mother of his older son and his own mother). All the horrifying information we presented, however, was still not enough for you to choose to keep my son safe.

I watched my son's body slowly shut down for nearly two days as I waited for the doctors to officially declare him brain-dead. As I watched my innocent baby boy die, I thought about you. I remembered how you told us you hated Family Court. I remembered how you blamed me for falling in love with a con man. I remembered how you talked about fairy dust and how you explained that my son would need to come home with cigarette burns before you would believe Joaquin was abusive. I remember how you rolled your eyes, appeared to fall asleep on the bench, and opened your computer as if to read your email—you did all of this as I pleaded with you to keep visitations supervised.

I'm now a mother without a child. My heart breaks every time I think about all the things my son will never do. You never got to meet Prince, but your decisions made a significant impact in his life. My son loved books. He loved to smile, to laugh, and was just starting to run. The week he died, he just started to say "ball". It was his first official word after "Mama".

Do you have children, Judge Jude? Grandchildren? You told us that you made your Custody decision based on what you would do if Prince had been your child. Would you have given your children to Joaquin in an unsupervised setting knowing what you knew about him? Would you have taken a closer look at that psychological evaluation or maybe appointed a psychologist to conduct the test if it had been your child? Would you've forced *your* daughter to send her child to this man as punishment for having been lied to?

One of the hardest things for me to deal with is that I will never again have the chance to protect my son. Nothing I can do will bring him back to life. I can't stop thinking about how my life would be different if I hadn't trusted you—if I had fled the country—if I had simply refused to comply with the court order. I will never get the opportunity to have a talk with my son. I will never see him have his first day of school. I will never see him graduate from High School and from college.

Since Prince was so young when he died, I'll never dance with him on his wedding day or hear him say, "I love you, Mama."

You said you hated Family Court—it showed. I hope you understand the incredible power you have and with that power—the unparalleled responsibility. If my son losing his life had little or no impact on your future decisions, I pray that you resign. If you still find yourself rolling your eyes in frustration and looking upon parents who sit before you with disdain, I pray for those parents who have no choice but to sit before you.

The laws are not designed to protect children, and they need to be changed. In my son's case, it appears as though death was the only threshold for denial of visitation. I knew how bad this could get. I *told* you how bad this could get. You didn't believe me.

Hundreds of scorned women must come through your court room. Maybe this has jaded or clouded your ability to see the truth. I wasn't scorned. I was afraid. I was a mother trying to protect her only child. How terribly sad it is that you have become so jaded that when a mother comes to you pleading for your help, you dismiss her concerns as merely those of a scorned woman. Prince deserved better than you gave him.

He deserved to live just as your own child would have. I have spent my entire career working to protect our country—to protect America. I wake up each day and fight for America—and fight for the freedoms you enjoy. I hope and pray that despite the system's failure, I can continue to take my job as seriously as you should have taken yours. It was your job to protect my son's basic human civil right to life. All the evidence was before you. All that was asked of you was to be cautious. You held the life of an innocent child in your hands—the life of my child.

You will forget me, Judge Jude. Of that, I'm fairly certain. I will, however, never forget you.

Sincerely, Hera McLeod (Prince's Mama)

Judge Jude has never responded to my letter nor any of my attempts to reach out over the years. But shortly before he was set to enter Family Court for his next mandatory 18-month rotation he resigned.

On January 24th, just as I drove into the parking lot of my condo building, the DA called my cell phone.

"Err, Ms. McLeod. How abouts you come on down to my office tomorrow. I would like to speak to you in person," the DA said, in a deep southern drawl.

He had a raspy voice and a tendency to mumble things under his breath. It was often hard to understand what he was saying, and I often found myself straining to try to make sense of it.

"Uh, oh course. Yes, of course I will be there. Thanks." I was taken aback by the phone call.

The DA didn't strike me as the type of person who often personally called folks to invite them to his office. He wouldn't tell me what he wanted to see me for, but it wasn't the type of invitation that I would have turned down. I was desperate for updates on Prince's case, and the DA was the belly button of that office. He knew everything, and when he called it meant that there was an update.

On January 25th, 2013, my father and I got in the car and took the hour-long drive to the District Attorney's office. I would have made the trip alone, but my parents insisted it wasn't safe. Since Joaquin was more afraid of my father than my mother, he came with me. We sat in the waiting room that day for what seemed like an eternity. Finally, we were called back to the office. As soon as I sat down, the DA noted that what he was about to tell us would likely be upsetting.

"The autopsy results have come back. The Medical Examiner has concluded that Prince was drowned," he said frankly.

My shoulders tensed. I wasn't sure I was ready to hear how my son died, but I needed to know.

"Ms. McLeod, they've determined that the cause of death was drowning," the DA said, with small tears forming around the corners of his eyes.

I'd only seen the DA a handful of times, but this was the first time I saw a tinge of sadness in his eyes. He knew this news would be heartbreaking. I appreciated this small piece of humanity in him. As soon as the news sunk in, my heart dropped. I immediately thought about how scared Prince must have been, how he must have been confused, and how incredibly painful it must have been to die that way. I was furious, and it took everything inside of me not to jump out of the chair, run to Joaquin's house, and kill him with my own bare hands. Had DA not followed up with news, I might have.

"Police are sitting out front his house right now. They are about to make an arrest, okay," he said, with a reassuring voice.

The DA must've known that fury would follow his disclosure of the autopsy results had he not informed me that the police were making an arrest. I audibly breathed a sigh of relief. My father and I sat in that office for at least an hour, as we waited for police to arrest Joaquin. The DA warned us that justice for Prince would be a lengthy, and painful process.

"I don't understand what you were doing with him. Good people don't hang around Joaquin," the DA said, while staring at me with a gaze that felt uncomfortable.

This comment seemed to come completely from left field but wasn't new—as it mirrored almost exactly what that police chief said months prior. It was as though he'd been thinking it for months but hadn't had the nerve to say it out loud until that moment. I could feel my brow curve downward, as I looked the DA dead in his eyes. I wasn't intimidated by him, but I also didn't feel as though I had to prove my "goodness" to him either. This was not the first time someone misjudged me based on Joaquin's criminal history.

"Well, sounds like you don't know all of us," I responded, indignant.

It was evident I wasn't going to change the mind of this stubborn, old man. I figured it would be more powerful if he saw the positive change, I was able to make in the world someday.

Minutes after I got into the car to head home, Michelle called.

"I just arrested Joaquin, and I got Prince's shoes" She squealed with joy so loudly that I had to move the phone a bit away from my ear.

The day Prince died he was wearing his first pair of shoes. I wanted them back, and she knew how much having a small piece of him meant to me. She later told me that the other officers on the scene laughed at her because she danced down the street after finding them.

When the arrest was over, I felt like I could finally breathe for the first time in what felt like years. I knew it was only the beginning, but it felt like a major chapter was ending. It was time to start doing more than just surviving. I felt empowered by Joaquin's arrest, because I knew advocating for justice had a hand in it.

Chapter 21
Wheels of Justice

The District Attorney was spot on when he described the time between the arrest and the conviction as an emotional marathon. The day Joaquin was arrested, it felt like a weight was lifted off my shoulders. I was so elated at that moment that I wasn't even thinking about the fact that the emotional turmoil might be far from over. I figured that if Joaquin was behind bars, I could at least rest easier knowing that he wouldn't be able to kill anyone else. I was blissfully unaware of how long the process between arrest and conviction would take.

A few months after Joaquin's arrest, the case went for pretrial. In the pretrial, the prosecution is required to prove to the judge that they have enough probable cause to move forward with the charges. This was a preview of the trial, but a good prosecutor only presents the bare minimum to keep the case afloat. Presenting the entire case would tip their hand and give too much information to the defense attorneys.

The prosecution was confident that the judge would allow the charges to stick, and that Joaquin wouldn't be offered bail. But I was a nervous wreck because my negative experiences in the justice system thus far tempered my expectations. I was afraid to be too confident. Especially when a dozen previous charges went nowhere. But unlike Shawn and Alma's cases, at least the DA was bringing the case before a judge this time.

The night before the trial, I couldn't sleep. I spent hours wondering how I'd feel when I would come face to face with my son's murderer. I also wondered how I'd be able to contain myself from having an emotional outburst at the mere sight of Joaquin and his attorney. McBride was back in the picture, and my experience with him had been so negative that I worried he'd infect my son's case as well. Whenever there was wheeling and dealing to be done, McBride popped up like a mole rat.

The morning of the trial, I woke up in a Virginia hotel and looked over the clothes I packed. I stood there staring at my suitcase, as though I expected the perfect outfit to jump out of the bag at me. Unlike my son's funeral, where I lifelessly went through the motions, I wanted to be an active part of justice. I needed my outfit to show the strength and fire that was brewing inside of me. I wanted both Joaquin, his attorney, and the judge to know that I wasn't going to back down and roll over.

Staring down at my clothes, I took a deep breath. This was a moment that didn't call for tears. My son needed me to be strong enough to put on a suit and walk out that door.

I arrived at the court in full-on mafia-like style. My huge family (who I sometimes jokingly refer to as "The Irish Catholic Mafia") walked alongside me. We're a non-violent bunch, which makes us not actually like the real mafia, but I can imagine we looked fairly intimidating that day due to sheer numbers. My father joined us later in the day, as well as Shawn Mason's family, who were also hoping that justice would finally be served. Walking in with all these people beside me, I felt proud to be Prince's mom.

Joaquin had no idea who he'd messed with when he came for Prince. If he thought we'd silently go into the night, letting him live off the proceeds of illegally obtained life insurance—he was wrong.

It was as though Joaquin had been pillaging through the woods a free man, and finally stomped on a pack of fire ants. We arrived to set his legs on fire and make sure he understood that he shouldn't have stepped there. I smiled as I thought about what we looked like walking into the court-house. My cousins in dark trench coats and all of us wearing stern and determined looks on our faces.

Shortly after I arrived, the media started filling into the empty seats in the courtroom. I took that opportunity to point them in the direction of Joaquin's only supporters, Roxy and Ronan. They sat behind the defense table. They were the only people on that side of the courtroom, except a few reporters. I immediately noticed Roxy clutching a suit-case. I presumed it was full of clothes for Joaquin, should he be released after the pretrial.

Given what Joaquin had slithered out of previously, perhaps they really did think he was coming home that day. McBride also walked into the courtroom with a confident swagger, his long arms swaying as though he was walking through the jungle about to grab onto a nearby tree and swing.

When Ronan saw me pointing him out to the media, he immediately called for police protection. This childish display was comical and reminded me of the pathetic antics Joaquin played in Family Court when he tried to make the world believe *he* was the victim. Hilariously, the court security officer looked at him and rolled his eyes.

As the judge entered the room, my heart started beating faster. A few minutes later, Joaquin came in. He was wearing an orange jump suit, and he looked like he'd aged ten years since I last saw him. His hair was matted to his head with frizzy pieces poking out all over, his skin had a grayish tint, and his face was puffy, as though he had eaten a few too many Twinkies while in jail.

I had to do a double take to even make sure it was him. It wasn't until I saw the familiar menacing look in his eyes that I confirmed. His eyes scanned the room, flashed a smirk, and he winked at Ronan and Roxy. He looked like a caged animal who'd just been taken for a walk by the guards.

Once I got past the first sighting of Joaquin, the entire day seemed a bit easier. No matter how painful it would be to testify that day, I was going to be able to walk out of the courthouse at the end of the day without Joaquin in my life. I wouldn't have to worry about whether he'd be lurking outside my house, and I wouldn't be looking over my shoulder for him. Now he was the state of Virginia's problem. They were finally holding him accountable, and this fight was now more than just mine.

After being sworn in, the other witnesses and I were told to leave the courtroom and wait for our turn to be called to the witness stand. I walked out of the courtroom confident that this day would be miserable for Joaquin. Family Court was full of second chances and pathological liars were given a stage and forgiven for any negative behavior in their past. Dishonesty is a parental trait we accept in America, but a reputation of dishonesty in criminal court could be the difference between freedom and the electric chair.

My testimony was simple. I explained my last morning with Prince. I told the judge how I let Prince sleep in that morning, and how he followed me around the house saying "Mama, Mama . . ." in his quiet little voice.

Trying to explain my last moments with my son in a way that showed the necessary emotion, without completely erupting into tears on the witness stand was hard. I didn't want Joaquin to have the pleasure of seeing the pain he caused. I didn't smile, held my tears, and felt tremendous pressure because my voice was the only way Prince could be heard. He was a part of me, and I brought him with me to court that day.

When it was time for cross-examination, McBride seemed as though he'd been misinformed. I wasn't entirely shocked by this, as Joaquin was clearly not inclined to tell the truth in this situation when he had never done so before. McBride tried to prove that Prince was terminally ill. He accused me of hiding a serious illness from Joaquin, which was far from the truth. When that didn't work, he tried to accuse me of having Munchausen syndrome. Being accused of making my son sick, for attention, made my skin boil. This was especially hurtful given how hard I tried to protect him from his murderous father.

After setting the record straight and informing the judge that I'd provided Joaquin with all the necessary information on how to care for Prince, McBride had nothing left to say. He fidgeted with his notes and stuttered that he had no further questions. His questions about seizures annoyed me. I wanted to scream that febrile seizures don't cause drowning, but I knew that this reality would be delivered more effectively from a doctor.

As I walked past the defense table, I turned and looked straight at Joaquin. He was actively avoiding eye contact, looking down at his bright orange jumpsuit and chained wrists. I felt so empowered walking past him. I finally wasn't afraid of him.

"Good riddance, baby killer," I muttered just loud enough for him to hear.

Once all the witnesses were called, we were all allowed back in the courtroom to hear the judge's ruling. The prosecution wasn't worried that Joaquin would be released that day, but one of the police officers warned me not to have an outburst once the verdict was read. I thought it was odd that he felt the need to warn me not to respond violently. Joaquin was free for three months after killing Prince and I didn't kill him then. I certainly wasn't going to do it now, in open court. I rolled my eyes, wondering if Ronan and Roxy said something that caused the officer to address me in this way.

"I think you should be more concerned about what the man in the orange jump suit will do than me, sir." I shook my head and turned away from the officer.

McBride raced through his closing statement. It seemed like he was trying to assert that he had more medical experience than the medical examiner. Unfortunately for him, this time the police didn't hand over evidence to Joaquin's defense team. The lead prosecutor on Prince's case, didn't appear fazed by McBride's statements. She elegantly and simply spoke to the judge and reminded the court why we were all there—the judge was only supposed to determine that a crime occurred, and that Joaquin was likely the person who committed said crime.

The judge quickly agreed with the prosecutor, noting that he believed the threshold had been met, and that the matter should be sent to the grand jury. When the judge's words sank in, Joaquin started dancing in his chair. Now he looked like a spoiled child throwing a fit when his parents wouldn't buy him a toy. A scorned look came across his face, as though he'd been the person wronged by the system. Most of the room erupted in celebration, as the realization hit us that Joaquin would remain behind bars at least until the conclusion of the trial. Finally, the pendulum of justice seemed to be swinging back in the right direction.

Joaquin was initially charged with first degree murder, and the trial was set for August 2013. On July 1, 2013, what should've been Prince's second birthday, I waited for a call from the DA. I hadn't spoken to him since Joaquin's arrest a few months earlier. When he said he was going to call me, I knew it was for something important.

That day, I was at the dentist's office. I had a standing appointment and wasn't sure when that call would come. When the prosecutor calls regarding the murder trial for your son's killer, you answer the call. My dentist initially thought that I was a doctor on call or waiting for some important deal to come through. I could sense that he was a bit annoyed at the potential distraction.

'At least I warned him,' I thought, as he raised his eyebrow and shoved the cleaning instrument in my mouth.

"Hang on," I mumbled, dental instruments still hanging out of my mouth.

"This is awkward, but I have to take this call. It is coming from the prosecutor who is handling my son's murder trial," I said with a casual tone that likely shocked the dentist.

I didn't want him to rush me through the call, so telling the truth seemed like the right thing to do.

As the dentist struggled to pick his jaw off the floor, I spoke to the DA.

"Heyya, Ms. McLeod? I wanted to run something by you. Uh, how do you feel about the death penalty?" The DA jumped right in without delay.

It was nice that he tried to make it sound as though the decision to upgrade the charges against Joaquin from first degree murder to capital murder would be my decision.

"I feel great about it if you mean it could be carried out on Joaquin," I responded without hesitation.

I hadn't thought much about the politics surrounding the death penalty before, but I certainly wasn't going to lose sleep over the Commonwealth seeking to kill Joaquin.

My initial elation was an indication that I had no idea what this meant for the case. Capital Murder meant that Joaquin could face the death penalty, but it also meant that Joaquin would get the best attorneys the public defense office had to offer. McBride could no longer defend him, so Joaquin finally admitted he was indigent.

Capital murder also meant that the judge was more likely to grant Joaquin's defense team whatever they asked for—more money for private investigators, several attorneys, and discovery beyond what was typically allowed. Capital murder carried an automatic appeal, so the judge didn't want a conviction to be overturned on appeal by some sloppy loophole.

Joaquin threw a fit about the first public defender who was assigned to his case. He didn't like him, and though

Joaquin had never been a taxpayer, he felt entitled to have the attorney of his choice. Of course, the judge allowed it.

For the first several years, Joaquin's attorneys filed multiple orders of continuance, delaying the trial. Every time we'd get close, another order of continuance came through to request more time for preparation. While the prosecutors tried to prepare me for how long this could take, spending years panicking that Joaquin could one day just show up at my door was soul crushing. The defense finally agreed to set a trial date in the Spring of 2015, but as the date approached, they filed another continuance kicking the can until Spring 2016.

Every taxpaying American should be sick with the amount of waste this type of trial causes. These attorneys weren't public defenders, the court allowed Joaquin to use taxpayer funds to hire private counsel—because the public defender didn't meet his standard. And the years it took for the case to go to trial was an epic drain on the system with his team of attorneys charging thousands and thousands of dollars monthly, which easily could've cost millions by the conclusion of the case.

Two weeks before the 2016 trial date, Joaquin's lead defense attorney quit citing an undisclosed medical condition that was exacerbated by this case. The new trial date was set for February 2017.

Rumor around the courthouse was that attorneys were trying to convince Joaquin to accept a plea deal. Despite the delay, I couldn't be mad at this lawyer. Many defense attorneys take the job to protect the law, and not necessarily to watch violent criminals go free. I'll never know exactly why this attorney chose to step down, but I can certainly understand how years on a case like this could negatively impact a person's health.

In the summer of 2016, Judge Johnson stepped down as the judge. He cited that his grandson was recently killed in an accident, and that he didn't believe he would be able to emotionally handle this case as a result. After he stepped down, I worried that we wouldn't find any Judge in the entire state of Virginia without some conflict

Two more capital qualified judges were passed over because they had conflicts—having been connected to either one of Joaquin's previous victims or Joaquin himself. The DA ended up having to look outside the county for someone who wasn't connected to a prior case involving Joaquin or otherwise conflicted. The absurdly frustrating reality was that none of these other cases resulted in conviction.

But in my opinion, bringing a judge from outside of the county was likely the best thing to happen to the case. I was relieved that the external judge was less likely to have any connection to officers involved in previous cases because those hadn't gone particularly well. And based on my dealings with the local authorities in that town, I had a healthy dose of mistrust in their ability to take Joaquin off the streets.

After the initial charges were brought for Prince's case, Joaquin was charged with over 20 other felony offenses, which were set to trial after Prince's case completed. My view on the death penalty changed throughout the course of the trial. While I look forward to a day when I no longer have to share oxygen with Joaquin, the money spent on death penalty cases alone seems like a miscarriage of justice. Joaquin should be forced to share a cell with a dangerous man, who happens to love children. And a public display of his death would be more ceremonious than he deserves.

Despite my extremely negative feelings toward Joaquin, for all the horrible things he did to me and to my loved ones, I now also look at him as more of a soulless shell of a man. He's responsible for what he did to Prince, but so are those in our justice system who enabled him along the way. These people won't spend the rest of their lives in prison, and many of them will continue working in the same capacity and making the same mistakes that put my son in harm's way. It's those people, and this broken system, that our country should be talking about—not Joaquin.

When I made a promise to Prince that I would get justice, I didn't just mean that I'd hold Joaquin accountable for his actions. My promise to Prince was a promise to get complete justice. The Commonwealth Attorney's office probably believed that all prior injustices had been corrected when Joaquin was arrested, but this is not how I saw it. If everyone just looks at Joaquin as the sole reason Prince died, the lesson wasn't learned. More children will be harmed. The safety of our society doesn't improve unless the public holds those who protect the law accountable when they fail. If I sat around and waited for someone else to scream about what happened to Prince, I'd die waiting for it.

Chapter 22

Accountability

Recently, I was called for Jury Duty in the Washington, DC Federal Court. After responding affirmatively to a Voi Dire question about whether I had strong feelings toward the police that could negatively impact my ability to be unbiased toward police testimony, I was swiftly dismissed.

"My son was killed by a serial killer, and I firmly believe that there are Virginia police officers who enabled this killer for years and are therefore accessories to the murder of my son," I responded to the judge's questioning, holding my head high.

The judge, whose mouth dropped open in surprise, exchanged a glance with the U.S. Attorneys.

"It would be dishonest of me to stand here and claim that I didn't have a particular bias against that particular branch of law enforcement," I continued.

I used to have naïve, blind trust in the institutions of justice in America—the police, the courts, prosecutors, and the law. My pendulum swung in the opposite direction after experiencing what I can only hope is a pack of some of the worst officers our country has produced. I went from blind trust to immediate distrust. In the seven years since I met Joaquin, I would be remiss if I didn't recognize the hope that's been sprinkled amongst the bad seeds.

Joaquin wouldn't be behind bars today if not for a few incredibly courageous police officers, social workers, judges, and private citizens. Bringing justice to my son's tragedy was not solely from the efforts of one person. These brave men and women, all whom I've mentioned in this book, took chances and weren't afraid to take on corruption and incompetence within our system.

Michelle Merritt actively fought attempts from other authorities to thwart her investigation into Prince's murder. A social worker from a Virginia Child Protective Services Department pushed through her investigation, after having to hire police protection because she believed she was being threatened. After Joaquin was formally notified of the child abuse investigation, his car was spotted loitering in the CPS parking lot on several occasions. She didn't let these terrifying circumstances negatively impact her ability to protect Sammy.

There were plenty of people throughout both the custody case, and the criminal case against Joaquin, who treated me as though I didn't deserve compassion. But there were also many people who went out of their way to show kindness. When Michelle rescued Prince's shoes, I felt an overwhelming sense of relief and gratitude. I have no doubt that Joaquin's arrest was chaotic. But even during that entire dramatic scene, she thought about how far this small act of kindness would go to earn my trust. She also never got too caught up in the police investigation to forget the human element of the case. Prince wasn't just a murder victim; he was my son.

While blind trust in our system is dangerous, so is complete despair. To restore my sense of justice and fairness, I needed to confront the police who harmed my family. I needed for them to recognize what they'd done wrong, and for them to convince me that they wouldn't repeat these mistakes in the future.

I regret not being strong enough back in 2011 to fight the police, after they maliciously and falsely charged me with a crime I didn't commit. At the time, I was so terrified that I was going to go to jail, and that I'd be separated from my son. I remained patient and trusted that the arc of justice would eventually swing in the proper direction. It never did, and it wasn't going to do so unless someone pushed it.

While the criminal case was dismissed against me, after the prosecution was unable to produce a shred of evidence, the process of having to defend myself against a crime I didn't commit was a damaging form of state terrorism.

Instead of going straight to the media, I gave the Virginia Police Department the option to redeem themselves and right the wrongs that their officers perpetrated. I went through the proper channels and filed a civilian complaint, demanding an internal investigation into the arrests of both me and my sister. During the first meeting, I met with a low-level officer who seemed completely clueless about my case. Not surprised, but disappointed that he hadn't bothered to read the file, I began to brief him on why I was there that day.

"You should know that I blame your department for the murder of my son, Prince McLeod. I suggest you search online for details about the case, as I think you'll realize the seriousness of what I am about to tell you."

I wasn't interested in starting out slow or adding fluff. This officer should also have done his homework before meeting with me, and my words meant to embarrass him for not doing so.

"Oh, um, I am so sorry, ma'am. I am sorry for your loss," the officer said.

He dropped his pen and looked up. From the sadness in his eyes, I suspected that he was a father. I wasn't angry at him. He was just doing his job. But I never lost sight of the fact that he was the messenger, and I needed for my message to be heard loud and clear.

"If I'm not satisfied at the depth of your investigation, I fully plan to utilize my media contacts and take this grievance outside of your department. My goal is to ensure that the dangerous behavior of your officers doesn't continue," I continued.

This was not a threat. I was simply being an honest broker, not sugar coating, and I was expectation-setting. I was finally an advocate. This is something I would never have been brave enough to do when this journey began.

The investigation lasted nearly a year, and, as I suspected, I was extremely disappointed with their level of diligence and transparency. My parents and I met with officers several times, provided court documents proving mishandling of evidence, and explained in detail the aftermath and consequences of their actions. My hope was that the investigation would provide an opportunity for the department to learn from the mistakes, hold those responsible accountable, and make changes to avoid repeating the behavior.

After nearly six months of no communication from the department, I received the following email from the captain:

Good morning Hera,

The investigation has entered the wrap up phase. The Lieutenant and I are finishing our investigation and will present it to our Chief for his review shortly. This investigation has led to several questions about staff performance. I cannot discuss what is under scrutiny, but those particular concerns are being addressed. You will hear from the Chief when he has reviewed the entire investigation. I cannot tell you exactly when that will be, but it will be soon.

In November 2013, the police scheduled a meeting between the Police Chief and I to discuss the results from their internal investigation. I tried to keep my expectations low but was hopeful that I would at least get an apology. I was also hopeful that maybe my report would bring positive changes within the department.

My daughter Estela was a newborn, and thankfully slept through the entire meeting that day. Looking down at her while at the police station, I remembered how thankful I was that she was in my life. I hadn't let Joaquin steal my joy forever. Remembering that Prince wasn't there, though, would always be a painful reality. Having his sister felt as though Prince had sent an angel into our family. I was so grateful for both.

Shortly before the meeting started, I turned on a recording device and hid it in Estela's car seat. I wasn't going to take the chance that the police would later deny what they said to us in that meeting. One day when I tell Estela about her brother, I suspect that she will be full of pride to know that even at her young age she helped that day.

My parents and I waited in a small waiting area at the entrance of the station for about thirty minutes before the Chief was ready for us. We all paced around anxiously. The sound of the police station radios was never something I would get used to. It always put me on edge, and my parents shared my impressions. None of us had extensive experience with the police before this situation, and the jarring environment of the police station was far outside of our comfort zone.

As we walked into the conference room, the Chief introduced himself. My eyes immediately shot to the Black police officer who was sitting on the Chief's right. While I imagine there are several Black officers in this department, I thought it strange that this was the first time I was seeing one.

"So, you brought the Black guy as back-up, huh?" I said, no longer afraid to call them out.

The Chief ignored my question and shifted awkwardly in his seat before introducing the Black officer. His name didn't register, and he didn't say a word beyond a cordial "hello" for the duration of the meeting.

"I would like to ask you not to blog about this discussion," the Chief said.

Without responding, because I planned to write about it, I smiled and waited for him to continue. He never asked me not to record the conversation, and I never agreed to keep it secret. I'd been burned by the police so many times that I needed evidence in the event we were mistreated that day.

In presenting the findings of the investigation, Hudson admitted that the department botched aspects of the investigation. He called parts "improper," "sloppy," and "with shortcuts."

He continued by stating that he was "disappointed" that the detectives "didn't pursue every possible means to either support the allegations or conclusions that they were reaching or disprove them."

Just when it seemed as though an apology might come next, the Chief stressed that it was his belief that women lie about rape, so it was important for his officers not to be too credulous.

He defended the officers by saying that it was only his "opinion" that police shouldn't have pressed charges, but that he believed that it was within their discretion to do so.

"It is not uncommon for people to make false, malicious, salacious allegations of sexual assault," the Chief said, "That does happen."

I didn't need to be educated on how women behaved, from the perspective of this man. I have a vagina and I know what it's like to live in a country that's strangled by rape culture and mistreatment of women.

I was shocked to hear so many words, laced with ignorance, come out of the mouth of a man who held such a powerful position. His negative opinion of women was palpable, and I immediately felt an overwhelming sadness for all the women who would be forced to face his judgment. He spoke to me as though he didn't believe I was as smart as him, or as worldly.

"How often do you think women just go around lying about being raped?" I asked.

I'm sure by now my facial expression was betraying my attempt to appear cordial. No longer able to fix my face, by painting a false smile, I glanced over to the Black officer.

I wonder what he was thinking as his eyes darted in every direction as though he was embarrassed at what his boss was saying. He was trying to avoid my gaze while I was looking right at him.

The Chief didn't appear to hesitate when he claimed that it was his belief that 10% of all rape reports were fake—a statistic that I found astonishingly high based on my knowledge that rape is typically under-reported, and false reports were not nearly that high.

According to the National Institute of Justice, in a study released in June 2016 titled "Reporting of Sexual Violence Incidents", most rapes in the United States go unreported. The National Sexual Violence Resource Center (NSVRC) reports that the prevalence of false reporting cases of sexual violence is low, but when survivors do come forward, many face harsh scrutiny.

I didn't go into the police station that day expecting to be shocked, but the words that came out of the Chief's mouth that day both shocked and appalled me. They were doomed to repeat the same behavior, because even though he was able to admit that things were improper, and openly blamed officer "fatigue" for the mishandling of evidence, he couldn't take the only logical step and admit that they needed to make internal changes.

Just before leaving the police station, I asked the Chief if he would be willing to release a public statement about the investigations, the findings that things were handled improperly, and a description of what they would be doing to ensure that these mistakes are not made in the future. Hudson said he would check with their media department to see if that was allowed. A few weeks later, Hudson told me that they were taking actions internally, but that he couldn't share what these actions were with me. He also noted that they were unable to make the findings of the investigations public or issue any sort of apology.

After such a dismal meeting with the department, where the Chief begrudgingly admitted gross negligence, condoned the deplorable behavior, and claimed that he wasn't sure he would have done anything differently the next time something like this should occur, I knew that I had to do something. At this point, it wasn't just about justice for my family, it was about justice for everyone else too.

I sat on my recording of that meeting for nearly a year because I wasn't sure how I wanted to go about using it. My sister hadn't yet been in a position of strength to tell her story, and I was not going to push her to hold these authorities accountable before she was ready.

In the summer of 2015, an acquaintance reached out to me and asked me if I had heard of a reporter named Katie Baker with Buzzfeed news. I'd never heard of Katie before, but my friend told me that she was a reporter who had done several well-done exposés about rape on college campuses. She suggested that my sister and I talk to her about what happened to us.

The first time we met with Katie, Lara was extremely skeptical. She wasn't sure she wanted to relive what happened to her, and the idea of challenging the police in a public forum was scary for both of us. Neither of us were sure we could trust Katie either.

Outside of Joann Armao at The Washington Post, I didn't trust anyone with a story like this. This story was fragile because it required a lot of research and it required someone who was sensitive enough to work with trauma victims. We met Katie at Starbucks in the Cathedral Heights area of DC. There weren't many places to sit, and the venue was small enough that we couldn't get into too much detail during our first meeting.

"You can trust me," Katie said.

She assured us that after she did all her research and wrote the article, if Lara didn't feel comfortable with it, she would agree not to publish. Katie was taking a huge risk on this story. It would require months of her time, and if Lara backed out at the last minute it could have likely cost her a lot in her career. I respected this about her because it made me believe that she would have to earn her right to tell this story.

In the fall of 2015, I handed the recording from our meeting with the police chief to Katie. Despite the Chief's unwillingness for the investigation to be public, it became very public in the fall of 2015 when the article went viral. The Chief resigned shortly thereafter.

Chapter 23

My Kind of Justice

On a warm summer morning in 2008, I visited a small Christian church in Lafayette, Louisiana with a good friend of mine. During the service, the pastor explained the parable of the flood. In this parable, a man is trapped in his house during a flood. He starts praying to God to be rescued. All his neighbors urge him to leave as the water is rising around him. They offer to give him a ride to safety, but he chooses instead to wait for God.

After the neighbors leave, a boat arrives, and the captain offers to pull him to safety. Again, the man declines and decides to instead wait for God to save him. A helicopter comes to try to save the man, and he still chooses to wait for God. Eventually, the flood water comes over the roof where he is sitting and sweeps him away. After drowning, he arrives in heaven and asks God why he didn't save him. God, probably both irritated and confused by this guy, reminds him that he'd sent a truck, a boat, and a helicopter for him.

God can only do so much, if you're drowning you ultimately need to take the tools God gives you and help to rescue yourself. Even back in 2008, before I'd encountered tremendous atrocity in my life, this parable spoke to me. Years later, I have called upon this very lesson to force positive societal change.

In my experience, Justice works similarly to this parable. No one is ever going to care as much about justice as those who've been harmed. After my son died, flags weren't flown half-staff and most of the world went about their day as though nothing happened. My son's murder taught me that to get justice, I couldn't wait for someone else to deliver it to me. It became clear in those first months after his murder that if I waited patiently, justice would never come.

So, I pushed for justice—I spoke out and I didn't let authorities choose chaos and ignore my son's murder. I was a thorn in so many people's sides for years, reminding them that I wasn't going anywhere, and I'd push until they did the right thing. Thankfully, I wasn't in the fight alone—I was surrounded by family and friends who were my rocks when I felt like I was spinning out of control. When I was drowning from trauma, God sent people who were willing to fight alongside me and keep me from sinking.

In August 2017, Joaquin was convicted of capital murder for the 2012 murder of Prince and sentenced to life in Prison without parole. Judge Randy Bellows issued a 62-page ruling, which he meticulously read aloud from the bench for more than two hours. Despite the expensive attempts Joaquin's attorneys made over the years, trying to prove that Prince died of natural causes, Bellows methodically dismissed this suggestion.

He concluded that Joaquin premeditated the murder and that over $500,000 in life insurance policies was his primary motive. Crime victims are entitled to make Victim Impact Statements just prior to sentencing. This is the statement I made to the court that day:

Dear Judge Bellows,

I've thought long and hard about whether I'd write a victim impact statement. I wondered whether I'd be able to express how my son's murder has impacted me in the format I was given. Words alone cannot possibly express how I feel, but I understand the importance of this process, and I'm writing to honor my son, advocate for his legacy, and protect my family.

The day my son was murdered was the worst day of my life. It wasn't just my baby who died that day, but a part of my heart and soul left with him. From the moment I became a mother, I changed. While Prince was alive, there wasn't a moment when I didn't think about where he was, who he was with, and how he was doing. After his death, I still think of him constantly. Instead of wondering where he is and how he is doing, I'm now faced with a lifetime of mourning for the man my son would've and should've become.

There's no way to quantify how it feels to wake up every morning and remember that your child with never again call your name, never have his first day of kindergarten, never again laugh, smile, or cry. I dreamed of one-day dancing with my son on his wedding day. I dreamed of all the moments we'd share as he experienced the world for the first time.

This pain is not something that comes and goes. I live with it—walk past it—go to sleep at night next to it—wake up face to face with it—and carry it out the door with me every single day.

In addition to the pain that I carry about my son's murder, I live with the fear that my family will never be safe from Rams. I fear that if Rams has frequent and unsupervised contact with other inmates (particularly those who stand a chance to get out of jail), or access to the Internet, he will use this access to further terrorize my family.

I've been informed by Virginia Police Officers over the years that Rams has offered to pay people to kill me. While I have no proof other than the police reporting this to me, I have no doubt that he's capable of doing this considering what he did to his own flesh and blood.

I want the court to understand the beautiful spirit that Rams took from this world. In the 15-months that Prince was alive, he made much a positive impact on so many people. He had a huge family who adored him—aunts, uncles, cousins, grandparents, and a mother who would've jumped in front of a train if it could've saved him.

Prince was the type of person who lit up rooms with his smile. He loved his people and his dogs. He loved to dance, and the artist Prince's song "Kiss" would make him wiggle with joy. His favorite singer was Adele, and he had an unusual crush on the news anchor Ann Curry.

In his daycare, he was known for being the child who would run to hug anyone who started to cry. He loved to play with cars, blocks, hide cell phones and keys, and he had a way with animals that gave him the nickname amongst family as the "animal whisperer". His eyes were so dark brown that they reflected light and had a shine that will be burned into my memory forever.

When he died, he was just learning to speak, and had only said the word "ball" for the first time a couple of days before his murder. I'm eternally grateful that I was able to hear him say Mama before I lost him, but I will also wonder what he would have said to me had he been old enough to have had the chance.

I want to make clear that I don't spend time thinking about Rams, and what his life will be like in the future. In fact, I actively try to not think of him at all. I feel blessed to have had the chance to be Prince's mother. I've had more children, will always carry a part of Prince with me, and am grateful for the wonderful life I live. Please don't think of me and people like me as victims—I am, and we are survivors.

Rams has ruined his own life more than he has ruined mine. Prince and Sammy were the two greatest gifts of Rams' life. They would've loved him no matter how flawed he was, and he was too sick to understand that his only hope in life was to be a good father to those boys.

Rams should remain behind bars forever not *just* because he robbed an innocent child of a chance of a full life, but because he's truly dangerous. I'll walk out of the courthouse on August 1st and forget about Rams, but he will spend the rest of his life trying to plot ways to terrorize those of us he believes have wronged him. I pray that you understand this, and that you protect my right—the rights of my family— and my son's memory, by letting us live in peace.

* * *

When I left the courthouse that day, a reporter shoved

a microphone in my face to ask me if I was relieved that "justice was served". I stared blankly at the bright light on the camera, blinking slowly for a moment before responding.

I explained that I was thankful that Joaquin was behind bars but that we still had quite a long way before full justice was realized. It was clear from all the documents I'd found since leaving him that Joaquin was a sick and twisted criminal. While Joaquin's entirely responsible for his behavior, true justice is only possible if we're willing to take cases like my sons and use them to critically examine our civil and criminal courts—with the intention of preventing similar tragedies from occurring.

Once Joaquin was convicted, most of his previous associates scurried out of the public eye and pretended as though they'd never been involved with him at all. While I'm not sure I'll ever know why so many protected him, I've spent years trying to figure out what went wrong with our justice system to allow someone like Joaquin to perpetrate a string of violent crimes for over a decade.

There is power in naming—not just for my son but for all the victims touched by Rams—that so many things went wrong here. There is power in naming the reality that so many victims deserved better from our system.

One of my hopes is that in the years since my son died, the people whose lives were touched by his story—both positively and negatively—have taken moments to reflect. I've spent countless hours wondering what I could've done differently to save my son. Instead of burying our heads in the sand, thinking that what happened here was a fluke that will never happen again—we must assume that it *will* happen again unless our collective actions change based on what we've learned here.

In the time it's taken me to write this book, I've given a lot of thought to the meaning of justice. When I started this journey, I believed justice was an attainable resolution for the wrongs that occurred. After chasing justice for over a decade, I've realized that the problem with justice is that she takes a different shape depending on the person seeking her and depending on the complexity of the issue requiring justice.

If Joaquin acted alone, without decades and dozens of enablers, justice would've been achieved when he was convicted and sentenced to life without parole. But if you've been following this story, you realize getting justice is more complicated here. Justice for Prince means more than just Joaquin ending up in prison because it requires a level of systemic reform that so many Americans just aren't ready to embark upon. It would require us to acknowledge that parenting is a privilege and not a right—children have a fundamental right to safety—and that the family court system requires a complete overhaul with federal oversight and accountability to ensure the sanctity of children's civil rights.

There are moments when I worry that I'll never get the justice I seek because our system isn't currently designed to learn from its own mistakes. When Alma Collin's was found dead in Joaquin's house, why did her body get released to him prior to the rest of her family getting notified of the death? By that time, Joaquin was already the sole suspect in another active murder investigation. Having looked at the police records and autopsy reports, I wonder how on earth this happened. And how it took my son's death to finally put Joaquin in prison.

But despite the giant hill still yet to climb on my mountain toward justice, I'll never stop climbing—searching—and fighting for true justice. I believe that it's often the constant search that paves the path of progress.

And while it comes at a cost, every time I walk through my trauma to educate those in power to make changes, I do it because I made Prince that promise. And I truly believe he chose me to be his Mama because he knew I'd never stop.

Epilogue

A few months after Prince died, I had a vivid dream about a beautiful toddler. I kept praying I'd see him in my dreams and was overjoyed. But this child had a dirty blond, curly baby Afro and was bouncing around the room. In the dream, was sitting on the couch in my den, watching the child intently and waiting for them to talk to me.

"Are you Prince," I questioned because the child only slightly resembled Prince.

As soon as the question escaped, the child ran over to me, grabbed my face, and said, "No. I'm a girl!"

Then, just like that, the bouncing toddler ran right out of my dream. I woke up from that dream knowing that I was going to be a mother again. I wasn't going to wait on someone else's fictitious timeline to start living. While the child in the dream wasn't Prince, it felt like both him and my future child were sending me a message.

I promised Prince that I'd fight for justice, but I also

needed to promise him that I'd do more than just survive. In choosing to live, I also knew that living my best life meant being a mother again—but this time on my own terms.

The biggest decision I made in the months after Prince died was to pursue being a Single Mother by Choice (SMC). I wasn't willing to wait to start the rest of my life. I also knew that I never wanted to be in the situation where a court could tell me that I wasn't permitted to protect my child. Using an anonymous donor ensured that Family Court would never be a concern.

Choosing to be an SMC has been one of the very best decisions in my entire life and one I've never once regretted.

"Why don't we just make a baby together," my friend Brian said over drinks at a local bar one night.

"Brian, aren't you listening to what I'm saying? I don't want to know the biological father. I want to be a single mother."

Brian took another swig of the glass of whiskey that'd been sitting on the bar in front of him. He didn't understand why I'd choose to bring a child into this world without a father. I understood his frustration with my choice. He believed I was making social commentary on all men, but this wasn't the case. I knew there were good men, capable of being amazing fathers. But I also knew that I didn't want to rush a relationship due to my strong desire to be a mom. And I knew that being a single mother without the drama of a toxic co parent was exactly what I wanted.

I was surprised by how many people shared their opinions with me on how I should grieve. For several months, I was in this strange, suspended life state where I felt like I was watching the world as an outsider. I was a mother, without a living child.

"Give yourself six months, a year, several years . . . celebrate with your family, visit his grave."

Everyone wanted to offer assistance and guidance, whether solicited or not. While infuriating, I would usually smile awkwardly and thank them for their concern. When I first told my friends and family about my decision to have a child alone, nearly everyone responded with concern. They were worried I was trying to replace Prince.

"Well, did my parents intend to replace my brother when they decided to have me?" I thought this response would help bring some sanity to that comment.

I knew my future children weren't going to be a replacement of Prince. And I was ready to be this child's mother too.

"Don't you think it would be best to just wait a few years until you find a man and have a baby the traditional way?" the fertility doctor asked, after telling me that my fertility wouldn't be an issue in a few years.

It was clear by that comment that the doctor didn't understand. I didn't want a traditional experience. Using a donor felt like the obvious path for me at the time, because I didn't want to be connected to a man through a child. Any man I met in the future would need to accept me as a single mother. I couldn't just erase being a mother, no matter how many people tried to convince me that I could.

When I first met Joaquin, one of my biggest flaws was not trusting myself and not listening to my gut. My decision to become an SMC was my first true act of trusting my gut and choosing what was best for me—despite how much it deviated from the norm. I was done with respectability politics and was ready to live my best life.

I'd been so afraid of single motherhood, that I stayed in

an abusive relationship for too long. Now, I was running
straight for the very thing I'd been terrified of. My fear
was not fear that I wouldn't be able to be a mother alone;
I'd been afraid of what other people would think of me if
I had a non-traditional family. After losing my son, what
other people thought about my life choices was no longer a
concern.

I was no longer a doormat for my abusive boyfriend to
leave his dirty shoes on. I was a strong, independent woman,
who was not going to let society tell me how I was supposed
to be a mother.

On January 25, 2012, the day Joaquin was arrested, I
started the process to have my daughter. I fell in love with
her from the moment I knew she existed, and possibly even
before if you count my dreams. Every time I saw her on the
sonogram, felt her swift kicks to my ribs, or thought about
her, my heart felt as though it smiled. I lived through one of
the worst tragedies imaginable, but part of honoring my son
was choosing love and happiness.

My decision to have another child didn't stop me from
also being a mother to Prince. I wanted to show my daughter that I wasn't going to bury my head in the sand and allow
our country to remain broken. I also wanted her to know
how much I loved all my children. Two weeks before giving
birth to my daughter, I waddled my pregnant body up the
steps of the U.S. Capitol and gave my testimony in a con-
gressional hearing. The hearing was a precursor to federal
legislation protecting abused children of divorce and separation.

"This isn't about mother's rights or father's rights. This
is about the basic civil rights of our children. I would have

gladly given up my rights if only my son had been allowed the right to live," I explained, tears welling up in my eyes.

In the years since Prince died, I continue to speak out against the silence. I've testified in front of federal and state legislators and continue to advocate across the nation for Family Court reform. My advocacy in the state of Maryland assisted in the ratification of "Senate Bill 17, Child Custody—Cases Involving Child Abuse or Domestic Violence—Training for Judges", which was signed by former Governor Larry Hogan in May 2022.

Despite what's happened to me, I still consider myself a fierce American patriot. And I love this country, and its children, too much to let the civil rights crisis against children persist.

I've had two daughters since I lost Prince, both via anonymous donor insemination. The day I met my son, I felt as though I was meeting someone for the first time that I had known my entire life. I felt this all over again with both of my daughters. It was as though they'd always been with me.

Losing Prince was a pain that I couldn't have ever imagined before it happened, and meeting my daughters was the joy that I didn't think was possible given what I'd survived. Every time I look at them, I'm so grateful that I get to be their mom.

The journey I took surviving an abusive relationship, trying to save my son, surviving his loss, and advocating for justice fundamentally changed me. While I still hope to find love someday, my eyes are now wide open. I love myself now—and I know that I'm capable of being loved with the same intensity that I love others.

When my son was alive, I often prayed for a day when we could walk off into the sunset together—safe from his father—and just live in peace and happiness. I'll spend every day and the rest of my life honoring my son's memory while also being the best mother I can be to my little girls. While I didn't get to walk off into the sunset with my son, I get to walk off with my two little girls. And my son is watching over us every step of the way.

Made in the USA
Middletown, DE
18 February 2024

49386196R00187